In Defense of
Political Correctness

In Defense of Political Correctness

Howard Kamler, Ph.D., Psy.D.

IPBOOKS.net
International Psychoanalytic Books

International Psychoanalytic Books (IPBooks)
New York • www.IPBooks.net

International Psychoanalytic Books (IPBooks),
Queens, NY
Online at: www.IPBooks.net

Interior book design by Maureen Cutajar (gopublished.com)
Cover design by Blackthorn Studio (blackthornstudio.com)

ISBN: 978-1-949093-63-6

To Toby and Merv,
fierce champions of conscience.

CONTENTS

Compared to Democrats, Republicans are pretty good political street fighters. Their disparaging wordplay seems endless: the "Democratic Party" becomes the "Democrat Party," the "Affordable Care Act" becomes "Obamacare," "Liberals" are forced to re-name themselves "Progressives," and so forth and so on. Yes, they really know how to give their opponents a good poke in the eye. In the final analysis, these sorts of rhetorical ploys are relatively innocent; clever word-mischief meant to annoy, nothing more. That said, however, I think there is another more mean-spirited and danger-ous kind of rhetorical strategy deployed by the political Right that is not only harming the opposition Left but also the American spirit. The ways in which conservatives have manhandled the term "political correctness" is a perfect example.

Mr. Trump and his cohort base have made much political hay with their harangue against all things PC. Trump has been rallying the troops to defeat all the weak-kneed, liberal, politically correct policies he claims are destroying our country. The Republicans' charge that the Democratic Party has been taken over by an ethos of un-American radical liberal philosophy is nothing new. What *is* new is the particular hammer Mr. Trump wields to drive this point home. For the past few years especially, he and his fellows have managed to pound into public consciousness the idea that all the evils of liberal ideology can be wrapped up in a pithy expression: the liberal is "just so very politically correct," or better, "*too* PC." In virtually every one of his rallies since winning the presidency,

1

Mr. Trump scans the crowd, sternly looks into the TV camera, aggressively points his finger at an imagined liberal Democrat, and finally sums up his scowling disgust (against the backdrop of his cheering base) with those two words. His accusation of all liberals as being "*too* PC" has been unrelenting. As a consequence, the expression has become so pejoratively charged that any clear literal meaning to it has been trivialized in the public consciousness, overwhelmed by the more incendiary emotional content that Mr. Trump and all of his fellow "*too* PC" critics have attached to it. "PC" becomes an emotional slogan standing for the idea that a terrible, evil violation has been done to the American psyche, one that needs to be dealt with severely. Indeed, all of Mr. Trump's God-fearing supporters are encouraged to quake in their boots and pound their fists about what political correctness has done to all good—all "real"—Americans. Their hero Trump promises to come to their rescue and lead the charge to defeat this dangerous public scourge once and for all.

Okay, you get the picture. We would do well to take a deep breath here and move a step back from all the *Sturm und Drang*. Despite all this emotional hand wringing, there is really nothing so dangerous about political correctness. As properly understood, the idea has a clear, inoffensive, literal definition, as much as Donald Trump and his conservative allies would like it to appear otherwise. Their harangue only serves as a smokescreen for something far more insidious that conservatives don't want the public to know; the true underlying motivation behind the critical charge of liberals being "*too* PC." (Spoiler alert: an extreme case of what the smokescreen is trying to hide has to do with white supremacy.)

*   *   *

In this book I will peel away the layers of the "*too* PC" phenomenon and get at what's really going on.[1] It will be a process. Let me say outright that I am an unapologetic defender of political correctness (as properly understood) who believes that *the ongoing attacks against the concept's viability will eventually subvert our democracy and its core ideologies.* A strong charge, I know; but one of which I hope to convince the reader by the end of this book. With the goal of putting an end to this subversion, I shall argue forcefully against all those who would demean the PC concept. I will discuss how most of today's debates surrounding political correctness, pro and con, revolve around what our laws, courts and culture-at-large norms have deemed as acceptable public behavior, beliefs and attitudes regarding the rights of minorities—that which is often referred to as politically correct minority social liberation ideology. In defending the pro side of this debate, I'll argue that the very same people who oppose political correctness are also the ones who have taken dead aim against the cause of minority liberation, along with the laws and cultural norms that support it. Actually, much of their anti-PC energy is a kind of displaced venom for the ideology of minority liberation. I will then unpack what I see as a three-pronged strategy used to attack both the idea of political correctness and the liberation ideology it supports. The main players in this triple assault are principled conservatives along with bigoted conservative forces of racism, misogyny, homophobia and more. They share an underlying complaint: that political correctness holds them back from fully expressing who they are—from being allowed to voice their principles and/or their bigoted attitudes against minority liberation ideology. With Mr. Trump's emergence on the current political scene as the stranglehold bearer of presidential power, constantly filling the airwaves

---

[1] As a research psychoanalyst, I am interested in exposing its psychological defects. As an academic philosopher, I am interested in the logic of the concept and how it is used in political discourse.

with his never-ending stream of hateful invective aimed at all causes liberal—all causes having to do with political correctness—it has become apparent that these people feel they finally have license for their unrelenting assault on people of color, women, religious minorities, the LGBTQ community and others, whether for reasons of principle or—as is more often the case—out of unabashed bigotry. As we find ourselves in the throes of yet another election season, present-day America is a world in which political correctness and minority liberation are still both fair game and still both the centerpiece of Mr. Trump's unending litany of complaint.

With all of this in mind, here is the outline of how I will proceed. My discussion will divide into four parts. Part I first provides some precision about what I mean and what I do not mean by political correctness—a definition, if you will. This is followed by a brief look at the broad context into which the concept of PC came into existence. We will see how political correctness grew up as a conceptual bolster for various forms of minority liberation ideologies. I then introduce some associated concepts that will provide both a richer understanding of the basic definition and, later, allow for a better overall understanding of the current-day debates about the worth of political correctness as it pertains to issues of minority social liberation.

The remainder of the book explores both understanding and critiquing the general harangue the concept of PC has come under by Mr. Trump and his ilk. Specifically, in Part II, I introduce the main players—generally speaking, social conservatives who find absolutely no value in political correctness—looking at their main complaints. In Part III, I shift the focus to examining the ways in which many of these same conservatives attack the minority liberation ideologies related to political correctness. Finally, in Part IV, I engage head-on in a defense of political correctness, wherein I spell out the many ways in which the social conservatives' intentional misunderstanding of the concept not only has done unfair harm to the various kinds of minority social liberation movements, but also has irresponsibly weakened our democratic republic. I end the book with the suggestion that nothing less than a reinvigorated commitment to the idea of political correctness can save us.

PART I

The Context of Political Correctness

CHAPTER 1

Defining the Term

The usage of the term "political correctness" has, throughout
its history, been something of a wild ride with lots of twists
and turns. In this chapter, I follow those movements, with the
goal of discovering a common thread in that history. Ultimately,
I will clarify what I see as the core meaning of the underlying PC
phenomenon and, finally, settle on the best definition of "political correctness" as it should be understood.

History of the Concept

The term "political correctness" is as old as the hills, dating back
to the late 18th century when it was used in rendering a decision
of the Supreme Court.[1] The idea was that, given the technical
precision required by the Court in doing its business, certain terminologies were more appropriate than others when making
claims before the Court. Political correctness simply meant the
right usage of words before the Court. Terminologies that did not
as accurately capture what the Court was discussing were
deemed politically incorrect.

The term wasn't used much afterwards until the early part of
the 20th century, in entirely different circumstances. It reappeared
on the world stage in the context of pointing out differences between competing socialist theories and competing communist

---

[1] See Chisholm v. Georgia, 2 U.S. (2 Dall.) 419 (1793), where Associate Justice James
Wilson first uses this idea.

theories. Claiming "political correctness" became a rhetorical debating device, where each side in the debate used the term to
proudly summarize the virtue of its position in the argument. To
be on the most politically correct side meant that the details and
language of one's theory expressed most accurately what ideal so-
cialism meant or what ideal communism was about.[2] It meant that
one's side was the most ideologically sound or pure, and thus the
side whose practice would be of greatest value for the masses. The
obvious unspoken assumption was that whatever was of greatest
value for the masses was the primary *desideratum* of the society.
In this regard, a political position's political correctness meant its
position was consistent with the primary *desideratum* of the society.
Sometimes these debates over who was most politically correct
would turn into heated confrontations. This was true, for example,
of the Trotskyites and Stalinists of the Soviet Union in the 1920s
and '30s,[3] where the stakes for being the most politically correct
were raised considerably. To veer from the Stalinist "Party line"
(and its image of ideal communism) especially was to be ideologically unsound, impure, inaccurate and therefore politically incorrect.
And to be politically incorrect often led to being "purged" in the night
or else sent off to the gulag. The Stalinists gave no quarter. Healthy
ideological debate turned into violence. Political correctness here was
an overly rigid notion with consequences: the true communist would
follow the absolute strictures of Stalinist theory, or else.

Interestingly, a similar kind of rhetorical debating strategy occurred in arguments between social and political conservatives
in the United States during the 1960s through '80s, first during
the Goldwater era and later on during the Reagan years...and the
memories linger on. Although certainly not identifying with

---

[2] See, for example, Leon Trotsky, "The Struggle for Cultured Speech," *Pravda* (May
15, 1923)

[3] Later on, Mao and Che Guevara would use the term in the same way.

anything like a Soviet-style violent confrontation, conservative thinkers did, nevertheless, vie for who was best suited to wear the conservative mantle. Although they didn't use the terminology, they did use the concept of PC, debating over whose program and policy agenda best embodied "true" conservative ideology. Whoever could argue best for their conservative bona fides were praised as being the most ideologically pure (politically correct), sending their opponents off to a metaphorical gulag of silence. Leftist liberals also acknowledged the importance of political correctness. In being true to one's liberal cause, one was being politically correct; to veer from the path was to be politically incorrect. The budding women's movement of the 1970s, for example, had special scorn for anyone straying from feminist ideological positions, with one school of feminist thought competing with another. Repentance and rehabilitation back to political correctness was the only hope for such sinners and for maintaining an air of political virtue.

These debates were all intramural: communist vs. communist, conservative vs. conservative, liberal vs. liberal. But while this was happening, there were concurrent extramural debates of anticommunist vs. communist, anti-conservative vs. conservative, and anti-liberal vs. liberal. On this other path, a very different, rather clever rhetoric around "political correctness" developed, most notably among the anti-communist thinkers and the anti-liberal (i.e. pro-conservative) thinkers. It amounted to turning the concept of PC on its head and using it as an *ad hominem* shaming device. The "antis" began using "politically correct" to abuse the character of their ideological opponents, invoking the term sarcastically and disparagingly. Political correctness: what had before been exclusively a laudatory term of political pride was now, through deliberate *ad hominem* effort, re-defined as a defamatory term aimed at silencing the opposition. In 1950s America, anti-communists, their tone dripping with sarcasm, demeaned communist thinkers as being *so very politically correct* ideologues. Where before a communist might take pride in being called politically correct for taking the ideology positions he took, now he was mocked for being *so very politically correct.* ("Yes, comrade. You're sooo very politically correct, comrade. Good for you, comrade.") No details of political theories had changed; only the attitude toward "political correctness" had been reconfigured. Confusing, yes?

By the 1990s, conservative Republicans were using the same rhetorical strategy to disparage liberal advocates of social liberation movements, mounting broadside attacks against liberal notions such as multi-culturalism and minority group rights. Conservatives wielded the *ad hominem* anti-PC charge against all of what they saw and continue to see as the liberal, politically correct speech-and thought-"police." Liberation ideology, especially as it was expressed on college campuses, was seen as "liberal fascism." According to the way conservatives understood liberalism, any speech that veered from liberal ideology was deemed politically incorrect (by liberals). Conservatives saw this as a closing off of ideological debates, a new McCarthyism. In short order, these ideas—"liberal fascism," "closing off debate," "new McCarthyism"—became fully associated with PC, and from the conservative's perspective, fully worthy of *ad hominem* disparagement.

The anti-PC charge has become so effective that today, Donald Trump has been able to press the issue even further, selling the public on the idea that PC is all about trying to keep the nation from doing what needs to be done to protect itself. PC is a kind of fifth column, stifling those patriotic voices that would make a call-to-arms in the face of the impending threats from abroad and at home. PC, in other words, is a national enemy, championed by citizens who either are intentionally trying to undermine the nation or are too stupid to see that they are being duped by the purveyors of these threats. Since Trump "doesn't have time" to deal with all the nuanced roadblocks PC puts in the way of dealing with our enemies, he takes it as his personal mission to eradicate the forces of political correctness—which amounts to silencing any liberal complaint about the things that come out of his mouth: "You're trying to stop me, but you can't. I'm too strong. I will prevail over political correctness. I'll say and do as I want." Never mind the *content* of what he says or wants to do as president; what matters to him is being "unfairly" called out on some of his claims—some of which are factually incorrect (e.g. the present-day "real" unemployment number is far lower than the media claims; illegal Mexican immigrants number as low as 3,000,000, or is it 18,000,000?; the Chinese attacked us with the COVID virus), while others are flat-out raw bigotry (no black person can be his accountant because they're too lazy; but those clever guys who wear yarmulkes everyday can[4])—and that this kind of criticism is nothing more than fifth-column PC-supporting of the enemy. After all, there are Muslim and Mexican hordes at the gates; and there is no time to wonder whether there's something politically incorrect about how we stop them. (See my discussion in Chapters 10, 11 and 12.)

This is abusive *ad hominem* arguing on steroids, aimed at disparaging the very concept of political correctness in order to shame and silence liberals. Where, in an earlier time, a conservative might have been shamed by another conservative for not being politically correct enough, now the conservative systematically shames liberals for being *too* PC. The whole project is extraordinarily effective. Get into an argument with a liberal? Lose your footing there a bit? No problem. Just accuse him of

---

[4] John R. O'Donnell, *Trumped!* Simon & Schuster, 1991.

being too politically correct and he won't know what to do. End of story. The accusation has become a main conservative trump card (no pun intended) when facing off against liberals. Sadly, far too many people today have come to see political correctness as a pejorative concept that the *ad hominem* attacks against it set out to create.

If, from the PC advocate's point of view, this wasn't bad enough, the anti-PC critic regularly goes on to use a close cousin of this argumentative strategy against the very idea of minority social liberation ideology. Not satisfied with merely having savaged the concept of PC with his *ad hominem* attacks, the critic of PC uses his success to also savage the ideology that current-day opponents of political correctness associate with the concept— that of minority social liberation. The critic moves from his *ad hominem* destruction of the PC concept to then conflating it with the idea of minority social liberation. In doing so, he takes the now denigrated property of the PC concept *per se* and assigns it to the minority liberation idea that the current-day cause of political correctness champions. It's as though the critic of PC is saying, "If the concept of PC deserves my *ad hominem* attacks, so too does any advocacy of minority liberation movements deserve a good *ad hominem* bop in the nose." This kind of argumentative strategy is known as *poisoning the well* (sometimes referred to as *guilt by association*). The *ad hominem* poison that the critic has established for the concept of political correctness *per se* she now applies to anything having to do with the social liberation movements that PC is intended to support.

Unfortunately—as has happened with the public *ad hominem* attack against the concept of political correctness— this *poisoning the well* onslaught has hit its mark; many who might otherwise have found some justification for some of the claims of social liberation are instead overwhelmed by the psychological power of the right's *well-poisoning* attacks. For those unsuspecting people, PC and minority social liberation have become full-on pejorative notions.

How does one address such anti-PC attacks that have been so effectively pejorative?[5] Is there any air left in the room for PC to even breathe? Well, yes. My primary mission in this book is to defend the good name of the PC concept against the smears. I believe that political correctness is fundamentally not only an acceptable idea when used in legitimate public discourse, but also a very praiseworthy and necessary practice. As I've said, I'm an unapologetic, strong defender of political correctness. With this in mind, I will see if we can take the brief historical excursion we've just been on regarding the evolution of the concept of PC and use it to better define the term; to capture its underlying essential meaning; and to use this new definition to defend against the forces stacked against it. I want to settle upon a definition of political correctness that demonstrates and embodies the common thread between the historic champions of PC and their assumptions of its meaning, and the assumptions and understanding of its denigrators.

Some Mistakes Made by PC Advocates

Before I get to setting—settling on—that definition, though, there is one matter I feel compelled to deal with first. In defending the good name of political correctness against, among other things, the kinds of *ad hominem* anti-PC challenges I've been describing, I don't want to give the impression that I think there's never anything about political correctness that can't be rightfully challenged or, rightfully criticized. There is. Advocates of

---

[5] Obviously, I am also concerned with answering to the anti-minority social liberation attacks (the *well-poisoning* attacks). But not yet. For now, we will focus only on the concept of political correctness.

political correctness have not always been squeaky clean in their use of the concept. And I am not about to defend those infractions that don't warrant defending. But having acknowledged this, I am also concerned about the critics who fallaciously savage the very idea of PC *per se* and who use the particular instances of where PC is *rightfully* criticized as proof for their more extreme view that *all* PC (i.e. PC *per* se) is without merit. And we simply cannot let this kind of move stand. Accordingly, then, let me make clear where the mistakes have been made by PC advocates and how the critics have jumped all over those mistakes in their rush to destroy altogether the concept of PC *per se*. Once I've cleared the decks in this regard, I'll finally be ready to get on to the job of setting down a definition of political correctness.

I have three sorts of PC-related situations in mind where mistakes are made. The first has to do with anti-PC critics claiming that liberals always advocate for political correctness solely "for political reasons." The second relates to situations where facts on the ground make it politically impractical to insist on being politically correct—that is, situations where the actual facts dictate that we override political correctness. The third involves situations where PC advocates are extravagant in their invoking political correctness when it is inappropriate for them to do so.

Here's what I mean by the first kind of mistake: the conservative, anti-PC critic claims that liberals *always* tout and support political correctness when it comes to minority issues and they do so for purely political reasons—i.e. solely for the purpose of getting themselves voted into power—not out of a genuine concern for the well-being of the population they claim to be advocating for. The anti-PC critic sees this as highly immoral. He believes that since this sort of callous liberal behavior goes on all too often, then political correctness is nothing more than a prop that liberals use for their own selfish purposes and, so, is deserving of total disparagement; i.e. PC as a concept is altogether worthless.

When liberals do in fact mention political correctness *only* for political reasons, they are indeed morally wrong. Having acknowledged this, however, there are two necessary provisos I would make: first, for the conservative anti-PC critic to say that political correctness is *always* in the service of political voting concerns—that advocating for political correctness is *always* done for political reasons—is patently false. That it happens sometimes can't be denied; and where it does happen, it is rightfully criticized. But to say that being or advocating for PC is *always* the liberals' agenda is simply not true. So, because a political representative supports a specific issue that his constituents deem to be praiseworthy, the anti- PC critic concludes that the representative's dependence on the favor of his constituents to get re-elected must certainly compromise him and the support he has given to the specific issue in question. While it is true that representatives depend on their constituents for re-election, it is also true that representatives quite often believe in the causes of their constituents; indeed, it is because of their sincere embrace of the constituent causes that their constituents elect them in the first place.

My second proviso about the charge that being politically correct always means doing things for political reasons is that while this infraction sometimes occurs, it only justifies the complaint that the PC concept is occasionally misused. It doesn't justify the conclusion that there is something wrong with the PC concept *per se*. Analogously, a person can misuse a certain tool in their toolbox on occasion without our having to conclude that there is something wrong with the tool itself. It is not the wrench's fault that it has been employed as a hammer.

Let's move on to the next PC-related situation where political correctness is sometimes claimed to be problematic—where facts on the ground come into conflict with being politically correct, rendering the concept politically impractical. Consider this: when we finally found Osama bin Laden, political correctness would have required that we give him a speedy and fair trial. Instead, he was immediately killed and buried at sea. The idea was that in doing this, there would be no specific place where his supporters could go to celebrate him and plot new attacks. In this case, a strategy favoring a practical political calculation outweighed the concern for political correctness. I have no problem with the devout politically correct bowing to this kind of calculation. Sometimes the facts on the ground really do outweigh consideration for being politically correct; this is something that reasonable people can always argue and disagree about.

Having acknowledged that there are situations in which concern for PC is impractical, I've heard critics, in their rush to completely steamroll the very idea of political correctness, insist that being politically correct is *always* unrealistic, that there are always practical considerations that outweigh what they see as unrealistic concerns for being politically correct, rendering the PC concept impotent. The critic thinks that for most advocates of political correctness, their unrealistic concern for being PC amounts to spouting impractical pie-eyed PC *ideals* in the face of what reality requires, while for other followers of PC, it amounts to their desire to follow whatever happens to be the political (PC) *fad* of the day even when that fad flies in the face of what practicality demands. The critic believes that there are always practical facts on the ground which always trump what the PC idealists and faddists are advocating for.

I disagree with everything the critic says here. For starters, I don't accept the critic's caricaturing assumption that most advocates of political correctness are pie-eyed idealists or faddists. As we will see shortly, they are actually clear-eyed patriotic upholders of social justice ideologies. Secondly, the critic is simply wrong that there are *always* practical facts on the ground that will *always* trump any concern for political correctness. While clearly there are such situations, facts on the ground don't always trump the requirements of political correctness. In fact, instances where facts on the ground outweigh PC concerns are actually few and far between and, in our default mode as political actors, we must be as politically correct as we can be. Arguing that there are some cases where facts outweigh PC and that we should therefore dismiss *any* adherence to political correctness amounts to throwing the baby out with the bathwater.

Now let's look at the third kind of situation where political correctness is sometimes claimed to be problematic. There are anti-PC critics who are right on the money when they note that there are instances in which PC is misused through extravagant overuse— that PC advocates sometimes invoke PC in situations that don't warrant that invocation. Once again, I agree with part of what the critics are saying but must disagree with the anti-PC conclusion they draw from their criticism. Yes, advocates of PC sometimes are extravagant in where they choose to invoke the concept. But that doesn't justify the critics' oft-heard conclusion that this misuse of PC proves that the very idea of political correctness *per se* is wrong-headed. So there have indeed been some extravagant claims made by defenders of political correctness against others as not being politically correct enough, meaning that others have said or done things that PC advocates find offensive, when the so-called offense really has nothing so much to do with the so-called offender as it has to do with an overly sensitive PC offendee. Where such uncalled for charges by PC advocates are made, they shouldn't be tolerated. PC in this case is rightfully criticized. But that does not make for a reasonable argument against a person's *ever* legitimately invoking the idea of political correctness.

Here is a clear case in which the PC infraction does occur and the objection is justified: imagine a person who, in the course of a conversation with someone, says "It's a nice day out today," and as a result ends up hurting the feelings of the other person because she doesn't like sunny days. For the hurt party to accuse the sunny day enthusiast as being politically incorrect—because, as far as he's concerned, hurting anyone's feelings is always, no matter the circumstances, bad and politically incorrect behavior—would clearly be beyond the pale. The extravagantly PC person has no reasonable ground to stand on. Moreover, were she to insist that anyone veering from this belief about ever hurting anyone's feelings is being politically incorrect and that this political incorrectness makes him deserving of condemnation, then that also would be beyond the pale. First of all, the belief about "*ever* hurting a person's feelings, no matter the circumstance, always amounts to bad behavior" is frivolous. To then invoke political correctness as some kind of protective shield against feeling offended only gives fuel to the anti-PC critic. By invoking political correctness to defend a belief that's clearly a lost cause, one is, in the critic's eye, effectively weakening the legitimacy of political correctness as an appropriate political stance. As someone who defends political correctness as an important and legitimate concept in political discourse, I certainly don't approve of this kind of improper invocation of PC.

So the "hurt feelings" example is an obvious, even silly example of political correctness overuse, PC extravagance; what a PC critic would call a micro-aggression. Frankly, to my mind, these sorts of trivial cases are the only clear cases of PC being extravagantly misused. As soon as we leave such trivial cases aside and go to more serious minded disputes involving political correctness, rightfully objecting to PC from the basis of extravagance gets far murkier. Consider, for example, what happens when two students argue over Israel's West Bank settlements. One says, "The Israelis need to get out of the occupied Palestinian lands." The other accuses the first of offending her. She doesn't care to have Israelis characterized as "occupiers" of lands that the Bible says they're entitled to. The two go back and forth. Finally, the defender of Israel tells the other that he is being politically incorrect. To some, this amounts to the defender of Israel trying to shut the other person down once and for all to his advantage— and that this sort of thing is more PC extravagance. To those who perceive matters this way, the critic's claim of people being "*too PC*" here would be justified. To others, however, the invocation of political correctness amounts to the defender's raising a good point—that using the term "occupiers" *is* politically incorrect and invoked to irritate and bait the defender. Obviously, if the defender of Israel is in fact using PC as a shibboleth to shut down all debate, then she is off base. On the other hand, if she does truly believe that the term "occupiers" is a loaded term that prejudices the debate from the outset, then she is well within her rights to claim that the critic of Israel is being politically incorrect in his use of language.

The upshot of the discussion in this section, then, is this: there are three general kinds of situations where advocating for political correctness can be problematic, though not fatal for the concept. While I believe that, when understood correctly, invoking political correctness in political debate is generally a legitimate political stance to take, I also believe that sometimes people are insincere about having a true concern for political correctness and instead are only acting *for political reasons*; and that sometimes they refuse to acknowledge that certain *facts on the ground* outweigh the *prima facie* requirement to be PC; and that sometimes they are *extravagant* in their use of the PC concept. All three sorts of people here abuse the PC notion. And where that happens, it's to be condemned. Truly, though, it is not always easy to know when a person is concerned with defending political correctness merely for political reasons and when he is genuinely concerned. Moreover, it is not always easy to determine when some facts on the ground really do trump political correctness. And it is not always apparent when PC extravagance has occurred. Certainly, in the case of extravagance situations, one person's extravagance is another person's acutely accurate take on reality. Therefore, when there's a difference of opinion in a given situation, the matter simply has to be hashed out, hopefully resolving (we should only be so lucky) which side of the line—i.e., the extravagant or the acutely accurate—PC has fallen onto in the particular case. Similarly, in the case of claiming that facts on the ground trump the requirements of PC, when there's a difference of opinion about whether this is really so in a particular situation, this, too, must be hashed out. And obviously, in the case of charging someone for being politically correct only because it suits his political agenda, only a very careful scrutiny of the individual's overall pattern of behavior around political correctness-related situations will be able to settle the matter.

Acknowledging all of this, however, has nothing to do with my larger point: to establish that there are clear cases of using political correctness solely to score political points, or that there are clear cases where PC has rightfully been trumped by facts on the ground, or that there are clear cases of PC extravagances, or that there are close ambiguous cases of any of these three that fair minds can disagree about, doesn't prove fatal for the concept of political correctness *per se*. That political correctness can be misused doesn't justify the critic's contention that PC is a worthless notion. Analogously, if a taxi driver gets into an accident, you don't insist that the company shuts down the whole fleet or that they stop making taxis altogether. You simply hail another cab and go off to your destination; it is an effective way of getting around. In the same vein, because political correctness sometimes is invoked inappropriately, that doesn't mean that we shut down the whole PC fleet. Rather, we point out the problem, do what we can to prevent mistakes in the future, and move on.

Defining Political Correctness

Having acknowledged, then, that PC advocates do sometimes go astray with the concept, let me now finally get to my main goal in this chapter and suggest what I take to be the proper definition of political correctness. To do this, we will look for the common thread in the examples of political correctness that we've discussed.

Let's begin with the 1793 Supreme Court introduction of the concept. It will be helpful to be precise about what was really going on with the political correctness claim in the particular case in which the Court first referred to the PC concept—*Chisolm vs. Georgia*. Here, the Court pointed out that in the typical course of business, the Court as a matter of linguistic habit had always referenced *the states* as the objects of their rulings rather than referencing what the Constitution intended to be the true objects of any of the Court's rulings: *the people*. Technically, in *Chisolm vs. Georgia*, the Court was now saying that going forward in their rulings, the Court should always talk specifically about the citizens rather than the representative states because the Constitution recognized *the people* as the central players. Moreover, the Court said in passing that any plaintiff's failure to conform to the literal political reality about who the objects of the Court's rulings were (the people) was politically incorrect. Political incorrectness therefore referred to making statements in the Court's proceedings that were inconsistent with the Constitution's ideological beliefs about the proper objects of the

Court's deliberations. This is the first known use of the PC concept. Going forward, political correctness would require litigants to use the most exacting language when arguing cases before the Court. According to the Court, this amounted to a terminology *consistent with the general ideological intent of the Constitution.*

The idea of a person's being politically correct (or incorrect) when using a term in a way consistent (or inconsistent) with the ideological intent of the Constitution is a good start for finding the common thread which will help us to understand the true meaning of political correctness. Let's see what else we can glean from other notable instances where mention of political correctness found its way into the public discourse. Specifically, let's look at the Communist, conservative and liberal ideologues and see what we can extract from their use of the term.

For all three types of ideologues, at one point in each of their histories, being politically correct was a good thing, a laudatory attribute. But what did each mean by political correctness? The Communist ideologue thought that within the power structure of world communism, a person was considered to be the most politically correct if his views about communist ideology were those that most consistently promoted the aims, norms and practical concerns of the world Communist movement, e.g. that most consistently promoted the ideals of Stalin's communist Soviet Union. The use of the term "most politically correct" evolved, however, and the ideologues dropped the comparative "most." "Political correctness" went from being a descriptor of a person (by virtue of the views he promotes) being the "*most* politically correct" to simply being a descriptor of being "politically correct" at all. The Communist touted himself and his ideological views as simply politically correct, meaning that he had consistently promoted the views embraced by world communism. Similarly, among American conservatives and liberals, to be politically correct meant to hold political views consistent with the aims, norms and practical concerns within the world of American conservative ideology (think of the example of Goldwater) and American liberal ideology (e.g. 1970s feminism). For a conservative or liberal person to be politically correct in virtue of her holding politically correct ideological views meant that her ideology-based views were accepted in the world of conservative thought or liberal thought and by the conservative or liberal powers-that-be.

I see the common thread in these cases as mirroring the essence of the original Supreme Court use of the term. Where the Court view has it that political correctness means using terms consistent with the Ideological intent of our nation's Constitution, the proud Communist, conservative or liberal ideologues are also saying that being political correct means to act consistently with one's preferred ideology and that the ideology is championed by the broader ideological power structure. In each case, there is a power structure that underlies and enforces—decides—the specific acceptable tenets of that power structure. The only difference between these cases, then, is that, in the Court situation, the Constitution is the power enforcing what is to count as appropriate—politically correct—word usage and linguistic convention; in the instance of the ideologues, it's the ideological power structure (e.g. a nation, a loose set of "major player" ideology leaders, the culture, etc.) that decides what are the appropriate—politically correct—ideological views.

What can we say about what PC means to the critics who have turned the concept into a pejorative? I refer to the anti-Communists who mockingly disparaged Communists for being "oh-so-very politically correct," as well as the conservatives who mockingly charge liberals with being "just *too* PC." Both of these disparagers assume the same idea of political correctness that the above PC advocate ideologues have had in mind. It's just that their *attitudes* about PC are completely different, pejorative. The anti-PC critics are simply upset that our national power structures have embraced certain ideologies of liberalism antithetical to their own ideologies and so they are upset with the political correctness that would support those ideologies as well.

As of this writing (2020), we are in the throes of a conservative culture war against liberal ideology. Not only do conservatives have at it with liberal ideology; they also attack political correctness as an evil support for that ideology. The culture war stems from conservatives' anger with the culture-at-large forces as well as the political and judicial powers-that-be, who celebrate and embrace the prevailing liberal ideologies. They are angry at the preponderance of the American citizenry who embrace and promote in their daily actions those same ideologies. In other words, the conservative war is a war against liberal ideology and the "politically correct" people (the predominant public) who enforce that ideology on a daily basis. Conservatives have not appreciated being on the outside looking in at the normal course of liberal affairs in the lives of most Americans.

It is now time to formulate a definition of political correctness, basing it on the aforementioned ideas:

> When, at a given point in time, a certain ideology that an individual respects and has proudly supported is also fully embraced by major decisions of the judicial system; by the main tenor of both the enacted laws and the publicly stated views of a consensus of the duly elected political establishment; and by a broad array of culture-at-large norms and traditions that are generally accepted by and absorbed into the lives of the great preponderance of citizens; then that individual—along with the individual's behaviors, attitude, and beliefs consistent with that ideology—can rightly be called politically correct.

Here are two other renditions of this definition that capture the same meaning in slightly different ways—the first zeroing in on the idea that an individual person is sometimes the entity that is called politically correct, the second focusing on the notion that it is a person's activities that are the entities deemed politically correct:

> To be politically correct means that an individual's behavior, attitudes and beliefs are consistent with a certain ideology that the individual respects and has proudly supported; where that ideology is fully embraced by a broad array of culture-at-large norms and traditions that are generally accepted by and absorbed into the lives of the great preponderance of citizens; by the main tenor of both the enacted laws and the publicly stated views of a consensus of the duly elected political establishment; and by major decisions of the judicial system.

Alternately:

> That an individual's behavior, attitudes and beliefs are politically correct means that they are consistent with a certain ideology that the individual respects and has proudly supported; where that ideology is fully embraced by a broad array of culture-at-large norms and traditions that are generally accepted by and absorbed into the lives of the great preponderance of citizens; by the main tenor of both the enacted laws and the publicly stated views of a consensus of the duly elected political establishment; and by major decisions of the judicial system.

While each of these definitions of PC is a mouthful, I believe they both capture the essence of what all the historical political types I have talked about have in common: that a person and his words and actions are politically correct when they are in step with a nation's prevailing ideologies. Political correctness is actually an *attitude* a citizen of any nation has that amounts to respecting and showing a full-throated support for the prevailing ideologies that the nation embraces. Indeed, citizens having this attitude of respect and full-throated support is the tight-knit fabric that holds a nation together in camaraderie, allegiance and common cause. It is the mesh of who we are. That attitude is central to what makes an American an American, a Frenchman a Frenchman, a Russian a Russian, and so on. Obviously, then, PC is pretty important stuff and not an idea to be trifled with. The attempt to cheapen and subvert it is tantamount to tearing at the fabric of a nation. In the case of the grand American democratic experiment, the anti-PC critic's attempts to cheapen and subvert the very notion of PC tears away at the camaraderie, allegiance and common causes that make us the people we are. With these ideas in mind, it should come as no surprise that, in the chapters to follow, I will confront the anti-PC critic as forcefully as I can.

Before I get to any of that, let me express a few more introductory thoughts about political correctness and ideologies. While my main concern in this book is to see how this notion of political correctness impacts the prevailing national ideology of social liberation—most specifically, minority social liberation—I should point out that there are many other prevailing ideologies that Americans abide by and aim to be politically correct about (as I have just defined the term); for example, political democracy, social egalitarianism, social freedom, political freedom and economic capitalism. More recently, we've also embraced the ideologies of multiculturalism, globalism and climate control. On a broader level, since the dawning of the Enlightenment, we have always abided by an ideology of objective thinking and scientific method—i.e. an ideology that requires the individual to respect impartial objective standards of evidence when arguing about and justifying factual claims about the empirical world around us, including the world of scientific inquiry. I mention scientific inquiry because, as we know, empirical thinking has come under attack during the past 50 years with the advent of postmodernism. It has currently taken serious body blows from Mr. Trump and his conservative followers, both in their attempts to paint much of the media as the "elites" purveying "fake news," calling into question the very idea that objective standards of news reporting are something to strive for and respect (Mr. Trump: "Don't believe what you see and hear; believe what I tell you"); and in their seeming objections to scientific thinking altogether, most especially as it pertains to climate science. Somehow, conservative conspiracy thinking has taken precedence over objective/evidentiary thinking in both the cultural and political arenas.

My point here is that these ideologies, together with the ideology of minority social liberation, are examples of ideologies that Americans have taken for granted as societal givens. The people, the culture, the political and judicial powers-that-be for the most part have embraced these ideologies. As citizens, we expect our fellows to be politically correct about them, to behave and think consistently with these ideologies.

I should also point out that there are times in history when opposing ideologies are almost equally embraced by the people, the culture and the political and judicial forces that be; and so, large swathes of the citizenry end up being politically correct about opposing views. This has pretty much been the case in America over the past 70 years regarding what might loosely be described as the ideology of social welfare vs. the ideology of pure capitalist competition determining who gets what in society. Liberal Democrats have championed the former, conservative Republicans have championed the latter. Some from each party have tried to square the circle by offering an amalgam of the two ideologies. But amalgams aside, both ideologies are embraced more and less by bare majorities at different moments in our nation's history. Therefore, we either vote Democrats or Republicans into national office, depending on the most popular sentiment. The two ideologies vie for a most favored status with the majority of Americans.

Within each of these popular ideologies, the people who consistently abide by the given ideology embraced by the culture and the political and judicial powers-that-be are "politically correct." On the other hand, when speaking of *competition between* the two popular ideologies for most favored status (for example, Trotskyites vs. Stalinists, different schools of conservative American thought vying for "most properly conservative," and social welfare vs. capitalism), we say that the ideology which at a given point in time has the passion of the majority of the people is the most favored. But this is a misnomer. What we are really discussing here is which of these ideologies, each of which has large numbers of politically correct advocates, is the most *popular* at a given point in time in the nation, not which ideology is the most politically correct. Ideologies are not politically correct; its advocates and their actions are. Saying that any two ideologies are vying for political correctness is just a figure of speech standing for which ideology has the most politically correct advocates. This general idea will take on special importance for us in subsequent chapters when we talk specifically about vying for correctness occurring between minority social liberation ideologies and the conservative ideologies that oppose them.

In any event, given our understanding of the relationship that political correctness has to a nation's prevailing ideologies and its ideological actors, I hope you can begin to see why I think political correctness is an indispensable notion that needs to be preserved and protected against the conservative onslaught that would eradicate it. Being consistent within the prevailing ideologies is good for the integrity of any nation. And it is a good thing for the individual who is a member of that preponderance of citizens who are politically correct; she is happy with her lot. As I've implied, in her being politically correct, she displays the essential quality of what it is to be a good citizen. Of course, those who don't approve of the political, judicial and cultural institutions embracing a given ideology aren't so happy. Therefore, they take issue with the politically correct behaviors, beliefs and attitudes around that ideology as expressed by the predominant citizenry. They go about the process of trying to dismantle the entire prevailing ideological edifice. One way to accomplish that is to undermine the concept of political correctness altogether in the ways I have described. The idea here is that if one can successfully disparage the concept of PC, then one will have effectively argued that the national institutions that support the ideology in question, as well as the people behaving and thinking consistent with that ideology, are all wrongheaded and in need of recalibration, an ideological re-education. This is precisely what today's anti-PC crowd is intent on doing.

Again, my mission in this book is to argue against this kind of anti-PC thinking. That means first understanding the forces set against political correctness as well as the ideology about which they are dead set against being politically correct. After those discussions, I will defend political correctness as an important tool for anyone who would be a good citizen of the nation. A nation's ideologies are its life's blood and, as I have said, championing them is what binds us together as a people. The maintenance of those ideologies depends upon people devoting themselves to the politically correct expression of them through their behavior, attitudes and beliefs. That's what is at stake in fighting the forces that would do away with the very idea of PC.

But I'm getting ahead of myself. It's important that first I provide you with some context which will allow the ensuing discussion of political correctness and ideology to come alive. First, I will clarify just what particular ideology today's critic of political correctness is most centered on—America's minority social liberation ideology; second, I'll discuss the nature of bias that preconditions so much of what motivates that anti-minority liberation criticism; and third, I will zero in on the idea of the culture-at-large that is the main power source championing politically correct ideology. Let's begin.

CHAPTER 2

Social Liberation

The '60s was not merely the era of sex, drugs, rock 'n roll and anti-war sentiment. They were also the years when social liberation for minorities in our country came of age. This was a time when many people of color, especially black people, said "enough" to racism; when many women said "enough" to sexism. Before this decade of change, people practiced discrimination (some reflectively, many unreflectively) against black people and women with abandon, denying many of them their civil rights, denying them equality. But the '60s saw black people come together to form a powerful political movement of liberation from racial bigotry. Feminists carved out a powerful political movement of liberation from prejudicial male bias. Both groups demanded that their rights be respected. Through various forms of social and political action (marches, occasionally violent protest, electing sympathetic legislators, political horse-trading, etc.), black people and feminists brought their complaints to public view. The general public could no longer avoid becoming consciously aware of our past and continuing discriminatory attitudes, beliefs and practices against the civil rights of minorities. Consciousness-raising was afoot. As a consequence, a new moral consensus began to take hold against such bigotry and bias.[1] As this consensus grew, so too were many forms of race and sex discrimination seen as immoral and eventually they became illegal as well.

---

[1] While right here I am using "bigotry" and "bias" as distinct terms, in fact I think bigotry can be defined as a specific kind of bias. This will become apparent in Chapter 3.

To my mind, the fact that minority social liberation became and continues to be a cornerstone ideology of our nation—that, at our core, we celebrate the formerly unacknowledged civil rights of minorities alongside of the civil rights of all citizens—is the centerpiece of what is so incredibly powerful in the American spirit. Of course, liberation consciousness hasn't only been aimed at discrimination against African Americans and women. Since the '60s, plenty of other liberation movements (LMs) have staked their claim. LGBTQ liberation has probably been the most vocal among these next-generation movements. Others, though, certainly share the stage—liberation from immigrant discrimination; other racial discriminations (against Latinos, Asians, etc.); economic discrimination; disability discrimination; age discrimination (ageism); ethnic discrimination (e.g. anti-Arabism); religious discrimination (e.g. anti-Semitism, anti-Islamism).

Most liberation movements typically work on two fronts: one aimed at changing oppressive beliefs and attitudes, the other at changing oppressive behavior. The latter is what most of the public debates over liberation tend to center on. A given LM exerts its political power in hopes of persuading legislators to pass the right kinds of laws ending oppressive prejudiced behavior. Indeed, since *Brown vs. the Board of Education*, many of our state and federal legislative bodies have tried to fine-tune and sometimes even broaden the boundaries of discriminatory behavior deemed illegal for an ever-growing number of protected classes of American citizens.

Influencing discriminatory beliefs and attitudes is a different story. Obviously, putting these sorts of things to bed would be a wonderful accomplishment. But it's hard to control what goes on inside a person's head. Beliefs and attitudes can't be legislated. So, what do liberation movements do to play to hearts (attitudes) and minds (beliefs)? How do liberation movements try to affect the psychology of people? This is where consciousness-raising comes in. LMs try to educate and morally persuade public consciousness by telling and re-telling stories of prejudice and oppression through literature, theater, film, music and the visual arts. The goal is to sway the attitudes and beliefs of a critical mass of the public, to the point where the culture-at-large finally absorbs the desired social changes as new social mores that are *givens*, established facts. Once that is accomplished, it is hoped that social forces exerted by these cultural mores will do the rest of the job and work its will on those still resistant to change.

Changing laws as well as changing hearts and minds—this is what liberation movements attempt to do. To the extent that these movements have been successful, liberation ideology has become central to defining who we are as a people. Furthermore, social liberation—minority liberation ideology—anchors our national identity. I also see it as a *continual social process*. Part of what America is about is our *constant expansion* of the rights of citizens. This sometimes means expanding rights for minority citizens against discrimination; sometimes it means expanding the rights of *all* citizens (think of healthcare, meaningful employment, affordable college tuition). Indeed, we have even gone to the mat to influence foreign governments to expand and honor the *human rights* of all citizens of the world. These are universal, inalienable, and indivisible rights that all people possess simply by virtue of being people. Examples include the right to life, liberty and the pursuit of happiness; the right to food, clothing and shelter; the right to work; the right to education; the right to freedom of expression; the right to equality before the law. Championing rights of all kinds—be they civil rights against minority discrimination, civil rights of all citizens, or human rights of all persons on the planet—is an ongoing process for our nation, undoubtedly well into the indefinite future. And in the case where we focus our attention specifically on the civil rights of minorities, there will always be *new legal rights* established and *new* moments of *consciousness-raising* aimed at having *new rights claims* become part of the mores—the givens—of the culture-at-large.

That is my basic understanding of how America's liberation psychology works. But there are a few auxiliary points I'd like to make. I've found a metaphor to be most helpful in doing this: social liberation as a kind of *frontier* activity. America continually blazes new trails for new rights claims to be heard. We have always been a nation of explorers, pioneers, and settlers—from Plymouth Rock to the Wild West to the "final frontier" of Space. Exploring, pioneering and settling are part of our historical legacy; not just aimed at opening new geographical frontiers, but new idea and technology frontiers as well.

Perhaps our greatest expression of this historical legacy is found in the arena of *civil rights*. We will always have a new frontier where new civil rights claims cry out for exploration, pioneering, and settling.[2] The explorer identifies new rights possibilities (e.g. the minority group that identifies and demands an end to certain discriminatory anti-rights biases and practices). The pioneer argues for their acceptance (e.g. the liberation movement that attempts to influence law and raise consciousness with the goal of achieving rights acceptance). The settler embraces them and fits them into the foundation of his life and the life of the nation (e.g. those of us who are moved and convinced by the explorers and pioneers to put what they say into practice).

---

[2] I realize there is a very unhappy irony here. Yes, blazing new rights frontiers is a wonderful part of who we are as a nation. However, the same can't be said about how we have blazed geographical frontiers. Much of our frontier activity of opening up new lands has been at the expense of oppressive rights infringement—and worse, a virtual annihilation—of native peoples indigenous to those lands and against black slaves who would work those lands.

The settler is precisely the politically correct citizen inasmuch as his behavior, attitudes and beliefs are consistent with these new rights claims that are advocated for and protected by the powers-that-be and the culture-at-large.

Of course, while I think that these ideas accurately describe America's passion for expanding rights, not everyone is willing to get with the program. Not everyone is interested in being politically correct. The idea of settling—fully embracing—new rights claims becomes an especially iffy proposition for some. On any new rights frontier, the general population, as *prospective* settlers, is challenged to acknowledge and honor the new rights claims that are being made. As with any kind of challenge, there will be some who accept it immediately and enthusiastically, some who resist for a short while but eventually fall in line with these "first generation" settlers, and some who dig in their heels, refusing to settle at all. This latter group insists on remaining attached to the long-ago established places that are part of their everyday familiar civilization; "the way things have always been"—e.g. the 19th century prospective settler nostalgically longing to be "back home in Boston" or the current-day version of this sentiment: "Make American Great Again." As far as tendencies go, I would put political liberals and middle-of-the-roaders in the first two categories and political conservatives in the third. Part of what being conservative *means* is having at least a *prima facie* recalcitrance to change. And that's as true for them on the frontier of new rights claims as it is anywhere else.[3] I think that both the conservative working-class person and conservative elitist intellectual feel no resonance with *anything* having to do with the opening of these

---

[3] I don't mean to reduce all conservative resistance to liberation mentality to this characterization (e.g. not all conservatives are zeroed in on "making America great again"). There certainly are other reasons conservatives have for opposing rights claims. We will come to them when we finally tackle the anti-PC agenda in Parts II and III.

frontiers. They feel no kinship with rights settlers, nor do they have patience for explorers and pioneers, and they have no desire to join with any of them. To conservatives, all frontiers-people are alien-seeming *others*. The conservative who would fight the national liberation spirit altogether doesn't want to acknowledge the ever-expanding rights frontier (populated by "those people") as having any legitimacy to it in the first place. So, of course, he won't honor (settle) the rights claims made there, either. He is only willing to accept rights as spelled out in the Constitution—i.e. our inalienable rights, our civil rights and our civil liberties as delineated in the Bill of Rights—and no more. In effect, he will fight the social force of the culture-at-large around the issue of expanding liberation along with any consciousness-raising activity and arguments pressed by rights advocates that go beyond what is literally referenced in the Constitution.

For the rest of us, when we find something new on the frontier of individuals and groups making rights claims that have been or are in the process of becoming absorbed by the culture-at-large, there are, as I've said, some who briefly resist but eventually come around as well as those who immediately welcome the rights-liberating activity. Among the former, their initial bias against a new rights claim is not, psychologically speaking, so deeply rooted that they never can evolve. When they hear stories about rights oppression and acknowledge sound arguments supporting rights acceptance, along with feeling the social force of the culture-at-large, their resistance is eventually transformed into an embrace of the liberation spirit; they join the cause.

Supporters (settlers) of any new kind of liberation come to realize that *prior* to arriving at their current cultural moment—where they now fully embrace some new rights claims—they had beforehand not even been aware of the rights claims in question; and so they weren't in a position, psychological speaking, to honor them either. Some of them actually might have been *consciously* biased against entertaining any potential rights claims of a particular minority (e.g. they might even have been consciously racially prejudiced or sexist) and consequently, when they eventually heard a rights claim made, it was so out of their ordinary experience that it didn't immediately register as legitimate. Others might not have had any prior opinions, conscious or otherwise, regarding the minority rights claims in question. That is, they might have been *"rights-blind."* Still others might have held *non-reflected-upon* negative value judgments, negative biases (e.g. unintentional, albeit still bigoted, racist views) that were inconsistent with the new rights claims. Now, however, looking back from the new cultural frontier, they realize that where they were before is incompatible with their current consciousness. With this realization, some of these people might also—counterfactually, as it were—bemoan and blame themselves for not coming to honor these rights claims sooner.

In sum, then, where an individual or a class of individuals belonging to minority groups make rights claims well before the claims were brought to broad public culture-at-large consciousness, there will doubtless be some members of the general public who blame themselves after the fact for their past bigotry or blindness, whether intentional or unintentional, to the rights claims of these minority groups. We should also point out that not all people who finally come to embrace the liberation of others react in any of these ways to their former selves. Doubtless, there are those who accept their past selves for who they were and simply "move on" to at least entertaining new rights claims as they are explored and pioneered. Regardless of how any of these people got to this juncture, the main point here is that they all now give rights claims their full attention.

There's a noteworthy corollary to these ideas that we might call "the *future* rights claim phenomenon." It's this: in a nation where there are ever-expanding rights claims and acceptance of those claims into the future, there are an indefinite number of rights today that haven't yet been claimed or even thought about by the society-as-a-whole. All this (the claiming of certain rights and the public's then becoming aware of those claimed rights) will unfold continually in the ever-expanding rights claims of the future. But precisely because none of these future rights claims have been asserted yet, *most* rights-favoring members of the public *right now* are insensitive to the genuine rights of others, while the rights-favoring public doesn't have the faintest idea they are being insensitive. Because the appropriate rights claims haven't yet been made by their bearers (indeed, the bearers, themselves, might not even be aware that they have the rights in question), the rights-favoring members of the public are either rights-blind or else holding some conscious or non-reflected-upon biases because they are not aware yet that those entities have the given rights that will come to light in the future. When the rights claims are finally made in the future and find their way into public consciousness, I can imagine the formerly insensitive rights-favoring public members looking back and self-flagellating ("if only I had known"). This condition (of rights insensitivity toward rights that will be claimed in the future) is true of *most of us* today, and it will be true of us again tomorrow and the day after that and the day after that.... There will always be something new about injustice—there will always be some new heretofore rights violations unearthed—that we are not aware of today. This is part of the human rights frontier condition.

If one were to take an historical broad view of how rights have unfolded on the frontier, this corollary has been illustrated again and again. Consider the wide sweep of the past 100 years. There was a time when it was commonplace for most people to either blindly, consciously, or non-reflectively denigrate entire groups of people as perverse homosexuals, silly women, inscrutable Orientals, savage Indians, shiftless ___ (insert unprintable racial slur here). These groups were communally (i.e. with the blessing of the culture-at-large) disparaged as inferior as a matter of course. This is just the tip of the iceberg. Certainly, as new rights frontiers were successfully opened, much has changed. Through cultural forces and consciousness-raising, many of our old attitudes have transformed, some even counterfactually bemoaned as old bigotries or insensitivities.

But that is looking at matters from a broad historical perspective. This same phenomenon happens daily, right up through the present; and it will likely continue into the indefinite future. The paradox is that at any given moment, we can't really point to definite examples of where this will happen on a future rights frontier. Although we are undoubtedly currently in a state of blindly or biasedly not recognizing someone's rights, it's also true that while a person is in such a state, he isn't aware that he's in such a state. That's because the precise frontier moment that would finally make him aware hasn't happened yet. (For example, before the expression "systemic racism" emerged, many if not most Americans—including some people of color—were unaware of their own collusion with this ongoing form of discrimination and oppression.)

Nevertheless, that we currently and unknowingly are either blind about or have negative attitudes toward individuals or groups of people that will later be deemed an infringement on their rights is, as I say, a definite characteristic of the rights frontier condition. Let me conclude this part of the discussion with an illustration of this idea. I want to describe a science-fiction sounding scenario whose very oddness will hopefully drive the point home. Imagine that 70 years from now, when computers and the science of artificial intelligence are well past "the singularity" point and the age of "machine consciousness" has gained general cultural acceptance, people will talk about how "those people 70 years ago were so incredibly prejudiced against the *rights* of primitive artificial intelligence computer devices, mistreating them as 'mere hardware' with no rights, and to be disposed of at whim." As bizarre as this image would undoubtedly seem to most of the current public, it's meant only to dramatically suggest the above idea—that at any given point in time in a culture that embraces ever-expanding rights frontiers, people do have blindness or biases (insensitivity) about rights that they are unaware of.[4] But, in time—through concerted efforts at consciousness-raising, persuasive rights arguments and subsequently changed cultural mores—rights do get recognized and embraced.

All right; I believe that what I've been saying accurately describes the terrain occupied by those of us who have a general respect for rights claims and who embrace the ever-expanding liberation frontier mind-set. But what about those who, from the get-go, don't buy any of this talk about how everyone should be on board with the idea of a rights frontier or the claims of minority liberation? They are not comfortable with anything I've been saying here. I am talking about the anti-PC crowd, the significant conservative public who don't accept a lot of minority rights talk and many of whom are even consciously and quite proudly dead-set against the mentality of a minority liberation frontier or ever-expanding-rights for all. We must come to terms with their point of view, not only so that we see exactly who these people are who would undercut the claims of minority liberation advocacy, relegating minorities back to a condition of second-class citizenry—but also because it is precisely these same anti-liberationists who have made the destruction of political correctness

---

[4] Could Animal Liberation possibly fit under this description?

their abiding concern. So, of course, we want to finally see what these conservative critics have to say.

But first, there are still more matters of context-building we need to speak to. It should come as no shock that, when people argue about ideologies—whether having to do with minority liberation or something else—very *deep biases* inevitably come to the surface and take over the discussion on either side of the ideological debate. I think most people understand that ideological positions are about differing biases, differing firmly held perspectives. This is certainly the case when liberationists and anti-liberationists square off. Ideally, any ideological opponents would be able to argue their respective cases rationally, but this is not the typical reality. Ideological debates are often quite emotionally charged; certainly when it comes to the biased debates between pro- and anti-liberationists. That's not to say that rational discussion between the two sides is impossible; it's only to acknowledge that there is a lot of emotion behind their respective biased points of view and that where there are emotion-laden biases, there is bound to be a strain on maintaining decorum. Consequently, because we will see later on how emotionally charged biases can take over any rational discussion between the two sides, it behooves us to get a handle on exactly what goes on when emotionally charged biases arise in ideological debate. Because these kinds of biases play such an important role in both the challenge to and the defense of politically correct liberation ideology, it is important for us now to turn our attention in the next chapter to these kinds of biases and understand what they, vis-à-vis their salient features, are all about. That understanding will prepare us for the PC/anti-PC and liberation/anti-liberation debates to come in the rest of the book.

CHAPTER 3

Strong Biases

Biases are kinds of beliefs and attitudes that can be formed at any point in a person's life. We all have them. They are the pro or con beliefs and attitudinal preferences--dispositions, tendencies—we have about many matters. For example, we have positive biases about our ideals, and we have negative biases against what we perceive to be evil in the world. Our biased beliefs and attitudes are our slants on life in the sense that they are a kind of mental shorthand device we use for judging a given matter whenever that matter arises; they preclude *prima facie* the issue of our having to rationally weigh considerations for the matter's favor or disfavor. We already favor or disfavor the matter. The value judgment (the favoring) about the matter has already been settled in the form of our bias—what we commonly call our prejudice, our pre-judgment.

There is a continuum defining the degree of impact our biases have on our lives. Among a person's biases, some are relatively benign—such as being biased toward rocky road ice cream and playing baseball or being biased against broccoli and watching soccer. These benign pre-judgments have relatively little impact on the lives of anyone other than the biased individual and her immediate surround. Moving toward the other end of the continuum, there are biases of increasingly greater import, in the sense that they can impact more than the individual and her immediate surround; for example, being biased towards voting Democratic or being biased against all members of a certain religion.

For what I hope are obvious reasons, there is a subclass of the latter "greater import" kind of biases that warrants a special mention: the negative biases of *bigotry*. These are biases aimed specifically at demeaning, devaluing and dehumanizing entire classes of individuals. The racist, the misogynist, the Islamophobe, the homophobe are clear paradigm cases. We are all familiar with what bigotry looks like when it is out in the open, i.e. when it is conscious and intentional. It seems the news is always filled with reports of outright discrimination, overt hatred and violence against certain groups. However, it is important that we also recognize that plenty of bigotry comes in the form of the people who harbor unintentional demeaning, devaluing, and dehumanizing biases against groups of others. Some people are just not aware of what they're doing, but they're doing it, nevertheless. However, too, I have no qualms about using the term "bigot" to designate biased young people (ageists) who demean, devalue, and dehumanize senior citizens; or to describe biased wealthy individuals who demean, devalue, and dehumanize the poor and middle-class people; or to call out biased, able-bodied people who demean, devalue, and dehumanize people with disabilities; and so on. There is all manner of bigoted biased people whose bigotry and bias are alive and well in our country, doing their thing.

There is also a continuum having to do with the strength with which we hold biases. On one end of the continuum, we have biases that are malleable and susceptible to change. For example, it wouldn't be odd to hear that someone who had a bias toward taking a certain route to a particular destination was talked out of taking that route—talked out of his bias—when shown a shortcut. There are other biases, though, which are not so easy to change. It is probably true of all of us that we find ourselves at different points in life having our biases challenged. And then we resist, resist, resist. Since it is these relatively change-resistant—strong—biases that are precisely the kind that play a predominant role in the anti-minority liberation and anti-PC debates—usually, though certainly not always, in the form of change-resistant bigotry—those are the ones that I will focus my attention on in this chapter.

Four Kinds of Change-Resistant Biases

(1) Biases conditioned by wholehearted approval or disapproval

There seem to me to be (at least) four basic kinds of strong (i.e. relatively change-resistant) biases. The first has to do with how we respond to the things we wholeheartedly approve of and the things we wholeheartedly disapprove of, however it was that we came to the state of approval or disapproval. It is not uncommon that we form change-resistant biases about both; these biases serve as a kind of backstop support for such approbation or disapprobation. They defend against our being shown to be wrong about our commitment, pro or con. And they do this by actually taking control of some of our cognitive processes having to do with the object of our approval or disapproval. For example, when we wholeheartedly approve of a political figure running for office, we invariably form a strong bias in her favor that has the effect of cognitively filtering out anything that would speak negatively to her candidacy and character and cognitively filtering in anything that would speak positively to the same. We are strongly biased in her favor. When we just as wholeheartedly disapprove of her opponent, we form a strong bias against the opponent that has the effect of cognitively filtering out anything that would speak well of the opponent's candidacy and character and cognitively filtering in anything that would speak ill of the same. We are strongly biased against the opponent. In the final analysis, these kinds of strong biases defensively serve the purpose of preventing the possibility of anything disconfirming our approval or disapproval—i.e. preventing us from ever being effectively shown to be wrong in our own eyes. Biases in the service of this sort of thing are notoriously resistant to change.

This kind of bias posture naturally comes into play on the liberation frontier. Many anti-liberationists don't want to even consider what a liberationist has to say. Nothing is to count against their disapproval of—indeed, their enmity toward—all liberation activity. They are cognitively set to see only the shortcomings of any new rights movement. It is also the case that many liberationists might be equally cognitively "impaired." That is, there surely are some liberationists who have biases that are so stilted in favor of their pro-liberationist beliefs and attitudes that it is virtually impossible for them to objectively judge what any anti-liberationist is arguing; so much the worse for them concerning some of the debates on the rights frontier.

(2) Biases conditioned by fear and trauma

A second kind of strong (change-resistant) bias has to do with how a person responds to extreme fear or intense trauma.[1] It's quite normal for a person to fear someone who victimizes him, or to feel traumatized by some event that has victimized him. It's also quite normal that the victimized person might then feel angry with the victimizer and also, depending upon the egregiousness of the victimizer's actions, hateful toward him. We say the anger

---

[1] Certainly, fear is a major component to any trauma. However, because there is so much more to trauma than fear, fear and trauma need to be treated as distinct concepts.

and possible hate would be justified, *rational*. On the heels of this, it wouldn't be unusual for the anger or hate to work its way into an intense bias against the victimizer. And we would think of this also as being a *justified bias*, a rational one. That is, being fearful of or traumatized by a victimizer legitimately *entitles* a person to being angrily or hatefully biased toward him. To be biasedly forewarned is to be rationally forearmed.

That's one kind of bias—justified bias. There are other situations, though, where we feel fear of or feel traumatized by people and we form angry or hateful biases against them, where those biases are *not justified* because, measured by any objective standard, those people have not done anything egregious to us in the first place. They haven't in fact done anything fearful or trauma-inducing to us. Nevertheless, because of the peculiarities of our own psychology, we feel fear of or traumatized by them. And in these situations, we're being *irrational*. In the spirit of our trying to make some sense out of—in trying to bring some semblance of reason to—these feelings, we typically then impose (or rationalize) a justification for them. We make up reasons for why the other person makes us fearful or traumatized. That in turn has the effect of justifying for ourselves the angry or hateful bias we have toward them, even though in fact it is not justified by the world beyond ourselves.

In both the justified and unjustified contexts, our bias serves a special psychological defensive purpose: fear and trauma are feeling states people would rather not ever experience. Therefore, we naturally try to defend against having such feelings as heightened states of consciousness. A time-honored way of doing this involves a well-known psychological defense mechanism of self-distraction[2] in which a person moves his focused attention

---

[2] Many psychoanalysts might be tempted instead to use the term displacement here. To me, though, there are subtle differences between self-distraction and displacement. But I don't wish to go into that matter here.

away from his heightened feelings of fear or trauma about an object and instead aims them at what he considers—sometimes correctly, sometimes not—a justified angry or hateful bias against that object; in effect he changes the subject for himself. He has become so focused now on his feeling justifiably biased against the object, that he is no longer so fully aware of his fear or trauma.[3] These two feeling states are no longer heightened states of consciousness. His angry or hateful bias has the effect of dampening or perhaps even calming and soothing—and thereby defending against—the severity of these feelings. So, when another person or an event has so negatively shocked us that we come to fear the person (perhaps even feel terrified of him) or feel traumatized by the event, such a mechanism could be triggered. And once triggered, it is highly resistant to change; that is, because fear and trauma are such relatively intractable and uncomfortable psychological states, the angry or hateful biases that then form as a defensive mollifying response to them not only have the effect of dampening, calming and soothing them, but also, to the degree that the biases are dampening, calming and soothing, they (the biases) have the quality of being that much more resistant to change.

We are all familiar with this kind of defense mechanism. The bully in the schoolyard frightens you again and again. Your fear becomes overwhelming. You correctly respond by feeling angry with him, this feeling working its way into a full-blown all-absorbing general hateful bias against him that feels righteous to you. Forming the hateful bias is an eminently rational response. But then, becoming *absorbed* in it and its righteousness serves the further defensive purpose of calming yourself in the face of such bullying. If you are so absorbed in your anger and you feel you are on the side of the angels in reacting this way, then you don't have much room in your consciousness for the disturbing feelings of fear. Obviously, your

---

[3] There are other common expressions capturing the same idea: "Better to be angry than scared" and "The best defense is a good offense" readily come to mind.

fear doesn't totally disappear, but it does subside in a comforting way. A feeling of righteousness (righteous anger) will do that for a person. And so long as the bullying continues to be present in your life, so too will your hateful (though comforting) righteous bias remain strong. That is all to the good.

Consider a different example, where a person is irrationally, unjustifiably fearful of all immigrants. Xenophobia has been known to lead some people to engaging in hysterical biased angry diatribes against the "other," a defensive consequence of which is the soothing of this otherwise uncontrollable feeling of fear. To the extent that their xenophobia was intractable—and that is the unfortunate norm for xenophobia—so too are their defensive biased angry yet soothing reactions intractable.

Those are situations of fear. What about situations of trauma? A paradigm case of this would be our national reaction to 9/11. We all were traumatized. And as a natural response to our feelings, we all had a hateful bias against Osama bin Laden and his henchmen. Our *immersion* in this hateful bias served to soften our feelings of trauma. Clearly, the bias also had an inordinate amount of staying power, commensurate with the staying power of the trauma that gave rise to it. Another example might be what's going on as of this writing during the coronavirus COVID-19 situation across the world. Certainly, in our nation, many people not only fear being infected by the virus but also justifiably feel traumatized by the very possibility of catching it. For some of us, the way we respond to these feelings is to immerse ourselves in anger toward the national leaders who strike us as incompetents, unable to do anything that can effectively protect the health of the nation (e.g. rolling out testing for the disease in a timely manner). While this anger doesn't eradicate the feeling of trauma, the immersion into the it as a righteous response does at least momentarily calm the trauma experience.

Defensive biases can on occasion turn into *generalized* biases against that perceived (whether correctly or not) kind of fearful person or that perceived kind of traumatizing event. For example, repeatedly seeing TV news reports of members of a minority group's criminal behavior has been known to make some people strongly and angrily biased against the entire minority group, suspecting all of them of being criminals. This is unjustifiable stereotyping, pure and simple, but you will never convince this angry, biased population of that. They likely had a pre-existing irrational fear of the minority group. And their new generalized, angry, criminalizing bias serves to make what in fact has all along been their unjustified irrational fear now (wrongly) seem justified to them. This angry stereotyping bias and the (mis)perception of justification that accompanies it have the effect of calming their pre-existing irrational fears of the minority group. The bias also has the effect of calming their new, irrational fears of being victimized by that minority group's potential criminal behavior. Both of those fears feel now that much more under control.

That is how fear and angry generalized (stereotyping) bias can manifest. How about trauma and generalized bias? Once again, 9/11 is a perfect example. While virtually all Americans were traumatized by the events of 9/11, some were traumatized to such a degree that they formed strong hateful biases not only against Osama bin Laden and al Qaeda but also against all Muslims, seeing all of them as terrorists. The trauma induced by the singular Islamist 9/11 terrorist act led to the generalizing stereotyping hateful bias that all Muslims are terrorists and all Muslim crimes—any unlawful events carried out by someone with an Arabic surname—are acts of terrorism. Once again, this hateful stereotyping bias actually had the effect of calming the intense feelings of 9/11 trauma they (the biased ones) had been experiencing. In this same vein, for example, it seemed to many similarly biased

Americans that the San Bernardino workplace shooting and the Orlando gay nightclub shooting must have been acts of Muslim terrorism as opposed to, say, heinous murderous acts carried out by psychologically disturbed individuals who, *after the fact,* happened to rationalize a devotion to Islam as their motivation, but who beforehand were actually motivated by a desire to settle some imagined score—in the first instance, with his workplace fellows and, in the second, with the gay public who triggered the shooter's conflicted homosexual feelings and subsequent self-loathing. Unwilling to entertain the actual motivations as even remote possibilities, the hateful and stereotyping biased population interpreted the shootings as being more acts of Islamic terrorism, thereby confirming their already strong generalized hateful bias. Having the generalized bias that these were both acts of Islamic terrorism had the effect of then calming their sense of feeling re-traumatized (in a 9/11 way) by these shootings. It is as though, if one could jump to the conclusion (via the generalized bias) of who the perpetrator was, then one would not have to feel the trauma as much as one would otherwise feel it.

It's obvious to me how many of these kinds of fear- and trauma-defending strong biases behave on the liberation frontier. If an anti-minority liberationist, for example, happens to be motivated primarily by fear of the liberationist "other" (however it is that he's come by that fear), then he is bound to bring with him some strong biases—all too often taking the form of hateful bigotry—against the liberationist "other" and all similar "others" as a way of mitigating for himself the severity of his fear. This is clearly the case for so many anti-liberation racists, where their irrational fears of people of color are most definitely distracted or deflected—dampened—by their hateful, and what they perceive to be righteous, anti-rights rants against those same people of color. As for what happens on the liberation frontier when the anti-liberationist has been traumatized by a liberationist "other," examples are not as easy to come by. Liberationists don't typically go out of their way to traumatize anti-liberationists. That said, there nevertheless are anti-liberationists who feel traumatized, if not by liberationists then by people with whom the liberationists are associated. Again, consider the example of 9/11: anti-liberationists certainly were as traumatized by the events as the rest of us. There's no doubt that many of them were precisely the people who responded to their trauma by forming the kinds of hateful biases against all Muslims that we just discussed. There's also no doubt that, were any liberationist to champion the cause of religious tolerance for Muslims, he would be met with extreme angry biased opposition by the anti-liberationist. The liberationist here was not part of the circumstances that induced trauma in the anti-liberationist, but to the extent that he now is associated with a cause working in the name of the people the anti-liberationist so vehemently hates (Muslims), the liberationist is nevertheless inadvertently re-traumatizing the anti-liberationist and inviting anti-liberationist hateful bias. The anti-liberationist's now being able to spread his hatred and what he perceives as righteous anger to an even wider target than before (now he is aimed at both Muslims and their liberation advocates) further distracts and deflects, calming his feelings of trauma.

Trying to put the shoe on the other foot now by looking for parallel fear- and trauma-defending strong biases on the part of the liberation advocate can go only so far. Liberationists are not normally motivated by fear of the anti-liberationist; by disgust maybe, but typically not by fear. But while fear is not typically part of equation, trauma induced by anti-liberationists against liberationists often enough is. I am thinking specifically of the liberation advocates who are members of a minority group that has been repeatedly victimized by anti-liberationist bigoted behavior and attitude to the point of inducing a sense of trauma. With this kind of trauma having played out so extensively in the victim group's past, it would be hard to imagine that its members would not respond with trauma-motivated bias against the anti-liberationist and the entire anti-liberation project. Nevertheless, one would still hope that reason and consciousness-raising would play a more central role than trauma-related bias does in this liberationist advocate's encounters with the anti-liberationist. That is, although trauma and the biases attached to it are certainly difficult to overcome or mitigate, that doesn't mean that a victim of trauma cannot also appeal to reason and consciousness-raising when advocating on the rights frontier. Indeed, to be a genuine advocate there would seem to require as much.[4]

(3) Biases that anchor self-identity

Let's look at the third kind of strong, change-resistant bias. This bias concerns a person's sense of identity, her sense of self. For many people, when they are living out their strongly held biases, they are fully and unapologetically being their authentic selves. Many Second Amendment supporters, for example, can't easily give up their identity-related bias for owning guns. What a comfortable place to reside; it's psychological honey. Any interference with this comfort zone is a cause for distress that people do all they can to prevent. We can extrapolate from this the following idea: *the degree of resistance to changing any given bias largely depends on the degree to which that bias is anchored in a sense of identity.*

---

[4] What's good for the goose.... What I mean is that if we can imagine a liberationist overcoming his trauma to the point where he can become rational in his dealings with the anti-liberationist, then theoretically so too can we imagine a traumatized anti-liberationist overcoming his trauma and becoming rational in his dealings with the liberationist. Theoretically this is true. It is just that as a matter of empirical fact, we rarely see the latter play out, while we often see the former occur.

Of course, not all of a person's biases are related to their identity or sense of self. But for the ones that are, this idea most definitely applies. In the case of anti-liberationists, the degree of the bias held is often extreme and deep-rooted. For example, the gun rights advocate is so identified with her bias in favor of a literal interpretation of the Second Amendment that it fully feels to her like an *essential* characteristic of who she is. And although it's not totally impossible, it's terribly difficult to challenge oneself to change when "this is who I am." In fact, that is the most demanding context in which people might even conceivably challenge themselves, because, in the extreme, the integrity—the experienced wholeness or unity—of the entire sense of self would be on the line. And, without a doubt, the integrity of a person's sense of self is our most prized psychological possession. Nevertheless, sometimes others will challenge our strong biases because they have perhaps equally strong *opposing biases* that anchor the integrity of *their own* sense of self. They might take umbrage at a particular strong bias that we've made public. And much to our chagrin, we are now forced to reflect on the bias in question; the integrity of our sense of self really *is* on the line. So, even though we reflect some on our bias, it isn't too long before we stop reflecting and begin to double down on our strong bias as a way of keeping our sense of ourselves intact.

A good example—one that will have special resonance for us later in the book—has to do with a person's principles. Principles are strongly-held, biased ideas that anchor a person's sense of self; they often come into play when someone else insists that contrary principles (which anchor their own sense of identity) should win the day in a dispute. We see this occur in liberation contexts when conservatives and liberals argue from their respective (biased) guiding principles. For example, the conservative will insist that questions of liberation need always pass through the filter of the principles of freedom and personal responsibility. She so self-identifies with these biases that she can't imagine settling questions of ideological policy without passing them through this filter. Likewise, many liberals insist that questions of liberation pass through their filter of the principles of minority equality and ever-expanding rights claims for all citizens. These are important biases that define their sense of self and must be addressed if they are to feel whole. It's theoretically possible that there might be the rare occasion where both of these conservative and liberal political actors could be satisfied. That is to say, questions of liberation might get settled in such a way so as to allow the conservative to see that the principles of freedom and personal responsibility have been served, while allowing the liberal to see that the principles of minority equality and ever-expanding rights claims for all have been served. More often, however, one of the two sides will not be satisfied. If, for example, they are looking at liberation ideology specifically in the context of the need to pass legislation for expanding welfare for the poor, the conservative will insist that in the name of principled "personal responsibility," we refrain from passing such legislation. The liberal, on the other hand, insists that in the name of the principles of social justice and equality, we pass the legislation. The issue on both sides is wrapped up in how their respective principles help define who they are; they will fight tooth and nail to preserve their identities as expressed by these positions.

We will see in the ensuing chapters how these along with other kinds of self-identity-defining biases play a decidedly oversized role in the debates between liberationists and their critics and the debates between political correctness advocates and their critics.

(4) Biases motivated by the need to socially belong

A fourth kind of strong bias is conditioned by a variety of social forces; the kind of change-resistant bias that begins in childhood as a simple though powerful mirroring phenomenon—specifically, the socially-attaching child's repeated imitation of the values she sees in the world around her. This repeated imitation (mirroring) constitutes the first iteration of a strong bias. Later, with the unfolding of still other social forces throughout childhood, adolescence and adulthood, the mirroring turns into biases that are even more impressively resistant to change.

During infancy and early childhood, we humans take our first (unconscious) stab at psychological attachment to others[5]—usually attachment to mother, other caregivers, siblings, authority figures, peers and eventually, to the culture-at-large. This is our first taste of sociality. One way in which the infant/child socially attaches to these other important characters is by way of forming primitive mirroring value biases. During infancy/childhood, we form biases that typically mirror the value norms of our parents and other authority figures. We copy in these primitive biases that which we see in the world around us, as a way of attaching to that world and becoming empowered by it. Once psychologically attached, we do everything in our power to maintain that connection through our primitive mirroring of value biases. That's a given about our sociality. It's also a given that these biases go unchallenged. Because the world (culture, parents, etc.) typically doesn't challenge its own value norms (being norms, they are experienced as *givens*), neither do we as children who mirror them as value biases. A person doesn't have to be a psychoanalyst

---

[5] There are whole literatures about "attachment theory" in psychoanalysis in particular and in psychology more broadly speaking. Obviously, those are beyond the scope of this book. My few words here about it will in fact suffice for my purpose.

to know the psychological truth that the more any such states go unchallenged, the more they get deeply ingrained in our psyche and the more resistant to change they become.

In sum, then, in the service of social attachment, people from their earliest days onward form, maintain and protect their most primitive mirroring change-resistant biases. Clear examples of this kind of socially conditioned bias can be seen among racists and sexists on the one hand (negative bias) and among idealists of various stripes on the other (positive bias). For many people, their racism or sexism took shape in their formative years as mirroring biases they copied from their immediate environment, from people who were important to them. Wanting to be attached to and just like his racist mom or sexist dad, the youngster mirrors these traits as perfectly as he can. Idealism may start out in a similar manner. Wanting to be attached to and just like her brave and loving mom or dad, for example, the youngster tries to mirror the trait her parents embody.

Soon enough, as we work our way through childhood, adolescence and into adulthood, our biases deepen even more with the introduction of other social factors. One of those has to do with the notion of social bonds. This initially appears to be simply a dressed-up version of primitive attachment, but actually, being attached and being socially bonded in fact are two different things. This is a subtle but genuine distinction. Primitive attachment is about wanting to become part of someone or something external to ourselves by taking in, as a *new* part of ourselves, part of who they are—in this case, taking in their value norms to become our new primitive value biases. Bonding with someone, on the other hand, happens by our sharing something *already established* in us—say, sharing already established beliefs and biases in common. It isn't about wanting to take in something from another person in order to make it a new part of ourselves but rather to take something the two of us already have in common and celebrate our commonality. The experience of bonding through sharing what is common to us is a basic social *desideratum* for everyone. This is as true about our shared biases as it is about any other shared ways of being. Sharing our biases with others solidifies our sense of *kinship* with them—with our culture, our family, our group of friends. Feeling these social bonds is another crucial part of anyone's essential humanity, the stuff that makes a person a person. It defines the closeness of relationships for us as social beings, something we all aim for. Because of this social force, then, most of us find bias change in this context extremely difficult. That is certainly true of anti-liberationists and their ideological kin who are typically loath to dropping their biases. And it is just as true for liberation advocates and their ideological cohort.

There's another social condition supported by strong biases that builds on what we have discussed. Most people actively *affirm* and *support* one another by applying shared value biases in making value judgments about other people. Sometimes a defining aspect of a given community will be precisely those value biases, the biases about others that we hold in mutual communal affirmation. Sharing biases in this way has the effect of bolstering one another's commitment to our biases. A feedback loop is created in which the sharing of biases has the effect of mutually reinforcing them and, accordingly, further strengthening and deepening our community biases. Interestingly, when people organize their sense of community around their biases, the community often enough will have developed a kind of shared shorthand for expressing those biases. We notice this when two people who totally affirm one another through their shared bias, merely have to look at each other's facial expression (maybe a subtle smile or wink) to see the common biased attitude they both have about some third person in their presence who is not a member of their preferred value bias community. No words need be spoken. We all know "the look" that affirms we're on the same team; a sense of ease comes from this sharing of value bias. Think, for example, of two racists in the presence of a person of color. Or think of what silently passes between the eyes of two conservative anti-liberationists while they listen to what some liberation advocate has to say. And think of what is conveyed but unspoken between two liberals while they listen to what a conservative anti-liberationist has to say. That is the force behind sharing mutually affirming biases.

Some General Observations About Change-Resistance

There you have it—four basic kinds of strong bias. While there are many other kinds of strong bias, in the context of the PC and liberation issues we're looking at in this book, these are the four that are most important for us to understand. Before we get to see how they play out in those issues, however, I want to make some final observations about the change-resistance nature of all four kinds of biases.

I hope it's obvious that all of these biases serve to support the various psychological and social conditions that, as we have seen, are related to them (e.g. biases motivated by the need to socially belong, biases that anchor one's identity, and so on). Moreover, depending on the degree of importance these psychological and social conditions have to a person, the biases supporting them will to a comparable degree become *change-resistant*—i.e. they will to that degree become stronger or weaker. So, if, for example, a given bias thoroughly anchors a person's sense of identity, then the bias's resistance to change will be quite high. If it doesn't serve as a thoroughgoing identity anchor, it won't be quite so resistant to change. If kinship is very important to a person, then those shared biases that cement it for her with another person will be to that degree resistant to change. If sharing that bias with another person is not so important, then the shared bias will not, at least for that reason, be quite so resistant to change. And so it goes in a similar vein for a person's biases and the rest of these psychological and social conditions.

There are a few relevant corollaries to this idea. One is that while there are degrees of change-resistance in every bias, all four kinds of bias contain what I call an inherent base level strength; they are all *strong* biases. As a matter of empirical fact, because the psychological and social conditions I have pointed out in this chapter all have a base level genuine importance in any person's life—soothing fear and trauma, anchoring identity, etc. are genuinely important issues for everybody—then all the biases that support them have a comparable base level degree of strength to them. Then, beyond that base level degree of strength for a given bias, its strength will increase (and never decrease below the base level degree) depending on the increased degree of its importance to psychological and social conditions.

I hope it is also obvious as another corollary that any of these strong biases can vary in depth (beyond the base level) from person to person. Psychological and social force considerations are different for each of us and so the degree of strength of a given bias can vary in a like manner between different people. Moreover, within the lifetime of any given person, the strength of any particular bias can vary from one occasion to another, depending on the changing behavior or the psychological or social conditions that her biases support.

The final corollary is an educated speculation on my part regarding ranking the susceptibility of a bias to change. Admittedly, this is based entirely on my clinical experience with observing these sorts of things in action. If there are studies regarding the same, I'm not aware of them. In any case, taken with the appropriate grain of salt, I would say that, to the degree that any of these biases are ever even *slightly* susceptible to change, the mirroring attachment bias is most susceptible. It's not *prima facie* susceptible; but it is susceptible under the right circumstances. I believe that in the realm of liberation debates, whenever someone with strong anti-liberation biases has been won over to the side of liberation, that person is usually someone whose strong anti-liberation biases were mirrored in childhood. They were anchored simply by the desire to be like some important person in their life. That is certainly a powerful motivation for most people; nevertheless, I have seen this kind of motivated bias crack, usually because the individual has been mirroring parental *behavior*, but with no internal attitudinal malice supporting it. For example, someone might say and do racially insensitive things—he might verbally behave and act as a racist, but with no actual racial fear, wholehearted disapproval, or internal racist anger or hatred behind any of it. He simply does what he does out of a mirroring behavioral habit formed long ago in support of his attachment to, say, one of his parents. This kind of biased behavior is not easy to change, but certainly possible. On the other hand, were this behavior supported by mirrored biased cultural attitudes and beliefs as well, change would be a far more difficult proposition but still possible. So, yes, any mirroring attachment bias is powerful, but, under the right conditions, is susceptible to change. And among all the change-resistant biases, I've seen these as being the most susceptible.

I won't expand clinically anymore on what I believe allows the other strong biases to be at all susceptible to change. And I won't go into the "why" of my ranking that susceptibility. All I'll do now is simply state the rest of the ranking as follows: after mirroring attachment biases, those next most susceptible to change are the shared biases that lead to a sense of social bonding and kinship, followed by shared biases that are mutually reinforced between people. Next would be biases that serve to distract and soothe feelings of fear or trauma, followed by biases that support a person's pre-existing wholehearted approval or disapproval of some persons or things. The least susceptible to change would be the biases that anchor a person's sense of self. Again, I am simply referencing my clinical experience. That certainly doesn't constitute an argument; I offer it only as something to chew on.

And with that, I conclude this chapter's discussion of strong biases. As I say, going forward, we will see the various roles they play in the kinds of debates that PC/minority liberation advocates and critics get embroiled in. Before we get to any of that, however, there is one final matter to discuss that I think will be important to more fully appreciate those PC and liberation debates. We go to this now.

CHAPTER 4

Culture-at-Large and Subcultures

The final matter that needs to be taken care of before we look head-on at the clash between the anti-PC critics and the pro-PC liberationists has to do with the general concept of the *culture-at-large*. In this chapter I will clarify both the concept and the connections between the culture-at-large and the other central concepts we've discussed up to this point.

The culture-at-large is a major ingredient in determining when a person is being politically correct or not. This is true by the very definition of PC we settled on in Chapter 1. The culture-at-large is one of the entities—along with the levers of power exerted by the judiciary and the political leadership—that through its full embrace of a given ideology, endows any person who champions that culture-at-large embraced ideology with political correctness. Obviously, then, when the anti-PC critic challenges the very idea of political correctness, he also challenges the culture-at-large that partly defines it. Best, then, that we be clear on what this central defining piece of political correctness is all about.

Building on our discussion about strong biases, we can think of a culture-at-large as constituted by the shared change-resistant biases that the bulk of the nation's citizenry hold at a given point in time regarding various aspects of various ideologies of the day. There is a sense of ease or comfortable social flow to these biases, contributing to a general spirit or mood of the nation—a *zeitgeist*. Together, these biases constitute a national web of sorts;

what is sometimes referred to as a nation's *mainstream thinking*, the thinking of "the people."

The weave of that web of biases is made of various interlacing threads. These threads consist of various bias *traditions* (e.g. the shared celebration of specific historical figures and events) and various bias *norms*. Among the norms are the people's shared *social custom* biases (for instance, a shared respect for national institutions such as the F.B.I. and news organizations,[1] a people's civil behavior toward one another, the kinds of language and logic the preponderance of people use in public discourse, the kinds of clothes that are currently fashionable); the people's shared bias toward certain *principles* (e.g., liberty, egalitarianism); the people's shared bias for certain *moral ideals* (the golden rule, the sanctity of the greater good); their shared bias toward various *economic, political and social ideologies* (such as biasedly favoring capitalism, democracy, minority liberation). These are but a few of the threads of our particular cultural web.

The shared threads of the biases of any culture create a singular whole web. Were one to pull hard enough on any one of them—in the sense of trying to damage or remove it from the overall woven product—that would have the effect of stressing the other threads to some degree. But at the same time, because all the threads together make for a tight weave, when one of them is stressed, the tight fit of the overall web tends to bring the errant thread back into place. It takes a lot to successfully destroy the national web of biases constituting our national traditions and norms. Put another way, the predisposition of any culture-at-large is for its prevailing tradition and norm strong biases to remain comfortably in place for the general citizenry, thereby successfully resisting

---

[1] Clearly, those two institutions have been under a withering attack by President Trump, but as of this writing it seems that, in mainstream thinking, they have so far withstood his barrage.

change. Most notable among the conditions that explain the tenaciousness of these biases are the social bonding and mutual affirmation such biases promote for the general citizenry. The critical mass of the culture-at-large—the mainstream, the people— maintain a kind of tradition/norm *inertia*; pointedly, a tradition or norm at rest relative to the culture-at-large tends to stay at rest. It's tough to supplant them once the great preponderance of citizens puts its stamp of approval on them. They are change-resistant.

Understand, too, that these truths about biases that are embraced by the culture-at-large are change-resistant bias *tendencies* only. Inertial rest is just a tendency. So although any of these cultural biases may be change-resistant, it's inevitable that some of them will eventually change. No cultural bias is fixed forevermore; any culture-at-large *vis-à-vis* its biases is *always evolving*. From the long view, a culture-at-large is always changing—at least incrementally—even though from up close it appears to be static. Historically, for example, certain culturally entrenched fashion biases eventually if slowly fall out of favor. People sometimes simply get bored with them—say, biases about the use of certain fashionable terminologies or slang ("Cool, man." "Twenty-three skidoo!") or about the current state of clothing fashion (zoot suits, bustles) or even once common yet mildly offensive fashionable slurs against minorities or women (which we need not mention). When a critical mass of the culture-at-large incrementally loses interest in these biases as bonding and mutually affirming social coinage, the biases fall by the wayside, leaving the culture-at-large to be defined by their remaining shared biases. This describes what I would call a relatively benign evolution of the culture-at-large.

But there's more to cultural evolution than benign activity. There always seem to be *new* candidate biases vying for eventual majority acceptance into the shared social flow, replacing certain of the current entrenched biases. Some of them are *consistent* with the current crop of biases overall, while some are not. In the former case, the new biases' eventual absorption into the culture-at-large usually happens without much fanfare because they fit in seamlessly, consistent with the existing culturally accepted biases. As more and more members of the culture, for their own individual reasons, adopt these new biases, a critical mass is eventually reached, and the biases are absorbed into the culture-at-large. By contrast, when vying biases are *not* consistent with elements of the existing culturally absorbed biases, they only succeed in becoming part of the culture-at-large if there is first a severe *disturbance* or *rupture* that calls into question and finally overwhelms and replaces some of the culturally reigning biases that are in opposition to the new competitors. Indeed, we've seen just such a turn of events in our nation in the recent past. Traumatic events such as war, economic depression, an out-of-control pandemic, the sudden appearance (shocking to the racist) of a black President of the United States and the subsequent appearance of a charismatic demagogue to fan the flames against him—have been some of the more recent ruptures. An extreme national paranoia about foreign enemies, terrorists and domestic subversion, along with a deep cultural divide leading to an intense distrust between broad swathes of fellow citizens, along with unceasing challenges to the sanctity of news reporting and our political institutions, are all cases of disturbances that have laid the foundation for a serious challenge to some of the old-guard biases of the culture-at-large.

Not only are the conditions of rupture and disturbance the most instrumental factors for the replacement of culturally reigning biases, the number of people holding the replacement biases matters, too. Any biases considered serious contenders for eventual inclusion in the culture-at-large are already held by large numbers of people, although not large enough to constitute a majority or critical mass, and so, not large enough to warrant inclusion in the general social bias flow of a nation. We say the population holding these vying biases constitutes a *subculture* that's defined by their holding of these biases, with its own smaller web of intermeshing bias threads.

I think there are some obvious observations we can make about how this understanding of the culture-at-large plays into the history of liberation ideology as well as on the current cultural scene. A majority bias toward a liberation mentality has had a firm foothold in the psyche of the culture-at-large going back to the 1960s. But the forces opposing this mind-set—most notably, those triggered by the twin social rupture events of 9/11 and its terrorist aftermath events, along with the economic depression events of 2007—2009 and their unemployment aftermath events, as well as the other triggering disturbances as listed above—now constitute a sizable portion of America[2]—not sizable enough to call it an attribute of the culture-at-large, but certainly enough to call it a powerful, oppositional subculture if not yet an ideological *zeitgeist*. Some of the subculture's inhabitants are clearly made up of all the anti-liberationists I cited in many of my examples in Chapter 3. Unhappily (for my taste), their numbers seem to be growing. Indeed, many of them tipped the scales in favor of Mr. Trump in the last presidential election. It's precisely because their numbers are now so great and their voices so loud that many social commentators refer to today's America as fully *polarized* regarding many political issues, not the least of which includes liberation ideology and minority rights. Importantly, the liberationists on balance (but only marginally) still control the levers of political power in the form of a bare preponderance of rights-

---

[2] I will be pointing out yet other factors in the chapters to come.

friendly people in national elected office, minority rights in-scribed law and Supreme Court rights-favoring decisions (although clearly with the ascendance of Mr. Gorsuch and Mr. Kavanaugh, it's anyone's guess as to whether the Court will continue to affirm minority rights claims). If the current bare preponder-ance of people and institutions favoring the rights of minorities were to change, it would go a long way toward anti-liberation ideology replacing the liberation mentality in the culture-at-large. Certainly it would indicate that the anti-liberation subcul-ture had become the ideology of the majority and that the other less official expressions of popular culture biases—ordinary citi-zen's beliefs and attitudes about minority rights being assumed as givens or not, the general news reporting slant regarding daily rights activity, etc.—were supplanted by a national wave of ordi-nary citizen's behavior, beliefs and attitudes expressing anti-liberation ideology…thus rendering liberationists a strong but relatively ineffective minority subgroup in America. The anti-liberationists would become the new inhabitants of the culture-at-large. And if the commentators on Fox New have anything to say about it—and it seems that they do have a lot to say about it—then these matters are closer than ever before to coming to fruition.

Of course, none of this has happened yet and, hopefully, rights-favoring citizens will become reinvigorated and rededicate them-selves in fending off the anti-liberation throng; for the latter have made it known in no uncertain terms that they are coming. They are pounding at the door of the culture-at-large with a heavy fist. "Change and replace" is their unspoken (well, sometime spoken) battle cry. They would like nothing better than to destroy libera-tion ideology and replace it with their own.[3] As we will see in Part

---

[3] This terminology sounds eerily familiar; a lot like those unsuccessful Republican at-tempts a few years ago to "repeal and replace" the Affordable Care Act. Their mantra:

II, for some, the replacement culture is all about a return to unbridled bigotry while for others, it's a return to certain conservative principles that they see as incompatible with liberation. In the process of pressing the case for social liberation's replacement, all of these people take dead aim at destroying the concept of political correctness that up until now has been a favorite rhetorical device for liberationists silencing the more offending bigoted aspects of anti-liberation ideology. They have all joined the battle.

One final point about culture-at-large: as I reminded us at the beginning of this chapter, a person behaves in a way that's politically correct when he is acting consistently with an ideology embraced by the culture-at-large and by the government's political establishment and judiciary. That said, I would stipulate that, while each of these three public entities embracing politically correct ideologies is a distinct player in the ideological dramas that have unfolded in our nation's history, I think the culture-at-large has been the main player. Like the general citizenry, most leaders and public figures get swept up in the strongly biased social flow of any culture-at-large ideology. When push comes to shove—although not always the case, but often enough—our politicians and jurists will first look to see which way the ideological winds are blowing in the culture-at-large and then determine how to adjust themselves to align with and advocate for those ideologies in order to stay in step with mainstream culture and truly represent the constituency. With this idea in mind, then...from now on, when I talk about these three public entities promoting politically correct ideologies, I will normally place my main focus on the role that the culture-at-large plays and only secondarily on the role played by the formal branches of government.

"Citizens don't have the *right* to healthcare." This is, in fact, a particular example of the broader concept—i.e. "repealing" the ideology of social liberation—that I'm talking about here.

Finally, with all that we've said about social liberation, strong biases and culture-at-large as a background—we are prepared to tackle the central concern of this book: political correctness. Any full understanding of this concept will require that we observe it where it lives; that we appreciate the cultural and political air, both clean and foul, that it breathes in the rough and tumble of our everyday life. And so, we'll turn our attention to an excursion into the history of liberation movements that embrace political correctness and upon which so many anti-liberation critics over the years have feasted. We will see the ways in which strong bias has impacted the whole scene, how the biases of anti-PC and liberation's critics have faced off against the biases of politically correct liberation ideology. We will look at how the forces of anti-liberation—in the persons of principled conservatives as well as bigoted racists, misogynists and homophobes—have done their worst in opposing the acceptance of rights for minority peoples that the culture-at-large champions; and we will see how the forces of liberation have answered their challenge. Lastly, I will add my two cents about why I think it is so very important that the anti-PC voices and the critics of minority liberation *must* be defeated if our nation is to survive.

PART II

The Conservative Complaint
Against Political Correctness

Getting the General Lay of the Land: The Central Thesis of the War Against Political Correctness

A s I did previously, I will begin this chapter by reminding us of what political correctness means. It is a person, through his behavior, beliefs and attitudes, showing respect and full support of the prevailing ideologies embraced by a nation—the legislation that upholds it, the courts that systematically rule in its favor and the culture-at-large. The latter refers to how those ideologies have been woven into a broad array of norms and traditions that are generally accepted by and absorbed into the lives of the great preponderance of citizens. It is in the air, as it were—on the social winds. It is a nation's *zeitgeist*.

Now, as it turns out, *prior* to the 1960s, when minority rights liberation ideology emerged on the cultural and political scene, the terms "politically correct" and "political correctness" did not enjoy much usage in the vernacular other than what I noted in Chapter 1 about the early Communists' celebration of their ideology and later, the sarcastic American disparagement of that same Communist ideology. Nevertheless, the *concept* or idea of political correctness *has always been in force in our nation's history*, even if it has not always been publicly designated by the term. Since our nation's founding, national ideologies have always come in and out of fashion in the political, judicial and cultural arenas, and there has always been a great preponderance of citizens whose behavior, beliefs and attitudes were consistent with upholding those ideologies; people were politically correct, even if they didn't use the term to designate this condition they in fact were exhibiting.

Among the bigoted ideologies that had always enjoyed large-scale acceptance were sexism and misogyny against women; a racist ideology that celebrated the superiority of white Anglo-Americans over the newly arriving immigrant minorities and over the people of color who were already living here; and the anti-Semitic ideology that has always dogged the Jewish community the world over. In time, the newly arriving white immigrant minorities would join the Anglo whites in touting their own gender, racial and religious superiority; white, male and Christian supremacy would rule the culture. Not only were these ideologies of discrimination quite firmly entrenched as cultural norms—*givens*—but neither did most politicians nor the court system do much to dissuade people from these ways of thinking. Some even enacted laws or interpreted existing laws to further cement the various causes of bigotry. Of course, there were always pockets of people who went against the grain, arguing for the rights of minorities and women—the pre-Civil War abolitionists and the 19th—20th-century suffragists, for example. But these moments paled in comparison to the thoroughgoing racism, sexism and misogyny that predominated the culture, males insisting with a wink and a smile that a woman always defer to their men and demanding that black folks "know their place."

There was that singular moment in our nation's history when the official national government position against slavery led to a Civil War. Unfortunately, there was no accompanying national effort to eradicate the ideology of bigoted racism. The slaves were freed, but they were still culturally shackled as inferiors by all the ideological players; and there were many Jim Crow laws put in place that guaranteed maintaining their second-class status. The attitudes, behavior, and beliefs of the general population were totally in alignment with this. And then there's the history of our ongoing anti-Semitism. Until relatively recently, Jews would only be allowed admittance to many popular institutions in accordance with strict quotas (neighborhoods, universities, country clubs, political appointment, and so on).[1] The last 60 years have been a pocket in time in this country in which Jews haven't had to concern themselves very much about discrimination. But clearly that window is rapidly closing.

Long story short: for a good part of our history, *being a bigot was politically correct*. While bigotries as prevailing national ideologies were in their heyday, the forces opposing them (during the aforementioned pockets in time) were nothing more than relatively silent subcultures that posed no serious threat to the reigning bigoted ideologies. However, matters started to change following the Second World War. The first serious challenges to bigoted ideologies began with the landmark ruling *Brown v. Board of Education* of 1954; the emergence of the 1960s Black Civil Rights Movement; and all the other social liberation movements that soon followed, not the least of which was the feminist movement in reaction to sexism and misogyny. Anti-Semitism had receded temporarily to the background of national consciousness. *Publicly* advocating for bigoted ideologies was no longer considered politically correct; advocating for social liberation eventually took its place as the presiding ideology of the culture-at-large. When this happened, a person became something of a pariah if he

---

[1] Even more egregious were anti-Semitic political actions such as Lindberg's popular America First Committee, committed to keeping Jews from immigrating to our shores. This movement was a reaction to what its advocates saw as the Jews having already "infected" the body politic by gaining monopolies in our banking institutions, the news media and Hollywood. Sound familiar? The more things change, the more they stay the same. Lindberg is clearly a hero of Donald Trump's. Indeed, a couple of years ago we heard from the white supremacists in Charlottesville (some of whom Mr. Trump famously referred to as "very fine people") that "Jews will not replace us."

spouted bigoted views too openly; it was considered poor form. Even for conservatives, touting liberal social attitudes became the new cultural norm—proclaiming, for example, "Some of my best friends are black (or female or Jewish)," even if one actually remained bigoted to the core.

Bad form or not, acceding social power to the advocates of minority liberation wasn't in the cards as far as the more virulent forces of bigotry were concerned. Bigotry, an abiding national ideology for so much of our history, refused to go quietly. In the early days of minority liberation activism, while the open national embrace of bigotry began to weaken, bigots fought hard to maintain dominance over the national psyche by portraying liberation activists as anti-American brutes—perhaps even Communists— hell-bent on destroying the country's (white, male and Christian) social and political structure. The national psyche was changing, however; the headwinds of liberation were too great to overcome. Having lost for the moment the battle for the conscience of the culture-at-large, bigotry nevertheless would proceed with what first started out as a rearguard assault but in short order returned as unapologetic head-on open assaults against minority social liberation. The committed attempt to slow the progress of minority liberation has been an uninterrupted undying passion of many of our citizens and remains so to this day. In the early days (the 1960s and '70s), their scornful mocking of the culture-at-large's enthusiastic embrace of liberation ideology was seen as the vapid behavior of "bleeding heart liberals," as though liberationists were nothing but a gaggle of irrational, overly-emotional ideologues of misplaced altruism, blind to the havoc their thinking was wreaking on the country. In time, the "bleeding heart" rhetorical battering device would give way to the "you're just *too* PC" mantra. Bigots shifted their attention from anti-liberation *per se* to anti-PC *per se*. As if these constant drumbeats of bigoted derision weren't enough, the bigots were joined by anti-PC fellow travelers in the persons of *principled* conservatives who upped the anti-PC, anti-liberation ante considerably by taking at least a pose of leaving bigotry in the shadows[2] and actually mounting reasoned principled arguments against the perceived enemy, political correctness.

This activity of PC disparagement, both by bigots and by some principled conservatives, seems very suspicious. There was never *any* popular objection to political correctness as a *concept* by these people or anyone else *until* the minority social liberation challenges to bigoted anti-minority discrimination began gathering steam, both on the political stage and in the imagination of the general culture-at-large. When bigotry had before been a reigning ideology in the culture-at-large, it was more than acceptable to these people (the bigots) that one be politically correct—i.e. that one proudly support the ideological norms. That's what being a good citizen demands and, of course, in the bigots' eyes, they were only being good citizens, doing all they could to keep their inferiors from polluting the cultural and political gene pool that white America had fought so valiantly in our short history to protect. It was only when social minority liberation came on the scene that these people, along with their principled conservative allies, got riled up about the PC concept and decided to turn it on its head, into a pejorative notion; interesting timing. The aim of conservatives has been clear: they have simply wanted to develop another rhetorical cudgel (the heir to "bleeding heart liberalism") to wield on the forces of minority social liberation.

This brings me to my central thesis about what's behind the conservative attack against political correctness as a viable

---

[2] As I will point out in Chapter 7, some principled conservatives are motivated in their anti-PC stance solely on principle, while others (the ones who are posing as people of principles) talk about principles while masking their underlying bigoted feelings.

concept in public discourse. There are three aims to all anti-PC ranting, three tracks on which all anti-PC action is found.

On the first track, the anti-PC activity consists of conservative bigots advancing *ad hominem* attacks against the idea of political correctness *per se* along with their efforts to make the concept and term seem so noxious to the body politic that, because of PC's association with minority liberation, the minority liberation well becomes *poisoned* in the public's mind. The dedicated aim is to destroy the concept of PC along with the public's confidence in minority liberation ideology; nothing subtle here.

The second track *is* subtle. It's a kind of subterfuge, actually. On this track, the anti-PC bigot's over-the-top angry *ad hominem* noise is really aimed at getting the public to be so focused on the evils of political correctness that it won't recognize the awful savaging that he is doing off to the side about minority liberation ideology. *Look here*—at the disgusting idea of PC—*don't look there*—at how I've all along been ravaging the worth of minority liberation ideology. On this track, attacking political correctness is a *smokescreen* for the attack against the real enemy: minority liberation. I believe that, when all is said and done, the *main* reason why the idea of political correctness has been so focused on and incessantly criticized by many of the conservative bigots is that it serves as a good whipping boy in place of the real target of minority liberation ideology.

And this takes us to the third track. Here, the anti-PC conservative *openly* attacks minority liberation ideology. No smokescreens. This track is populated by three sorts of political actors. One kind is the conservative who argues openly and dispassionately against both PC and minority liberation on principles, the principled conservative. Another kind is the unapologetic hateful conservative bigot who, unlike the bigots on track 2, has never in the first place felt tempted to hide his feelings of disgust for PC, minorities and the liberation ideologies they espouse. The third kind of political actor is the bigot whose previous comfort zone *had* been in making angry anti-PC noise as a smokescreen for his true feelings but who now has chosen to leave all of that behind and instead engages his disgust with political correctness, minorities and liberation ideology out in the open.

Interestingly, many of these third track bigots feel deeply victimized by the social expectation that their feelings stay in the shadows; by having to bow to the cultural prominence of PC and liberation ideology. In reaction to this unwanted expectation, they center their attention on openly loathing political correctness and minority liberation ideology. All things PC and liberation-related are definitely on their minds. For many other bigots of this third track ilk however, thinking about PC at all simply falls away, leaving them to focus their conscious venom on the real enemy, minority liberation ideology. Political correctness no longer plays any part in the equation. They might in passing complain *pro forma* about PC; but that's no longer where the action is for them. Instead, their focus is squarely on opposing liberation ideologies. In terms of public displays of anti-liberation bigoted attitudes and behaviors in this country, there's not really an inch of distance between them and the bigots of yore, prior to the coinage of the term "political correctness."

In any case, the overriding goal of this three-track project is to so destroy the public's confidence in political correctness that the minority liberation ideology it supports will be ripe for displacing with anti-minority liberation as the preferred national ideology. Conservative bigotry, which has always been alive and well in our country, will—to the extent that it has been in the shadows for the past 60 years or so—finally be able to come out of those shadows and once again reign supreme.

Let me flesh out a little more here the critic's three-track strategy, understanding that a full discussion will take place in the rest of the book. Recalling Chapter 1, track 1 refers to the idea that the anti-PC bigoted critic begins by mounting her ceaseless abusive *ad hominem* attacks against the idea of PC *per se*. With anger and contempt, she sarcastically levels the charge, "I know it's not politically correct, but...." (Meaning "it's just *too* PC.") She turns PC on its head, taking the old laudatory sense of the term—when competing intramural schools of a given ideology would proudly vie for whose programs and policies were more praiseworthy and ideologically pure and therefore most politically correct—and transforms the concept into a pejorative one. Suddenly, there's something very wrong with being politically correct. The bigoted critic uses the term as a defamatory shaming device, exposing it as a shibboleth of old liberal thinking that's no longer deserving of respect. The very way she suffuses her speech with sarcasm and contorts her face with contempt when she utters, "you're just *too* PC" is an attempt to silence those who insist on political correctness . The ultimate abusive *ad hominem* becomes, "Oh, your view is just *so* politically correct," as if to say, "You sound exactly like those silly, sanctimonious (and dangerous) 1950s Communists."

Leveling the anti-PC *ad hominem* attack is the bigoted critic's first move in track 1. She then turns her attention to *poisoning the well*. She does this by conflating the idea of PC with the overall ideology of minority liberation and borrowing PC's now besmirched name as evidence that minority liberation is also a defective idea. To the critics' way of thinking, since it's the liberationists specifically who insist that people be PC about practicing the ideology of minority liberation, then they (the PC liberals) and the ideology of minority liberation they champion are just as bad as the PC concept; guilt by association. The well-poisoner typically next uses what she considers the now-established defective nature of minority liberation ideology to come back around at PC and smatter it yet again with more contempt.

It might look like this: a bigoted conservative engages you (an imagined pro-liberationist) in her *ad hominem* rant against political correctness. Then she associates PC with people on public assistance and thus concludes that welfare is as terrible as political correctness. The well has been poisoned. Not yet satisfied, she goes on to immerse herself in a colloquy about all the evils of the welfare state. I can imagine, for example, such a critic pointing to a news report about a member of a minority group who has been guilty of playing the system or worse—maybe wanton drug use or criminal activity. The critic rhetorically asks why she, a taxpayer, should have to furnish the upkeep of these freeloaders taking advantage of the liberation ideology. Why should *those* people get welfare payments, food stamps and affirmative action, and then abuse the gift by buying illicit drugs or by robbing hardworking people like her who have provided them with this handout? From here, the critic jumps to the conclusion, "Everyone (every minority person) is taking advantage of the liberation ideology-backed system." Then, focusing on her conclusion that vast numbers of minority persons are abusing the system, she points out how unfair it is to the rest of us who neither ask for nor expect a handout. Citing what she believes to be the legions of people unfairly taking advantage of liberation ideology in this way, she then leaps to blaming it all on too much political correctness: "If you liberal snowflakes weren't so PC, freeloaders would never get away with their thievery." She's taken all the poison she's infused into the very idea of minority welfare and circled back around to infuse it into the idea of political correctness; a kind of **reverse** *poisoning of the well.*

I'm sure we're all familiar with this scenario. The point I want to make about it is that the critic often uses her contempt for liberation ideology to then further disparage the idea of political correctness; since minority liberation ideology is even more defective than we first thought, then since we newly associate (conflate) the ideology with the cause of political correctness, political correctness must also be even more defective now than before, when we originally *ad hominem*ed it to death. More guilt by association. Bad argument? Yes. But it's unfortunately one that is often all too effective.

Now let me elaborate more about the second track of my thesis about PC and minority liberation, the smokescreen scenario; the idea that all the preferred conservative attention placed on the concept of political correctness is a case of intentionally missing the liberation ideology forest for the PC trees. The real enemy was and still is the culturally entrenched ideology of minority social liberation. As I've said, that's what the bigoted conservative complaint against political correctness really is all about, although the complainants won't explicitly say so. They don't want to claim publicly that they are *still* fighting *those* particular wars (of anti-liberation)—even though they still are, with a vengeance—when those wars have already been decided and absorbed by all the cultural and political forces that matter. What's a conservative critic to do? The answer: create a bogeyman. Insist that PC is a kind of thought-and-speech-policing mechanism intent on stifling our First Amendment rights; go on and on about the evils of thought-policing. Take the public's attention away from the conservative critics' bigoted disgust and disparagement of minority liberation ideology. It's actually the various generally accepted projects of minority liberation ideology that the critics feel muzzled by but are hesitant to complain about straight out. I don't mean that they are hesitant to be actively hostile against the cause of minority liberation; the pursuit of that cause goes unabated. The conservative war against minority social liberation

continues to be a hot—at times, violent and vicious—active enterprise. It's just that the warriors don't want to take public
responsibility for this pursuit, as they most assuredly would have
to if the public were to focus on how they really feel, their ingrained bigotry. So they mount their smokescreen war against
the concept of PC instead of revealing their bigotry.

Of course, not all anti-PC anti-liberation critics are smoke-
screeners. As I've already noted, a growing number of conservatives are choosing to level their complaints out in the open. Many
of these people are principled conservatives. But many others are
bigoted conservatives who either never had concerned themselves with smoke-screening in the first place or else had
formerly been concerned but now have chosen to move beyond
that enterprise. In either case, at the present moment in our nation, there are indeed many openly bigoted conservatives
espousing the anti-liberation sentiment who could care less
about hiding their true feelings about PC and minority causes.
The Trumpists—think white supremacists—are all too willing to
spout hatred out in the open; they want the PC public to hear
them loud and clear. They are proud and quite happy to take responsibility for their thoughts and deeds.

But while more and more of these openly bigoted folks are
coming out of the woodwork, I think it's still the case that most
bigoted anti-liberationists don't want to be too public about the
anti-liberationist activities in which they happily engage. I would
divide this group of people into two classes. One class includes
anti-liberationist bigots who knowingly use their outward complaints against PC as a smokescreen for their attempts to stifle
the cause of minority liberation. They are dissemblers, disingenuous, pretending not to understand why anyone would accuse of
them of bigotry, smiling internally at how clever they are—wink,
wink. The other class includes people who genuinely are not

aware that they are using smokescreens to cover their true intent, when in fact they are doing so. Having for the time being lost the war with our national ideological tilt toward minority liberation, they unconsciously or non-reflectively avoid talking too publicly about their bigoted activities aimed at destroying minority liberation ideology. They are unaware of using their very public complaints about PC as a cover for this other activity. Many are bigoted conservatives who don't want to hear any criticism aimed at their bigotry; in our culture, no one likes to be called a bigot in public. Unknowingly, they pick on something that in fact is nothing more than an avatar for their underlying intentions. For example, when someone complains that PC liberal thinking is a new McCarthyism that insists on strict conformity to prescribed liberal ideas, it's really *any liberal ideas at all* that they have problems with, not simply that those ideas might or might not be politically correct. They are not aware of *why* they are creating smokescreens or even *that* they are. When called on it, they are puzzled by the claim and genuinely deny it.

The following is an example of how haranguing against PC can be done in the service of moving public attention away from underlying bigotry. Certainly, President Trump and his acolytes don't want to take responsibility for their bigoted activities and they don't want to be *called* bigots; it sounds so distasteful. Instead, they dodge, deflect and rail against PC, doing all they can to deny their bigoted anti-liberation activity when it gets called out. I think many of these people—perhaps most of all, the President—come out of the first class, the dissemblers. They will distort reality and language in order to get off the hot seat, and they know exactly what they are doing. Consider Jared Kushner; when he complains that his father-in-law has been mistreated by the oh-so-politically correct "media elite" in their condemnation of Trump's tweets and retweets of anti-Semitic and anti-Latino imagery—first during his presidential campaign and continuing regularly ever since his election—he (Mr. Kushner) decries the media's actions by saying things like this:

> In my opinion, accusations like "racist" and "anti-Semite" are being thrown around with a carelessness that risks rendering these words meaningless....

> If even the slightest infraction against what the speech police have deemed correct speech is instantly shouted down with taunts of "racist" then what is left to condemn the actual racists? What do we call the people who won't hire minorities or beat others up for their religion?....

> I know the difference between actual, dangerous intolerance versus these labels that get tossed around in an effort to score political points....

> It doesn't take a ton of courage to join a mob. It's actually the easiest thing to do.[3]

Kushner's complaint that politically correct people are just trying to score political points[4] amounts to what I see as his very conscious attempt to deflect attention from Mr. Trump's racist and anti-Semitic anti-liberationist behavior. So, Kushner feigns annoyance with what he calls the media "speech police" and its liberation thinking and its misplaced ideas about racism and anti-Semitism. He then shares with us that his grandmother and her family suffered mightily during the Holocaust—that they experienced *true* anti-Semitism. As for what Mr. Trump does by comparison— according to Mr. Kushner, what are a few careless

---

[3] Jared Kushner, "The Donald Trump I Know," *The Observer*, 7/6/16.
[4] Recall from Chapter 1 that this idea of scoring political points is a problematic use of the term "politically correct."

politically incorrect words or some inelegant anti-Semitic or anti-Latino imagery compared to "real" anti-Semitism and "real" racism? As far as he's concerned, people are being *just too PC* about Mr. Trump's language. It's all the fault of the PC police.

Mr. Kushner (above) asks, "What do we call people who won't hire minorities or [who] beat others up for their religion?" He assumes that surely Mr. Trump wouldn't advocate either of these behaviors and asking this rhetorical question is supposed to prove that any of Mr. Trump's behavior couldn't possibly be placed in the same category as the "real" bigots, since Trump doesn't advocate beating anyone up. I disagree. To me, both the "real" bigots and the Trumps-of-the-world who don't quite meet up to Mr. Kushner's definition of "real" bigots are indeed racists and anti-Semites. What Mr. Kushner calls "real" racists are merely racists who have gone a small step further than Mr. Trump's racism, although he's not so far behind—it's well known, for example, that he won't hire black people to do his tax accounting (he says they're lazy and not smart enough). He actually said, "Black guys counting my money! I hate it. The only kind of people I want counting my money are little short guys that wear yarmulkes every day." And Kushner thinks that Mr. Trump couldn't possibly be considered racist and anti-Semitic? Seriously? This is a racist anti-Semitic twofer if there ever was one.

All of Jared Kushner's linguistic gymnastics around what counts as "real" racism or anti-Semitism—along with all his complaining that the PC police are working overtime—are meant to distract from the underlying racist and anti-Semitic anti-liberation behavior of his mentor, Donald Trump. This is a paradigm case of the second track of the anti-liberationist smokescreen. Since bigots don't want to be called bigots, they change the subject and move on to harangue against political correctness. Such harangues are not atypical of PC's critics, but the aggression level of the anti-PC harangue is so over the top in order to mask what's really gnawing at the critics—minority liberation. Like Mr. Kushner and his father-in-law, instead of focusing public attention on their real target of liberation ideology, the anti-PC critics instead scream bloody murder about the very concept of political correctness.

Enough said about all of this right now. Of everything I've talked about in this chapter, the main takeaway should be the reader's understanding in broad strokes of the three strategies (the three tracks) through which conservatives advance their opposition to PC and minority liberation ideology. With that in hand, then, I'm going to devote the next four chapters to filling in some detail of how these strategies get played out. So Chapter 6 will be a brief excursion into the conservative bigot's track 1 and track 2 attacks against political correctness; Chapter 7, on his conservative cousin's principled open offensive (track 3) against the same. Chapters 8 and 9 will move the discussion to both kinds of conservatives' open assaults (track 3) on minority liberation ideology, where Chapter 8 will focus on the bigot's behavior in this arena and Chapter 9 will zero in on how the principled conservative conducts himself against the same enemy.

CHAPTER 6

The Anti-PC Bigot

The bigot is so overtaken by her animosity for minorities that she can't help but engage them by levelling the anti-PC flawed line of attack—the "*too* PC" pejorative—with as much viciousness as she can muster. She feels that she's in a zero sum game where everything is on the line in her total opposition to the politically correct liberationist. She defends herself against a liberal system of thought—a politically correct checklist of acceptable and unacceptable (i.e. proscribed) behaviors, attitudes and beliefs—that would have her renounce her bigoted biases that doubtless are conditioned by the kinds of psychological and social underpinnings we discussed in Chapter 3. What I am going to do now in this chapter is offer a general characterization of what I see as the most important of these psycho/social conditions, and follow that up with characterization of the kind of track 1 and track 2 arguments that typically flow from the bigotry which those conditions foster.

I begin by commenting on the psychological elements that factor into her strong anti-PC biases? For one sort of bigot, the underlying issue pertains to her need to maintain her sense of self-identity in the face of the PC advocate's checklist of demands and proscriptions. For the anti-Semite, the racist or the xenophobe who *defines herself* in terms of her believed superiority to minorities, the checklist's demands and proscriptions are experienced as challenges to the very being of her psychological self as a unified entity. It's a challenge that is invariably met with an ever-deepening bigoted bias that gets expressed through verbal *ad hominem* aggression. "You want me to change *who I am*? No way. You ask the impossible. Silly you. But what else would I expect from someone like you who is *just so PC*."

For another sort of bigot, the PC checklist would have her renounce hateful biases that soothe her intense fears of minorities, exposing her psyche to the experience of full-on dread. For example, intense fear of African Americans drives so much of what we hear from the anti-PC crowd. They insist they won't be silenced about their so-called politically incorrect certainty that black people harbor murderous intentions against all whites. Contrary to the facts, they insist that the black-on-white murder rate is soaring. They use this false belief to justify their feelings of terror, which in turn drives the intensity of their anti-PC bias. Imagining themselves sitting alone and psychologically undefended against such feelings is simply unbearable to them. And once in place, their intense bias against black people gets associated with the cause of political correctness (i.e. a kind of **reverse** *poisoning of the well* that I alluded to in the previous chapter), the result being that they now feel they have reason to despise the very concept of PC *per se*. This is an example of the kind of reverse *poisoning of the well* that I alluded to in the previous chapter.

For another bigot, the PC checklist would have her renounce biases about her wholehearted disapproval of minorities and, thus, also have her renounce her cognitive filtering belief system organized around disparaging the value of minorities as human beings. For example, the Breitbartiacs or the Alex Jonesians of the world hold the viewpoint that, along with the international bankers and Hillary Clinton who are all plotting to bring down American democracy, there is also a cadre of people of color, immigrants (code for "the inferior Latinos and Muslims"), Democratic and Republican "elites" and "the Jews," all out to destroy any conservative opponent of political correctness. Their disapproval of and hatred for these people shuts down their cognitive ability to process reality accurately. Instead, in the service of maintaining their comfort zone of bigotry, they distort reality and allow paranoia to rule. They have concluded that their lives are about "us versus them," where the so-called politically correct "them" is out to get the conservative politically incorrect "us."

These particular examples of a wholehearted disapproval of minorities in effect characterize more reverse *poisoning of the well*. The characters in these examples, so hated by the bigot, are first associated in the bigot's mind with the championing of minorities, something he already hates. This all gets muddled with the very idea of political correctness *per se*, the result being that the Breitbart and Alex Jones bigots of the world also believe that the associated general cause of political correctness (attempting to protect Jews, immigrants, people of color, gays) must be deficient, too.

Often enough, building onto the kind of wholehearted disapproval/cognitively distorting bias displayed in these examples, there is also a social component having to do with bonding and mutual affirmation. In common cause, many such anti-PC misogynist, homophobic, racist and religious bigots feel kinship with one another, solidified by their mutual bigotry and shared paranoid view of reality. Moreover, these are also often the people I alluded to in Chapter 3 whose strong anti-PC biases are in a mutually-affirming feedback loop with their fellow anti-PC critics. The more they engage with one another in denigrating political correctness, the more worked up they all become. They feel more and more affirmed as individuals and increasingly empowered to attack political correctness en masse. And it all builds on itself, further solidifying their biases. Such are the workings of the mob mentality aimed at taking down political correctness and the minority rights it promotes. Sadly, this mob idea well describes what has come to be known as the conservative "echo chamber" of conspiracy theorists who are caught in a feedback loop of shared "fact free" paranoid stories—made-up scary stuff about what they see as un-American, often corrupt PC liberationists who are out to get them. They use the internet blog— think Breitbart again, Drudge Report, Alex Jones' Infowars—as one medium of choice for their mutual reinforcement of one another and their fantasy views of the world. They use Twitter as another way to reach out, tweeting, and re-tweeting, trading and reinforcing stories of their preferred anti-PC reality, one that hasn't much to do with objective evidenced-based reality. For them, reality is what you make it, what you construct. So, there really is no such thing as man-made, carbon-emission-caused global warming. Science is a matter of opinion. The Holocaust never happened. People of color are intent on taking over the nation. The Clintons are murderers. Hillary presided over a child sex ring out of a pizza shop while she was running for President. Many Mexicans really are drug dealers, and even the ones that aren't are out to take jobs away from the "hard-working white Americans." Godless liberals truly want to take away everyone's guns. The Russians didn't hack into the 2016 Presidential election. COVID-19 isn't nearly as bad as liberals make it out to be. To think otherwise about any of these matters would be to bow to what these people see as anti-reality; the "real" reality is the one they have constructed, while political correctness is aimed at enslaving our thinking. *Hey, it says so on the internet and in our tweetstorms.* Ultimately, of course, this feedback loop of mutually shared reality serves only to feed itself and justify for its members their underlying bigotry.

When these are the sorts of psychological and social forces working on the typical conservative bigot's hostility to political correctness and its checklist, it's no wonder that the bigot is so intent on turning political correctness on its ear and using it as a sarcastic *ad hominem* cudgel to try to thrash the PC advocate into shamed silence; it's no wonder that he also often enough falls victim to reverse *poisoning the* PC *well* thinking. When what's at stake is exclusive to these kinds of unadulterated strong biases, going straight for the PC jugular is the order of the day. This direct bashing of political correctness is clearly tough stuff; and it has been effective in putting PC pro-minority rights advocates back on their heels.

No one, however, has been quite so an effective basher of PC as our own president. Indeed, he is the perfect model of how a skillful bigot bobs and weaves on tracks 1 and 2 with his attacks against PC. Accordingly, what I'm going to do now is use the rest of this chapter to show how his very unique skill set quite aptly illustrates the typical assaults found on each of these tracks.

For starters, Mr. Trump has convinced himself and his followers that PC is public enemy number 1, and that if this fifth column ideology of political correctness is allowed to survive, our nation won't. As he firmly believes, "We don't have time for it (for political correctness)." And so, he attacks PC head-on and, by virtue of his straightforward *well-poisoning*, he attempts to compromise the idea of minority liberation, too (track 1). But not wanting to admit that he is in fact *well-poisoning* minority liberation, he keeps his and public's focus squarely on his *ad hominem* assault against PC. Of course, in doing so, he is really about using his attacks against PC as a *smokescreen* (track 2) for what truly moves him the most—a fear and hate-driven animus for minorities, none of which he will ever admit to ("Hey, some of my best friends are _____."). And what he's actually doing with his clever linguistic jiu jitsu is *giving himself license to say and do whatever he wants, while taking no responsibility for any of it.* In the name of finally putting an end to the dastardly concept of political correctness, he says and does things that just happen to consistently work against minorities, though he would never acknowledge the latter as his true motivation.

Since, according to the anti-PC conservative, political correctness aims to muzzle Trump and his cohort through its demands and proscriptions, and since PC is the dangerous public enemy number 1 that needs to be fought and ultimately destroyed if our nation is to survive, what better way to engage in the battle than to actively demonstrate how little regard they have for anything on the PC checklist. Mr. Trump creates a bogeyman out of PC and then promises to save the world by showing he's not afraid of the villainous bogeyman. He demonstrates his fearlessness by throwing his bigoted views right in PC's fifth-column face. The sole purpose of his invention is to use it as a foil for his claims of courage in the face of this supposed powerful, malevolent, scary PC force.[1] And he expresses his courage by saying and doing the very things that this malevolent PC concept opposes. What better way to show one's courage than to do the opposite of what the enemy wants—to spit back in PC's face the very bigoted things PC is most against? What a clever cover, to create an imagined enemy for no other reason than to enjoy license to do and say anything he wishes.

In his battle against the loathsome PC scourge, Mr. Trump has quite simply become the poster child for bigotry gone wild. While

---

[1] As an aside, we often hear the claim by his followers that Trump is a *strong and decisive leader* and that he acts *courageously* in fighting Washington's "swamp" and "deep state." I believe that for many of his followers, these are displaced descriptions for how they see him fighting against the forces of minority liberation advocacy—that is, that they really like the fact that he is assaulting the power of minority liberation ideology; that when they see him as being strong, decisive and courageous, they see him through this bigoted lens as their champion. And, of course, none of them would admit to having any such bias.

there seems to be no limit to the number of politically correct groups of people he and his followers resent, there are four that he has continually hammered away at and who have every reason to live in fear of his screed: Muslims, Latinos, African Americans and women. Trump's history of sexual assault against women "who are at least 8's" is legendary. Woe to *Access Hollywood* and woe to the women like E. Jean Carroll who have come out of the shadows to expose some of his sexual misbehavior. His history of discrimination against black people is equally legendary. By now, everyone knows about his unwillingness to rent apartments or any other properties to African-Americans or (with the notable exception of Apprentice star Omarosa Manigault, who briefly worked for him in the White House) having them in his employ as anything other than menial workers because they're "lazy," they're "thugs," under Obama they had "never done more poorly' and, the "well-educated" ones aside, they can't be trusted: well-documented views of his that stretch back at least to the 1970s. He has also told us that he knows it's not politically correct to say so, but he thinks that many in the black community are inherently killers who are shooting up the inner cities. He'll take care of it, though; indeed, he says, "*Only* I can fix it." So woe, too, to the black community, other than the one fellow who travels around to the rallies and, during the 2016 campaign, Trump referred to as "my African American"…and the few black politicians, professional athletes and celebrities he considers to be smart or wealthy enough.

Then there's the Latino community for whom he seems to have a special enmity, seeing them as "drug dealers, criminals and rapists." He took his opponent Jeb Bush to task for having a Mexican wife and for speaking "Mexican." And can anyone wonder what the Muslim-American community or Muslims nations around the world think of this president? To him, they are all terrorists until they can prove themselves otherwise. Certainly, they don't deserve admittance to or inclusion in our White Christian nation—the

Muslim travel ban will see to it!

Since ascending to presidential power, Donald Trump and his most stalwart followers are itching for a confrontation with the forces of politically correct minority liberation, even though that ideology is still embraced by the culture-at-large and much of the political and judicial establishment. But as I pointed out earlier in Chapter 4, as of now, Mr. Trump and his cohort only constitute a subculture fighting against a very strong biased tide for politically correct minority liberation. But he is determined to change things in that regard. Recall in Chapter 4 where I commented that the *primary player* in determining which, from competing ideologies, will be a nation's prevailing ideologies is the culture-at-large, and that the political class and the judiciary usually follow suit with what the culture-at-large has decided. Mr. Trump is trying to reverse the order; making the political class and the judiciary the prime movers of determining popular ideology and have the culture-at-large—the people—the secondary players. He wants to challenge the age-old convention of the primacy of the culture-at-large in matters of determining ideology by having more of his supporters appointed or elected to political office and by demeaning the current liberal elements of the judiciary while hoping to eventually replace a sizable portion of it with right-wing judges. He's determined to have the political and judicial tail wag the culture-at-large dog, as it were, to have his programs of bigotry ascend to the status of national prevailing ideologies.

Let me elaborate: as representatives of the people in our democratic system of government, our legislators are supposed to mirror the thinking of the culture-at-large. This is as true for the people's currently popular ideologies as it is for specific political issues of the day. Even those politicos who don't necessarily personally agree with popular thinking often enough go along with it; haltingly and privately holding their noses, they legislate and lead in ways consistent with the views of their constituents in order to hold onto their jobs. In a similar vein, the way in which the judiciary interprets and executes the law reflects the general cultural bias of prevailing ideologies. This is partially true because in many states, the people elect the judges. Like politicians, elected judges—in order to keep their jobs—typically interpret the law in a way that reflects the current culture-at-large ideologies—i.e. they follow the will of the people. In other states, judges are appointed by elected officials. Because these politicians are already serving the will of the people, they typically appoint judges who abide by their same ideological philosophy, the effect again being that the way they interpret and execute the law typically follows the will of the people. (Today we are seeing more and more politicians and appointed judges going against the cultural grain, following their personal anti-liberation conservative ideologies, public opinion be damned.)

Then there's The Supreme Court, with its justices in office for life if they wish. We have seen historically how many of them follow their own ideological hearts, interpreting the law through their own biases, even when their ideologies are not always in line with the general will of the people. And so, with Judges Gorsuch and Kavanaugh ascending to the Court, the majority has taken on a decided conservative cast.

It has become eminently clear that Mr. Trump is intent on challenging the convention that the culture-at-large normally holds sway over the political and judicial landscape. The revolving door of appointees and nominations for government positions; the individuals with whom he has packed the Supreme Court and lower courts; and many of the policy positions he has floated through Congress or created through executive order go contrary to current-day culturally-approved political correctness and the minority liberation ideology of which PC is an

expression. He is trying to turn his anti-PC anti-minority liberation subculture ideology into mainstream thinking; to see if he
can single-handedly change the culture-at-large liberation *zeitgeist* back to that time when, he claims, America Was Great—
openly bigoted, with no concern for being politically correct in a
minority liberation sort of way.

I think that Mr. Trump's behavior will be a test case for my
thesis about the culture-at-large as the primary player in matters
of ideology in our democratic society. Certainly, he has engaged
a sizable anti-PC anti-liberation subculture base of support that
he hopes, with the help of all his new governmental actions, will
change our culture's thinking.

But Mr. Trump has even more demagogic arrows in his
quiver. Consider the ways he has attempted to create what I referred to in Chapter 4 as social *rupture* events in order to displace
the reign of minority liberation ideology. Examples include the
mass deportation of Latino immigrants or Muslim-Americans;
the implementation of torture in fighting the war on terror; his
very ascension to the presidency; and perhaps most frightening,
his incompetence as a leader and his mindless way of thinking
and talking, the possibility of his getting us into a war or putting
many more lives at risk (delaying aid to blue states, suggesting
the internal use of Clorox!) than necessary during the COVID-
19 pandemic. These are all rupture events, aimed at exploding
and undermining the confidence of the citizenry, with the goal
of implementing measures to supplant liberation ideology with
his preferred ideologies, his preferred cultural *zeitgeist.*

In addition, Trump is clearly interested in causing what I've
referred to in Chapter 4 as cultural *disruptions.* He does this by
installing an administration that flexes its powers in mounting a
racist and misogynist challenge to the dominant PC minority liberation culture—for example, when he chose a tried-and-true

racist Senator as our Attorney General, and when he threatened to publicly humiliate the women who came forward before and after the last presidential election to tell their stories of his sexual abuse.

Sadly, many of these shenanigans have gotten Mr. Trump some of his desired results. His ginning up his base through these kinds of ruptures and disruptions has moved many base members to more openly express their disdain for the reigning liberation ideologies. It is certainly no coincidence that the number of openly hateful racist incidents in our country (e.g. Charlottesville, Orlando.) has skyrocketed since his election. It's no coincidence, either, that the state of Ohio a few years ago passed a law banning abortions after six weeks of pregnancy, aimed at nullifying *Roe v. Wade*. Indeed, it's no coincidence that *Roe v. Wade* itself will soon be challenged directly in the Supreme Court. No doubt this is just the beginning of the fight to try to defeat the cultural norms of politically correct minority liberation.

Thus ends my commentary about Mr. Trump's bigoted behavior and how he is a perfect model of track 1 and track 2 antipathy toward minority liberation ideology. But I would like you to remember that, even after all his gyrations, Mr. Trump will swear up and down that he has no animosity at all for minority liberation ideology. (As he has claimed, even though he has failed to disavow the Ku Klux Klan, he is "the least racist person that you have ever met.") Rather, it's just political correctness that bothers him. It's hard for most of us to imagine Mr. Trump keeping a straight face when he says that he's only opposed to political correctness and has no bad feelings about minorities and the ideologies that support their wellbeing. Luckily for him, he's shameless about being disingenuous. Not so lucky for us.

This concludes our discussion about the bigoted anti-PCer. We have seen that he is someone whose fires are stoked by strong biases and the psychological and social elements that condition those biases. He is out to eradicate the PC checklist of minority liberation requirements. To do so, he has mounted track 1 and track 2 arguments to lead the charge. Having achieved some success, he feels more than excited at this moment in our nation's history because he now also has the backing of the President of the United States and the power that the holder of that office wields in his attempt to change the prevailing national ideology away from minority liberation into that of unabashed bigotry. I will have much more to say in coming chapters about Mr. Trump and his mission to destroy political correctness altogether and replace it with all the forces of bigotry. For now, we will look at what transpires on the third—the out-in-the-open, direct—track of arguing on which the principled conservative lives as he critiques political correctness.

CHAPTER 7

The Anti-PC Principled Conservative

L et's stipulate that there are two sorts of principled conservatives relevant to our discussion. One sort of them has no truck with bigots or bigotry; he is driven solely by his principles to oppose PC and many causes of minority liberation. But the second kind argues his anti-PC case on principle but has, lurking in the background, the same kinds of bigoted feelings we've discussed. He is just as motivated as the avowed bigot to use the *ad hominem "too* PC" pejorative rhetoric and the *poisoning the well* and *smokescreen* logic. However, when presenting himself as a person of principle, he mimics the behavior of the first kind of principled conservative by explicitly *avoiding* using any track 1 or 2 strategy for opposing PC and minority liberation. He doesn't want to appear as crudely biased as the kinds of bigots we looked at in the previous chapter; he typically doesn't go directly for the throat. Instead of aggressively playing oppositional anti-PC *ad hominem* hardball, he starts off in a more civil manner, looking at the PC checklist of preferred pro-liberation behaviors[1] and framing his argument directly against them (no *ad hominem* attacks, no subterfuge) and in language that's respectful, calm, sincere, honest and rational. In other words, he *openly* opposes political correctness; he lives on track 3: he says he wants to see where the logical consequences of the arguments go. Only later, if the debate doesn't go well for him, does he give up the ghost and join his bigoted anti-PC comrades-in-arms to mount their more direct mocking

---

[1] I will save a full discussion of the detail of this checklist for Chapters 10—13.

attack against the politically correct checklist of the politically correct liberationist.

We will see in Chapter 9 how this transition back to the *ad hominem* gutter plays out for the second variety of principled conservative. At present, we will focus exclusively on the principled conservative in the pure form. What does arguing against PC and minority liberation directly (track 3) and *strictly from principle* look like?

Let's get clear on what a principled conservative is in the first place. Obviously, she stands for principles. She places them front and center in her opposition to minority liberation and the PC agenda. What does it mean exactly that she stands for principles? What is a principle at all and what does it mean for the principled conservative—or for any other kind of principled person, for that matter—to have a principle that she appeals to?

What Are Principles and Principled Debates?

In the context of our discussion, let's think of a principle as a fundamental—i.e. foundational—guiding belief or support for an ideology. So, for example, the minority social liberationist is guided by the principled belief of advocating for civil rights, with an emphasis on the rights of minorities. Then, too, principles are ideological beliefs that act as abstract dispassionate standards telling the adherent of the ideology how to behave. They are the reasons the principled conservative acts as she does; and so they become her rational justifications for her behavior, in the sense that, in the world of objective judgment, this is how a reasoned person behaves dispassionately. This is in contrast to the person whose behavior instead is motivated by self-interest. There's nothing dispassionate or rationally justifying about self-interest.[2]

---

[2] I know that some (Adam Smith, for example) would claim that self-interest itself is a principle. The way in which I understand the idea of a person's acting from principle

Indeed, acting dispassionately means, at least in part, that a person *explicitly sets aside* any considerations of self-interest. Moreover, self-interest is not rationally justifying; for in the public arena of objective argumentation, while appealing to self-interest might *explain* why a person sometimes acts as he does, it doesn't rationally *justify* anything. Whereas were she acting on a principle, in the arena of public objective argumentation, that *would count* as rationally *justifying* her action.

One more thing that relates the concepts of principle and self-interest: a principle is what an individual is supposed *to stand for and defend regardless of personal consequences*—regardless of any concern for self-interest. Of course, on occasion, people have been known to have principles but then fold (about defending their principles) under pressure (the pressure of self-interest). But in that situation, we say the individual has abandoned his principles. A person of principle, by contrast, does stand up for them. In addition, in the public arena, standing up for one's principles is considered a proud, noble thing to do.[3] Whether we agree or not with a person's principles, we respect her for her standing up for what she believes. Finally, as I suggested in Chapter 3, it is also true that principles are fundamental guiding beliefs that are *strongly biasedly held* inasmuch as they anchor a person's sense of herself and define part of who she is.

So, we have the gist of what goes into having a principle. A reasonable question to next ask is, how do these strong biased, dispassionate, rationally justifying, fundamental guiding beliefs come into being in a person's psyche; and how does the principled individual behave as a result? First of all, a principle's taking hold of a given individual's thinking has to do with the wholly causal vagaries of her biological, psychological and social history.

---

renders that usage of the term self-contradictory.
[3] But see what I say later about "white privilege" as an "*organizing* principle."

That history causally determines (that is, she doesn't rationally choose her principles into existence) what principles will "naturally" appeal to her; which ones she will be disposed toward. In other words, it's about the luck of the genetic and psycho/social draw. Once her principles have been formed, they become central to who she is as a character. Because they now define part of who she is, principles in turn become part of her repertoire of biases. Furthermore, as per our discussion in Chapter 3, these biases are strongly resistant to change—we say she is highly partial to them, she's a partisan for them because they are part of what anchor her sense of character self. Her principles are strong biases so central to her sense of self that they are not open for debate. So, since she is not responsible for their causally having been brought into existence nor for their anchoring her sense of self, it's not appropriate for someone to challenge *that* a person has the principles she has or that she is wrong to hold onto them. In the normal course of human interactions, people do get into disputes over principles. But those disputes usually are about which competing principles are more *apt to the situation*, not that a person is wrong for having the principles she has at all. So, let's take a look at how those disputes—where two people holding different, competing principles—typically proceed and the kinds of considerations that people typically bring into play when they argue from different principles.

Consider an example of two people debating about issues having to do with a particular ideology, where one person supports the ideology and the other is critical of it. I can imagine that a principled pro-minority liberationist and a principled conservative critic of minority liberation might each be willing to discuss whether some minority group is genuinely entitled to making a claim about certain rights they think they should have; one dispassionately stands up for the minority liberation cause and the other dispassionately stands up for ideological considerations that are incompatible with the cause of minority liberation. Say the latter individual is a majoritarian who believes we should always look to see what benefits the majority of people, even if it means neglecting the concerns of minorities. This is a difference in principles, period. How do these people talk to one another? What do they bring to bear in their *dispute*?

First of all, they each would claim that their particular principled support of their ideology position simply is more appropriate to the situation of the particular rights claim that the minority group is making. But that argumentative move typically goes nowhere fast. In trying to persuade the other that her principle is more fitting to the particular situation, one opponent might try to make the point that her principle in some perfect objective world is a kind of *first principle* which, in her mind, should outrank and defeat all other considerations. Or if that doesn't work, she might try to persuade the other person to accede to her principle by pointing to the *beneficial consequences* of abiding by her principle for the general population. If, for example, adopting her principle would benefit the overall sense of social harmony in our nation—better than it would were we to adopt the competing principle—then that's a justifying point for her principle. If there are other societal consequences that would be beneficial—say, the economy would flourish more than it would under some competing principle—then so much the better for her principle. If that fails to persuade, then perhaps each opponent would try to educate the other about the importance of their respective principles. So, I can imagine the pro-liberationist trying to educate her opponent through consciousness-raising techniques—say, suggesting books to read or movies to see about the history of the oppression of the minority group she's advocating for, or, perhaps, arranging for her opponent to experience first-hand the oppressive conditions that the minority group lives in. Her opponent might try to educate her, in turn, about the advantages for a nation when people look out for the majority of its citizens. But if neither hits paydirt on any educative considerations that finally work, once again they are at a stalemate. The two might even agree to settle the matter by appealing to a mutually-agreed-upon impartial third party to adjudicate—say, a professional judicial arbitrator. Such things are quite common in a democracy; and even though their difference in principles about minority liberation divides them here, their shared respect for another principle—the principle of impartial adjudication in a democratic society—unites them as "loyal opponents."[4]

But what does it look like for any of these attempts to resolve principled debates to actually succeed? Suppose one of the disputants convinces the other that certain agreed-upon desirable consequences really will accrue if her principle were to win the day and that social and economic disaster would occur if the opponent's principle were to win out. To the extent that good evidence for this claim could be provided, the advocate of the latter principle (the one where economic disaster would occur) might very well feel she has to rethink her commitment to her principle for this particular situation. She still holds her principle, but she is no longer as certain as before that it applies here. On rare occasions, she might even doubt

---

[4] The idea of loyal opposition started becoming seriously frayed for conservative Republicans during Reagan's presidency and totally ceased to have any meaning for them during Obama's presidency. The same thing is happening now for liberal Democrats during the Trump administration. With the demise of a "loyal opposition," we have become a totally polarized nation where both sides of the conservative/liberal principled and ideological divide no longer accept that the majority should rule the day. While "majority rule" still does technically reign supreme in Congressional decisions, the disparagement of it is all too apparent. It's as if to say, "We are who we are—our principles—and our only political imperative is to choose which side of any ideological debate we want to be on." The only "decider" here will be "might makes right." Clearly, we are in a terrible fix in this regard.

the general efficacy of her principle at all. In this context, a person's change-resistant principles have been *troubled*; because principles are the kinds of biased beliefs that are *so* strongly entrenched as parts of a person's self-identity, the principled person typically would try to self-soothe by looking for extenuating circumstances that would explain the troubling consequences as anomalies. Because she feels on thin ice here, she looks for anything that would help her rationally hold onto her principle. Perhaps she would appeal to "the Founding Fathers" as an ultimate justification backstop in the face of the troubling evidence, even if everyone else could see that this citation was irrelevant. Unfortunately, this sort of behavior is clearly a kind of weak rationalizing in order to maintain what's biasedly entrenched in her. Any of us who have been alive long enough will eventually get to rationalize some of our principles, even if we're not aware that we are doing that or we are not willing to admit it. A person's strong bias toward her principles has the last say, even if that means creating rationalizations to support them, especially since maintaining our principles is so wrapped up in our sense of identity.

The Anti-PC Principled Conservative

That, then, is my sketch about what principles are and how they generally function in debate. Now I will focus my attention on how the anti-PC principled conservative behaves; recognizing that some of these people, in addition to having strongly biased principles, might also harbor other kinds of strong anti-PC anti-minority liberation biases; most pointedly, I'm speaking about the strong bigotry biases so blatantly expressed on the political scene today. We can say that the anti-PC anti-liberation stance is over-determined. I will have plenty to say about this later. For now, what can we say about principled conservatives who act *entirely* out of principle? Out of devotion to their doctrine and in defense of their sense of self, they refuse to buy into the politically correct liberation rights checklist that's so integral to the culture-at-large. They can't entertain the notion of America's being the frontier of ever-expanding rights claims and acceptance; that picture offends their sensibilities. But while they feel at odds with the mainstream culture, they differ from their anti-PC comrades who are solely motivated by bigotry in that they feel an obligation to justify themselves. We know that principles require that much.

In opposing political correctness, they hammer away at the idea that the minority liberationist PC advocates are offending some very important American principles that they (the anti-PCers) valiantly defend. Of course, they are not the only ones on the battlefield with principles. The PC liberationists have their sacrosanct biased principles as well, their reasons for advocating for minority civil rights and every other right on the crowded PC checklist. But the anti-PC principled conservative advocates primarily for *personal liberty*, individual freedom. This, too, concerns a right, but a very specific one: the First Amendment of the Constitution, which endows all citizens with the right to free speech, free religious belief, freedom of the press, freedom of assembly and the right to petition. The principled conservative's focus is on citizens as free individuals. As such, her attitude is dead set against government or any other institutional entity's intrusion on these freedoms. According to her interpretation of the First Amendment, the government's sole focus should be on doing whatever best promotes the well-being of the overall community—e.g. raising an army to protect the citizenry from foreign incursion. Freedom (liberty), though, requires the individual be left alone to do what she wants, just so long as that doesn't infringe on anyone else's liberty (à la John Locke). So,

when the government passes laws that interfere with the individual's liberty, the principled conservative cries "foul."

This is precisely what the principled anti-PC critic's debate is
about: crying foul, foul, foul. The constant opening up of new rights
claims and the enactment of those claims into laws which mandate
"oh-so-politically correct" behavior is seen as intruding upon her
freedom to behave as she pleases. When political correctness demands that the individual monitor the very language she uses when
conversing on the liberation frontier—that she need watch out for
the "word police"—that becomes "just *too* PC" for her liking.[5] Making matters even worse, the culture-at-large exerts a social pressure
on all of us to conform—not only in behavior but in attitude and
belief as well—with the PC checklist agenda; it feels to her like yet
another intrusion by an entity (the culture) over the individual. She
experiences a heavy hand of political correctness in the form of the
law, linguistic conformity and the force of culture all favoring the
claimed rights of classes of minorities over the liberty of the individual. And when the claimed rights of some come into conflict
with the liberties of the many (*qua* individuals), then PC or not, she
opts for individual liberties every time.

I should point out that there are a couple of other favorite
principles the conservative anti-PC checklist critic often appeals
to. One is the principle of *individual responsibility*. Revisiting an
example from Chapter 3, when the liberationist talks about helping struggling poor people by passing legislation extending their
welfare rights, this raises the hackles of the conservative who insists that passing such legislation would in fact rob poor people
of their opportunity to take personal responsibility for providing
for their own sustenance. The conservative actually sees the liberal's contrary position as an assault on the poor person's

---

[5] I will have much more to say about this in Chapters 10—13.

character; an offense against his humanity. Obviously, the liberal sees this matter differently, but it's something the two sides can have a genuine well-intentioned difference of opinion about. As far as one of these principles being *ultimately* more important than the other—that's a nonstarter. They are both important. Each side has something valuable and valid to contribute; which biased principle wins the day can only be determined by looking at the particular circumstances in which the principles are raised on a case-by-case basis.

Another principle the conservative anti-PC critic often appeals to has to do with *fairness, justice*. It's the idea that not only are politically correct rights claims being favored over personal liberty, but the amassing of ever-expanding new rights for minority groups under the principle of affirmative action is *unfair* as it favors those now "protected" groups over the rest of the citizenry. As this principled critic sees it, in the name of political correctness, the rest of us are not being treated as equals. Sometimes she even trots out the old racist and sexist rationalizing trope of "reverse discrimination."

While I do in fact believe that the critic espousing the principles of liberty and personal responsibility at least has a valid argument to make (although, finally, I'm not persuaded by such arguments), I don't feel the same way about the critic's pointing to reverse discrimination as proof that justice is not served by the forces of political correctness and minority liberation. In fact, for reasons I will explore later, I believe that the concept of reverse discrimination is bogus. But because I believe that the principled conservative has nevertheless so often pointed to this bogus concept as an important reason to defeat political correctness and the ongoing cause of minority liberation, I want to take some care to explain just how egregious is this conservative claim of unfairness—that "reverse discrimination" is somehow proof that the principle of fairness trumps political correctness and minority liberation.

Indeed, when all is said and done, the principle of fairness (justice) does lean in favor of minorities and their rights and should do so indefinitely into the future. Although I am sure that there must be some principled "reverse discrimination" advocates who are sincere in their complaint about this "injustice" that the "politically correct" supposedly promote, I firmly believe that many more of their kind are instead disingenuous in their complaint. Regardless of their motivation, to put the principled charge of "reverse discrimination" as an injustice up against the principle of redressing the injustices of our nation's long history of vicious racism, misogyny, religious discrimination and homophobia; and then to say that the former is on a par with or worse, outweighs the latter—is patently ridiculous. I'm not going out on a limb when I say that the hundreds of years of various forms of bigotry on the American continent far outweigh any feelings of being passed over—of being "reverse discriminated" against—as in the complaints of some white workers or men who didn't get a certain job before the black person or some woman. For the conservative to say that disadvantaging white workers is no less unjust than creating policies advantaging minorities who have been victimized by systematic and intentional discriminatory practices of the past and present is a false equivalence to the nth degree. I'm not celebrating the fact that a qualified white or male worker doesn't always get the job he wants because government or a company's affirmative action policies mandate that a person of color or a woman sometimes gets priority in hiring. In a perfect world, we would *all* get our heart's desire. What I am saying is that it will take many *generations* (perhaps hundreds of years) of tilting social justice in favor of these historically aggrieved minority groups before our nation can consider the score even close to being settled as far as our historic egregious treatment of minorities is concerned.

Twenty years—that's in fact how long it took before the principled conservatives began complaining about the politically correct yet discriminatory injustice of affirmative action mechanisms such as minimal workplace quotas for minority hiring, fair housing, university admissions and the like…20 years of politically correct affirmative action set next to hundreds of years of material discrimination against minorities as well as the unrelenting psychological war waged against them as "inferiors" that has had such a devastating effect on the mental health and sense of self-worth of so many in the various minority communities.[6] "Cleaning up" that unforgiveable mess is not an overnight—or even a 20-year—psych project. And, yes, the least of it should entail our re-vitalizing affirmative action for generations to come and supporting it with all the politically correct energy we can muster.

That said, I don't mean to imply that anything goes in terms of affirmative action. We've certainly seen, for example, that telling minorities that they are an *ongoing victim class* and should *define themselves* as such serves no good purpose and in fact diminishes them. We've seen the unintended consequence of actually robbing some minority citizens of their sense of self-empowerment. That can't be good for anybody's mental health. Then, too, there's the example of welfare programs that have ballooned into a subculture where generations of members of disadvantaged populations have come to rely on public assistance as a mental habit, an internal expectation for how they are to live their lives; a part of their self-definition. Because this has become internalized as an expectation, family members in these situations may

---

[6] I will have more to say about this later when I discuss Black Lives Matter in Chapter 13.

lose the motivation to seek employment; with nothing to do each day, some fall into drug addiction, compounding the very economic problem that welfare was originally intended to help. But the conservative who then concludes from this that "these people" are inherently lazy or inherently weak-willed totally misses the point. With the best of intentions, our liberal policies aimed at redressing past and ongoing economic discriminatory wrongs done to minorities and the poor have created another wrong—a welfare policy that has the effect of sapping the very motivation to work for some of its recipients.

This is not to say that there are not many people who are in genuine need of welfare programs. Discrimination still runs rampant and "affirmative action" has become a nasty phrase, the result being that some minorities (as well as many poor whites) are once again the recipients of economic disadvantaging. As long as they are in this situation, justice demands that they receive a helping hand. However, for those able to work but who have become habituated to welfare as a way of life, we need to find new ways to motivate them toward work; to provide them the real opportunity to compete for meaningful employment and to develop more effective programs to wean people off of public assistance and/or off of drugs. President Clinton's policies aimed precisely at these things were a step in the right direction. The problem with those programs was that, as a result of a mean-spirited campaign waged by principled conservatives to denigrate political correctness and welfare policy *per se*, *anything* having to do with welfare programs soon took on a negative connotation in an otherwise liberal mainstream culture-at-large. I would argue that, quite to the contrary, there is nothing wrong with welfare *per se* as an affirmative action program if it is targeted at those who are truly in need and about whom justice demands they not be penalized for the historical and present economic discrimination they've experienced.

115

Conservatives who point to the unfairness of "reverse dis-crimination" and to the flaws of welfare as proof that all affirmative action is an unjust social policy that penalizes whites looking for employment and anyone who doesn't want their tax money going to support "those lazy, drug-addled people" are simply off base in their thinking. Acknowledging that there might be some problems doesn't then justify the suspending of all forms of affirmative action. But enumerating in detail what would go into a smarter version of affirmative action is a whole other discussion, something that would take us far afield from the central focus of this book.

In any case, these are the kinds of issues that principled con-servatives raise against liberation ideology and its politically correct checklist. I should point out that some (though not many) of these same principled anti-PC critics who wish to stay on the right side of legality have over time grudgingly come to accept the minority rights claims that have already been enacted into law. This is as po-litically correct (wince, wince) as they are willing to be, although some of them no doubt wouldn't mind if Mr. Trump's new Supreme Court were to reverse much of this established law. Whichever the case, though, it's clear that these people don't want any more new rights laws passed, so they rail against the remaining parts of the political correctness checklist that would require even more behav-ioral change on their part. They condemn what they see as a decaying culture-at-large that would have them sacrifice their prin-cipled attitudes and beliefs on the altar of protected minority rights. It's as though their sense of themselves vis-à-vis their principles of liberty and fairness is being squeezed tighter and tighter. The result: they hold all things PC in utter contempt. Any new rights claims that are embodied by the PC checklist become the enemy. So many enemies, at that; enemies they would like nothing better than to ex-cise entirely from the culture-at-large.

That, then, is what the principled anti-PC critic generally looks like. And this brings to a conclusion my discussion in Part II of how conservatives generally attack advocates of political correctness. In Part III, we will see the ways in which they mount their open opposition to the minority populations and liberation ideologies that proponents of political correctness defend.

In Chapter 8, we will look at the unabashed bigot. We will dissect his behavior, focusing on his abusive speech and actions against minorities through the years; and what he says and does today regarding the liberation ideologies created in reaction to that abusive history. Then, in Chapter 9, we will see how the principled conservative directly and systematically engages with the anti-minority liberationist in extended debate about liberation ideology, as well as how he sometimes lapses back into old habits of *ad hominem* and smokescreen arguing.

PART III

The Conservative Complaint
Against Liberation Ideology

CHAPTER 8

Bigotry and Liberation Ideology

To the extent that many bigots have debated minority liberationists *openly* since the ideology of liberation took
prominence in the public conscience, the general character of
that debate has not been pretty. Minorities, as we discussed in
Chapter 6, have historically been victimized by overwhelming
discrimination—unconscious, covert or openly, ranging from
subtle to overt violence in the extreme. For obvious reasons, minority liberationists and bigots simply don't like one another.
Respect and civility are hard to come by. However, in any ad-
vanced society, while respect is not a requirement and only can
be hoped for, civility is very much required. And so, the two sides
in this argument attempt to make a show of civility to remain in
the good graces of the culture-at-large. The minority liberationists have nothing to lose in making this show because they
already have the culture-at-large on their side ideologically. The
bigots, however, have a tougher row to hoe because they are
fighting against the prevailing ideological tide. What does this
battle look like for them?

Front and center is the idea again that the bigot's self-identity
is defined in part by her sense of superiority to minorities. For
her to even contemplate engaging a liberationist in civil debate
pushes up against her strong biases that anchor her sense of self.
Expressing her racist or misogynistic biases are part of *who she
is.* Add to this the fact that the typical bigot so very much loathes
and in many cases fears the minority group whose rights are

being championed, a not-uncommon response to the liberation-ist who actually *demands* that the bigoted critic mend her ways is that she momentarily dissociates—a kind of fugue state of cog-nitive/emotional short-circuiting—followed by fits of laughter over the minority group's presumptuousness that its members have any kind of legitimate rights claims at all. Furthermore, while minority group members expect to be treated fairly, re-spectfully and civilly, demanding that the critic stop her oppressive, often demeaning and dehumanizing prejudiced be-havior—the critic will have none of it. She's certain that the minority group members deserve her treatment of them; that the central traits of the group members—whether their skin color, their gender or their sexual preferences—are valueless; so, they have no right to freely exhibit those traits. Since the minority group members can't help themselves because those traits are part of who *they are*, then—according to the bigot—they shouldn't expect anything more than continued scorn. We all know the 60-year old history of how this has played out in big-otry's battles with black and brown liberation, women's liberation, LGBTQ liberation, etc. Any anger and protest on the part of the liberationist is eventually buttressed by civil efforts at consciousness-raising, argumentation, and forceful social and political activism. For the bigoted anti-liberationist, unbridled fury and powerful political backlash in the guise of "law and or-der" has been the typical response. Given the psychological forces at play in the bigot, civility for her is a terribly difficult position. Some have been known to rise to the occasion, however all too often disingenuously.

When we then add to the equation the social pressure of the culture-at-large that embraces the cause of minority liberation, the bigot feels up against it. It's hard to fight City Hall. But, as these matters go, there's been the rare occasion when some of these people not only force themselves into civilly engaging with the liberationist, they actually begin to give up the ghost of bigotry and the sense of certainty they once had about who's of value and who's not. Their bigoted biases begin to lose the change-resistant stranglehold on them that had been in force and they begin to soften. Clearly, if they can begin to question their beliefs, these are people whose sense of superiority and entitlement couldn't have been quite so central to their identity as it is for their remaining cohort of bigots. They are therefore ripe for the efforts of consciousness-raising and the influence of the culture-at-large, finally able to actually hear and grasp the meaning of the lessons of minority liberation. Depending on how they process this information, they might come to accept and respect the rights claims of the minorities they have forever spent their energy hating...or not. Whichever side of the debate line they finally fall on, at least civility has been genuinely achieved.

That's one (rare) possibility for how a bigot could respond to the pressure of the culture-at-large. More common is the great preponderance of bigots hearing and understanding the call, but, because of the overwhelming intensity of their strong anti-minority liberation biases, they once again reject the call. Expecting a comfortable civility from them would be a fool's errand; a significant number of conservative bigots will simply remain as they were, more than ready to engage again in barely civil confrontation. Again, the reasons for this vary from individual to individual; for some, their bigotry is fully tied up with their self-definition, while for others, the sense of kinship they share with strongly-biased anti-minority liberationists simply is more important to them than wanting acceptance from the minority liberation-celebrating culture-at-large. For still others, the intensity of their enmity or fear of the minority "others" might overpower and color their understanding of any conceivable pro-liberationist consideration at all. Whatever the motivation for their sentiments, these strongly biased people all genuinely believe that the members of a particular rights-claiming minority group are inferior human beings and, so, are not entitled to claim equal (what bigots would call "special") rights. Obviously, then, bigots feel that they shouldn't have to be attentive to minorities in the public arena or to think about any rights that the liberationists and their advocates say they are entitled to. Most emphatically, bigots feel that they *shouldn't have to justify themselves about these matters.* Their deeply-ingrained bigotry is its own justification.

Unhappily for the bigot, though, if she's to live alongside the culture-at-large, she is called upon to behave civilly and she can't avoid the call of justification. So, while she might not feel that she has to justify herself within her safe subculture, the norms of society require that she does. The culture-at-large that she lives alongside of demands that she fight her impulses, watch her words, and provide convincing reasons for her righteous opposition to minority liberation. Perhaps as recently as 10 years ago, this kind of cultural demand might have seemed so powerful that she might have been hesitant to publicly speak her mind at all in the presence of the powerful culture-at-large. But today—especially with the unending hateful polemics of Mr. Trump—challenging minority liberation ideology head-on seems once again to require no deflection or smoke-screening; many feel permission to go right for the minority liberation jugular. A few years ago, for example, Congresswoman Ilhan Omar, the well-known Somali representative from Minnesota, while riding in a taxi from the White House to her hotel, was sworn at repeatedly by the cabbie, threatened with physical harm and the forced removal of her hijab because, as he insisted, she must be a member of ISIS. She has repeatedly experienced similar kinds of threats.

The incidences of this kind of overt racist attack have skyrocketed since Trump's election. As I commented in Chapter 4 and then again in Chapter 6, even though they don't yet constitute a subculture that can displace the minority liberation ideological culture-at-large, the bigoted anti-minority liberation population has nevertheless risen to the status of "the other powerful pole" in our politically and culturally polarized nation. The inhabitants on the bigot's side of the ledger have grown large enough in number and loud enough in mob rage that many of them now say whatever vile things come to mind. They are happy to confront minorities and their allies head-on because they now unashamedly get to say their piece, express their full-throated bigoted biases and then bask in the glow of their like-minded fellows; they've finally broken free of the culture-at-large constraints that once smothered them. Thank you again, Mr. Trump.

So, the shackles are off for many bigots today, but not fully for all of them. There are some who still feel so much in the minority vis-à-vis the culture-at-large that they don't yet feel license to vent their rage publicly. They are what we might call the "shy bigots" who, while they might listen to what the minority liberationist has to say, there's not a snowball's chance in hell of ever changing their bigoted biased beliefs and attitudes. Though their sense of certainty (i.e., the absolute strength of their bigoted biases) hasn't weakened one scintilla; nevertheless, they haven't yet quite internalized permission to be themselves in the way that the Trumpian acolytes have. They don't yet sense enough power in their subgroup that would embolden them to speak out publicly. They fear the censure of the culture-at-large. Consequently, when pressed, they carry on a dialogue with the liberationist—empty and *pro forma* as it is—with a disingenuous smile, going through the motions of considering the merits of what he has to say, as much as their impulses would have them behave otherwise...but internally, it's "La, la, la, la, la—I can't hear you!" On occasion, they might go a step further and pretend to agree with the liberationist line; to go along to get along, anything to keep their rage from showing itself to a disapproving public culture-at-large. I would imagine that, in addition to the *non*-bigoted tribal Republicans and the *non*-bigoted angry white working-class Democrats and the *non*-bigoted anti-PC anti-liberation principled conservatives who supported Mr. Trump in the 2016 election, there were a good number of so-called "silent" Trump voters—those who came out of the woodwork in droves to vote him into office—among this group.

So, yes, there are some bigots who are "shy" about being full-throated with their true feelings. But the legions of proud, out-in-the-open bigots are growing daily. With that reality, then, as a prologue, I will now present an extended catalogue of the various kinds of concrete present-day, out-in-the-open, no-holds-barred, unapologetic anti-minority, anti-liberation bigotry, displaying each kind in full relief and seeing how they came to be.

Bigotry—Exhibit 1: Latinophobia ("white privilege" and more)

I'll begin with the bigotry of racism, focusing first on the racists who simply can't stand Mexican Americans, or any other Latinos. They are strongly and disparagingly biased against them. In league with their spokesman, Mr. Trump, they happily go on and on about the need for "the WALL" and mass deportations while they continue to devise new ways of disenfranchising the Latino voting public. These behaviors are only the tip of their venomous, racist spear. How did this come to be?

Latinophobia—a fear of all people of Latin American descent—goes back to the Anglo U.S. settling of Texas—the Texas Revolution in the 1830s—when fear, hatred and discrimination ran rampant against both the native Mexicans of the region[1] and those who freely moved back and forth across the new Texas borders. Of course, Texas, before the incursion by white Anglo settlers, *was part of Mexico.* So Mexicans, after the incursion, *didn't see themselves* as crossing any U.S. borders in the first place; they were just moving freely across what they had always considered part of their *homeland.* Just as North American Indians were indigenous to all American lands, so too were the mostly brown[2] Mexicans native to these newly-designated "Texan" lands. A similar pattern of Latinophobia took hold in the rest of the North American Southwest region, as Anglo settlers tried to displace the native Mexican inhabitants. In what eventually became New Mexico, California, Arizona, Utah, Nevada, and Colorado, white settlers discriminated both against the native Mexicans[3] living on the land in those territories which later became states[4] and the Mexicans who moved freely across the Mexican/United States border.

---

[1] By "native," I mean people who were born there and whose ancestors had lived on those lands. While the country of Mexico wasn't founded until 1824, people of Spanish descent had lived in the region—including what came to be known as Texas—since Spain's conquest of the Aztec nation in 1621. So when I speak here of "*Mexicans* who were native to the region," I'm referring to anyone who lived there from the time of the Spanish conquest and beyond—Spaniards and Native Americans who would later become Mexican Nationals and non-citizen Indian minorities living on the land. Many of the people living in Texas at the time of the Texas Revolution had an ancestry dating back at least two centuries to the Spanish conquest and were designated officially as Mexicans since, at that time, the land had most recently been part of the nation of Mexico. Those were the people who were discriminated against.

[2] While some of these "Texans" were white people of Spanish descent, most were brown-skinned, of "mixed blood" descent from white Spaniards, black slaves from various nearby Caribbean colonies and the United States, and various native groups such as the Nahuatl, the Huichol, the Yucatec, the Toltec, the Maya and others indigenous to the geographic region of Mexico.

[3] Here, too, while some Mexicans living in this region were white people of Spanish descent, most were brown-skinned or of "mixed blood."

[4] These became U.S. territories after they were "land granted" to the U.S. by the Spanish colonialists.

Again, however, Mexicans didn't see themselves as "illegal immigrants" coming into a foreign nation; historically, they had always moved freely over those lands.[5] So, what the law today calls "illegal immigration" is, from a historical perspective, considered by these native people to be their birthright. As such, this makes the current-day Mexican illegal immigration different from all other instances of illegal immigration of people from other geographically foreign lands. When viewed through the lens of long historical practice and an appreciation that these lands were part of the Mexican nation and Mexico's historical legacy dating back to the early 17th century, the question of whether it's proper for the United States to call Mexicans crossing the borders "illegals" is a fuzzy one at best.[6] But however one interprets the legality of Mexican immigration, the Anglos inhabiting the Southwest lands considered the Latino as the alien "other" to be feared and diminished.

That's the long view of how anti-Mexican bigotry and Latino-phobia unfolded in this country. How did we get to the current moment of mass deportations, "the WALL," and the full-on bigoted anti-liberationist hatred and discrimination against Mexican Americans and the "illegal" immigrants that "the WALL" represents? Prior to our nation's current polarizations, prior to having any awareness at all of some Mexicans "illegally" coming across our southern border, and prior to the current ascendance of a

---

[5] Again, to be clear, by "Mexican history," I'm referring to the history of the Latino peoples living on these lands dating back to the Spanish conquest.

[6] I don't suggest that we look at matters of "illegal immigration" of Latinos from Latin-American nations other than Mexico in a similar way. For instance, Salvadorans or Guatemalans are *not* indigenous to the American Southwest lands, so when they move across our borders without providing official notice, they can rightfully be considered illegal immigrants. That said, I do think there are certainly *other* considerations we could raise in favor of the idea of "open borders" for many non-Mexican Latinos (e.g. those seeking asylum).

Latino liberation ideology absorbed into the culture-at-large, many anti-Mexican-American bigots grew up in a subculture where it was open season on all Latinos, especially Mexican-American citizens. Not surprisingly, because of demographic patterns, this happened mainly in the Southwest. But as Mexican Americans moved to other parts of the country, bigoted behavior followed them. In short order, whites began having a passing acquaintance with Mexican culture, which was unfamiliar and significantly different from their own. For some, Mexican-American culture was exotic and therefore interesting. For many white people, however, the same cultural differences were alien and fear-inducing. That fear stimulated the kind of defensive strong bias formation in which one's focus on his hateful bias against the Latino served to pacify and relatively silence what for him had been an uncomfortable conscious fear of "the other."

As time passed and the anti-Latino bigots grew in number, so too did the intensity and sharing of their bigotry, creating a feedback loop of mutually affirming Latinophobia. As their numbers grew, so too did people find *more reasons* to hate the Latino "other." For example, bigots saw that many Mexican Americans made their livelihood from low-wage or service-oriented work: grape pickers, dishwashers, gardeners, maids, handymen, nannies and bus drivers. Among the bigots, many middle-class whites who were economically better off than these Latinos began seeing themselves as "superior." This sense of superiority became part of their white self-definition. In addition, many low-income working-class whites competing with Mexican Americans for low-wage jobs began fearing for their own livelihood. Once again, the same kind of defensive, hateful bigotry began to form among them. To make matters worse, the white public now was sufficiently motivated enough to notice that in addition to Mexican-American citizens, many Latinos vying for the same jobs were actually "illegal" immigrants; people they characterized as swelling legions of "criminals and rapists" *invading* our southern borders. Such hysteria has even led to paramilitary groups sprouting up, its members wielding AK-47s while patrolling our southern borders, ready to defend against and kill the invaders. All this lather has resulted in many anti-brown racists emotionally collapsing the distinction between "illegals" and "Mexican-American citizens," further intensifying their already ginned up hatred. On an emotional level, they began generalizing—stereotyping—that all Mexican Americans are illegal immigrants until proven otherwise, rendering "those people" objects to be loathed and feared all the more. As these things go, through social contagion, this stereotyping led to even more people joining the racist cause.

Throw into this mix a demagogue president who makes use of these popular prejudices and false claims and you end up with a vicious formula for the uncontrolled anti-Latino bigotry we see today. Racists now have permission to wholeheartedly disapprove of brown America. The system of their bigoted beliefs and attitudes has been so thoroughgoing that they and their subculture kin can never really imagine that Mexican Americans are anything but the lesser species of humans they assume them to be. The bigots can't get past their fear of "the other" enough to see that the moral worth of a person has nothing do with the kind of employment he has, the cultural customs he lives through, or the kinds of negative stereotypes into which he's been pigeonholed. Indeed, contrary to the negative stereotypes, devotion to family is far greater in the typical Mexican-American community than it is in the typical white American community; the commitment to work is stronger for the typical Mexican American worker than it is for the typical white worker; the allegiance to law and order is more solid in the typical Mexican American community than it is in the typical white community; and on and on.[7] What's more, anti-brown bigots are so locked into the irrationality of their bigotry that they can't even imagine that, in terms of life circumstance, the vast number of Mexican-Americans are in most ways *just like them*—rich or poor, smart and creative or dull; some can play in the Major Leagues and some can't throw a ball; some are liberal and some are conservative; some are exceedingly accomplished professionals and some are of modest endeavors; some can cook a meal and some can't boil water. The fact is, they all tie one shoe after the other, *just like everybody else*.

Many of these bigots see themselves as part of a subculture that is equal to the culture-at-large which embraces Latino liberation, or at least close enough to feel entitled to hatefully challenge Latino liberation head-on. They've steamrolled past their former complaints against pro-Latino political correctness right onto the main playing field of a very public collision with Latino liberation ideology. Now that they have finally been able to take over the levers of official political power and are moving at warp speed to do the same with the judiciary[8], they are chafing for a fight, itching to enforce their racist will on the nation and, more specifically, on the Latino minorities. The unhappy fact is that they are in full-on *disruption* mode with their aggressive behavior in the form of very vocal anti-Latino immigration protest rallies (especially in the context of Trump's pre-COVID neverending campaign rallies), increasingly violent anti-Latino threats made by alt-right white supremacy groups, the aforementioned paramilitary groups dedicated to "defending" against the invaders and, generally speaking, what seems like a total breakdown of

---

[7] Am I suggesting *positive stereotypes* here?

[8] That appears to be the current Senate Republican majority leader Mitch McConnell's main mission in life.

civility toward any and all people in the various Latino communities. All of this *disruption* activity is aimed at their demand for a prominent seat at the culture-at-large ideology table, along with their less vocal but no less biased "shy" anti-Latino brethren. In short, they are attempting to displace Latino liberation ideology in the culture-at-large with their own not-so-uplifting ideology of bigotry.

There's one more layer of bad news (as if the foregoing weren't bad enough): unbeknownst to themselves, there are many people who actually advocate for Mexican and Latino liberation but who nevertheless harbor biases that work against it. Specifically, many white liberals promote brown liberation but are, at the same time, unconsciously—or in some cases, non-reflectively—fully biased toward their own sense of "white privilege," sometimes at the expense of the brown minorities. This is such an important phenomenon for us white liberals to get our heads around if we are to continue to advocate for pro-Latino ideology with a clean conscience. So, even though much has already been said by many others about "white privilege," I will now put in my two cents on the issue.

As a preliminary matter, though, I will try to clear up something very troubling about the concept of "white privilege" and how it has fared since its arrival in public discourse. It's interesting that, even before the recent emergence of head-on racist challenges to Latino liberation ideology, the idea of white privilege has been a favorite whipping boy of the conservative forces looking to take down political correctness. The critics have pounded away at the idea that white privilege is a fabricated notion of the politically correct elite; that there is really no such thing as white privilege, but only a made-up notion whose sole aim is to keep white people from their due in life. When they use the smug. sarcastic "*too* PC' sledgehammer, they aim to destroy the notion of white privilege along with it; another instance of *poisoning of the well*. The normal strategy here of the typical anti-PC critic goes like this: if you can disparage over and over and over again some concept—be it political correctness or white privilege or any other target concept[9]—you can effectively plant in the mind of anyone paying attention that the concept in question is hackneyed and hopelessly passé. The goal is to get the public to feel too embarrassed ever to use the term or think about the concept again. The idea is that the minority liberationist and the observing public will do anything not to be disparaged and screamed at anymore. Once again, the strategy is very clever and, unfortunately, very effective.

Obviously, this situation is intolerable. We liberals need to have a thicker hide. The conservative bigot's repeatedly shouting us down is certainly not an acceptable way of doing business when it comes to ideological debate. But we shouldn't allow ourselves to be rolled over. We need to fight this kind of racist onslaught when it's levelled against the concept of political correctness, as well as to inoculate ourselves against falling for the shaming trap as it's applied to white privilege. The concept of white privilege is all too real and all too pervasive; it should never be swept under the rug.

That said, how are we to understand my claim that there are white liberals supporting Latino liberation who unknowingly harbor feelings of white privilege? Clearly, these people are not white supremacists, but they have grown up in a white world with a feeling of entitlement. I can best explain this by making some distinctions, relating back to my earlier general characterization of

---

[9] The most recent concept to take its turn at being sledgehammered is "identity politics." It's been quite successfully disparaged in the public's eye. One should realize, though, that identity politics is nothing other than politics that champion the liberation of minorities. Attacking the former is just a masked way of assaulting the latter.

the concept of *principle*. The assumption of white privilege is actually a biased *principle* of the white person. This can cut two ways. First, unlike the white liberal who unconsciously or non-reflectively assumes this principle, there are other white people who make the assumption of white privilege quite consciously. Those people *are* white supremacists. They consciously embrace white privilege as a fundamental guiding principle for, among other things, how they are to engage with all people of color. Such people would include, for example, the anti-Latino racists we've been talking about, who openly and proudly attack liberation ideology, taking full responsibility for their principle.

This kind of fully conscious biased principle needs to be distinguished from what psychoanalysts call unconscious or preconscious "organizing principles," biased principles that a person is not conscious of holding but which nevertheless are foundations for entire patterns of how she thinks and behaves. So, in the case where white privilege is an unconscious organizing principle of the liberal,[10] the assumption of white privilege organizes what she brings to the table when she engages with people of color, even though she doesn't realize that she assumes the principle and that it is one of her foundations for how she thinks about and behaves toward minorities. Moreover, *because* her assumption of the principle is *unconscious* in contrast with the white supremacist, she can't or isn't willing to take responsibility for it.

---

[10] Of course, there are many conservatives who also unconsciously assume white privilege and sometimes display it unintentionally, all the while eschewing any form of overt racism. However, as it is with the white-privileged liberals who advocate for minority rights and end up partly defeating that advocacy when their sense of white privilege infects some of their interactions with minority people, I will focus only on them in my discussion. Obviously, everything I say here about the psychological components of liberal white privilege applies equally to this particular kind of principled conservative.

And then there's a third way in which a person can assume the principle of white privilege. I have in mind the individual whose privilege flickers in and out of conscious awareness; it doesn't stay in focused awareness long enough for him to get a firm grasp on the fact that he holds the principle. We say the assuming of the principle is held in his preconscious mind. Accordingly, then, he too doesn't take responsibility for holding the principle.

The white liberal lives in either of the last two camps. Whichever of these two ways it sits in his mind, his assumption of white privilege borders on his having a feeling of "white superiority." He is the one who comes first, the one of greatest importance. He is the one most entitled to the best jobs, the best educational opportunities, all that comes from social and economic advantage. I've seen all too often—indeed, on occasion, I've been just such a person—how this expression of white privilege jumps out of many liberals when they least expect it. And when it does come out of their mouths and they truly hear themselves, they are so momentarily horrified by it that they typically then bottle it up as quickly as possible. They call it a mistake—oops. And they're right, of course. But it's not a benign mistake, as in "an innocent slip of the tongue" (although to us psychoanalysts, those are never really innocent, either). It's quite impactful. When a white liberal unintentionally says things that make his white privilege apparent, his words have the effect of subverting the cause of liberation. How so? I think a biased or assumed sense of white privilege comes close enough to an assumed sense of superiority that we can't help but see it as another form of bigotry, albeit unintentional bigotry. It's not bigotry of the hateful kind, nor is it the dehumanizing kind. Instead, it has the unintentional effect of demeaning a minority person—in the present context, this means the brown person—in terms of his worth relative to that of whites. I've never met a Latino or a person of color who wasn't aware of this phenomenon. The best that can be hoped for is that white liberals who unconsciously or non-reflectively hold onto white privilege come to terms with themselves so that they can stop conveying an attitude of superiority to the very people whose cause they champion. More easily said than done, of course, as many of these liberals would sincerely deny that they have any anti-Latino bias. And in a sense, they're right, at least as far as what's in their conscious minds. I'm certain that for many, they either have grown up with or have developed over time a strong pro-Latino rights bias that they feel in their conscious bones. So how could they be considered bigots? Again, this bigotry is a qualified one, in which the liberal is unintentionally demeaning. This is different from being biased *against* Latinos. These liberals harbor no ill will toward Latinos and they give their sincere unconditional support to Latino liberation. Rather, they are *biased in favor of their own special white privileged position* relative to Latinos.

I want to be careful to clearly characterize this reality for white liberals, because I think they find themselves in precisely this same situation with regard to *all* race-related liberation movements they support. Their situation is one of a *"double-consciousness."* They have both a bias that slants toward pro-liberation for racial minorities and an opposing qualified bigoted bias that slants in the direction of their assumption of white privilege. The first kind of bias is conscious; the second kind is unconscious or non-reflected-upon. This complicates matters when trying to mount a common defense by all liberationists against the forces of bigotry. Finally, all one can do is bring the problem into the light and hope that this will have some influence on eventually remedying matters.

One final wrinkle: even some Latino cultures have a bias relationship to white privilege in a way most of them would not like to admit in an ideological discussion. In some Latino cultures, it's Latinos who unconsciously hold the assumption that whites are privileged—that they're superior—and that that's okay. They are unconsciously biased in favor of whites. Take, for example, the Mexican-American community of Los Angeles.[11] When there's a birth in a Mexican-American family, it's not uncommon to hope that the infant will be light-skinned rather than dark-skinned. It is said of a light-skinned little girl, "*que bonita; esta huerita, blancita*"—"she's white, so beautiful." Brown or black skin is seen as relatively inferior or less attractive. This same preference permeates the culture, giving the light-skinned person a leg up in many social contexts where Latinos informally rank one another preferentially. Other things being equal, who is going to be favored for the job opening? Which girl will attract all the boys? Which "homeboy" is going to be the leader rather than the follower? (He might proudly leave his tagger signature, "El Huero," "White Boy.")[12] And what's common to all of these biases is that the Latinos who show such preferences and are aware of them are typically not aware that these preferences amount to an acceptance of the idea of white privilege. Their acceptance of white people as superior and entitled is unconscious.

Psychoanalysts call this sort of phenomenon the defense mechanism of "identifying with the enemy." The Latino has been systematically victimized by demeaning white bigotry and needs to defend himself against the feelings of inferiority and shame that the hateful bigot ultimately wants him to feel. One kind of defense is this identification. The Latino here (it could be a light- or a dark-skinned Latino; both in fact do it) takes on (unconsciously identifies with and internalizes as his new self-definition) the very trait that the victimizer uses in demeaning him. So, when the white-privileged white bigot sends the brown victim the message:

---

[11] I'm only referencing here the Mexican-American community of Los Angeles.
[12] Thanks to Alex Miramontes for this, personal communication.

"I am white and, because of my white privilege, I am better than you. The core of my personhood is superior to who you essentially are as a soul."

Then, in order to defend against this devastating proclamation, the Latino victim actually accepts the trait of white privilege *as his own* bias. Celebrating white privilege unconsciously becomes part of who *he* is, how he sees himself. He has the *unconscious fantasy* that if he becomes biased against darker-skinned Latinos and biased in favor of lighter-skinned Latinos, then he will not have to experience the pain of discrimination that his victimizer wants him to feel. In other words, the fantasy is that if he assumes that whiteness is privileged, just as the victimizer assumes to be the case, then he is being agreeable to the white person. In being agreeable, the victim and victimizer are socially bonded around their shared bias for white privilege. So (as the fantasy goes) the victimizer will be more favorably disposed to accepting the victim and, consequently, will not hold as harsh a bias against the victim as he had before. The fantasy also has it, then, that the Latino victim will actually feel soothed in the presence of the white bigot because (in his fantasy) the white person will no longer see him as an insignificant victim, but rather as a colleague-in-arms via their shared bigoted bias against Latinos. Of course, all of this is unconscious fantasy. In reality, the white bigot could care less about being identified with in this way—that the Latino is using white privilege to discriminate against other Latinos. Nevertheless, with this unconscious fantasy, the Latino has inoculated himself against the pain of victimhood. He feels soothed in the victimizer's presence.

An especially unhappy instance of this phenomenon characterizes the profile of some Latino backers of Mr. Trump. They've unconsciously identified with him and his white privilege and are actually calmed—soothed—in hearing him speak his white privilege bias against Latinos. And even though, in his case, the bias is a *conscious* white supremacist bias (no matter how insistent he is in denying such a thing), they refuse to perceive him this way, as that would most likely lead to an overwhelming (and rational, justifiable) sense of fear. Rather than invite that terror into their consciousness, they opt instead to perceive Trump as just another white man—albeit a powerful one—with a benign sense of white privilege, one they, too, internalize and identify with. Furthermore, like Mr. Trump, when they actually discriminate against darker-skinned Latinos and in favor of those with lighter skin, they feel just as empowered and superior to their victims as Mr. Trump does when he discriminates. Sadly, this comes with a price. These Latinos, too, inflict a terrible bigotry on their own people, with the added likely consequence of passing it on for generations to come. The terrible truth is that in unconsciously assuming white privilege for oneself and then using it to show bias against one's own darker-skinned brothers and sisters, one is helping the unapologetic white racist to get the job done—to make the brown Latino feel inferior and defeated.

Where does this leave us? Unconscious white privilege of both the white bigot and the anti-Latino brown bigot adds a bit more fuel to the anti-Latino liberation bonfire. Along with the more overt unapologetic elements of anti-Latino bigotry that we looked at in the first part of this section, the Latino community has a lot of forces stacked against it and the liberationists certainly have their hands full in marshalling an appropriate response. What's the appropriate response? The sad truth is that most people on the Left—and many in the Latino liberation movement—have been caught off-guard. When an ideology such as minority liberation ideology amounts to an entire social belief system that is firmly entrenched in the culture-at-large (as it has been in ours)—when it has been so much a *given*, so much part of the social flow—there is no reason to reflect about what to do were there a serious challenge. The person who rightly takes his pro-liberation stance for granted as the accepted view of the culture-at-large never expected that there ever would *be* a serious challenge and is unprepared for it. But when there is as emotionally charged a *disruption* to the ideological norms as our nation has been recently experiencing around anti-Mexican American feelings, the culture-at-large needs to be shaken awake. That's not to say that the entire Latino public (the Mexican-American public especially) has been sound asleep; since the 1960s, the various iterations of the Chicano movement (El Movimiento) and Liberation Theology have advocated for the civil rights of Latinos. They've long resisted the forces of bigotry that would try to "send them back to where they came from." It's the rest of us who are sympathetic to the cause who need to wake up, giving our full attention to the challenge, following the lead of Chicano leaders and, at the very least, coming to terms with and expunging our own sense of white privilege from the equation.

Unfortunately, I think it's clear by now that while the normal modalities that the MEChA-like Chicano and CFMN-like Chicana movements have used in trying to educate a stubborn public—consciousness-raising activities (theater, literature), rational argument, La Raza-like political action, and applying culture-at-large peer pressure—have enjoyed some success in converting some whites to the cause, those same modalities simply won't work on the kind of deep-seated, threatening bigotry that comes out of the mouths of Mr. Trump and his fellows. I don't pretend to have answers for this ugly turn of events. I'm only trying to clarify what I think the contours of the bigoted challenges to the Latino community look like. It is incumbent upon committed activists on the Left to come up with new responses to these challenges so that the Latino liberation ideology has a chance to survive as a cultural norm.

Bigotry—Exhibit 2: Racist Hatred of Black People (the "silent majority" and more)

Let's next consider our nation's ubiquitous anti-black racism as it comes up against the very powerful culture-at-large black liberation movement. All that I've just said about bigotry aimed at Mexican Americans and other Latinos applies at least equally to the bigotry aimed at African Americans. After all, anti-black bigotry has been around for a lot longer. The acts of horrific violence against black people over the past 400-plus years and the legacy of those acts are notorious in the annals of our national shame. And what have been the white racist attempts at justification for such horrors? The unapologetic white racist in effect has always said, "We are higher beings than they are—we are superior to them—and so we do what we must to bring them to heel." Although I will have a lot more to say later in Chapters 10—13 about present-day racist bigotry against black people and the black liberation response to it (notably, Black Lives Matter), in this chapter I will reserve my discussion to observations about the character of racism as expressed over the past half-century in our country and how it came to be.

From the beginning of anti-black racism in our country, one constant has been the intense and irrational fear of "the black man." Just as the racist white anti-Latino dreads the Mexican "drug traffickers, criminals and rapists" overrunning the nation, so too the anti-black provocateur has always stoked the flames of fear of the oversexed and murderous black man plotting to prey on the virtue of the white man's wives and daughters and to indiscriminately rampage the white community. These negative stereotypes are certainly still alive and well among the current batch of anti-black racists. These racists constitute a very powerful and unyielding sub-culture that has continued to make the lives of many black people miserable. But it is still just a subculture; in an earlier time, it was part of the culture-at-large, when most white people invoked white superiority and racial supremacy. Anti-black racist ideology was the *given*. It wasn't until after the second World War that some of these whites even began to express any sensitivity to the plight of black Americans. Those who finally became sympathetic with the cause of black liberation were still decidedly in the minority. They were part of a liberation movement that was decidedly a subculture vying for inclusion in the culture-at-large.

But then the '60s happened and payment came due. First, the rupturing events of the Black Civil Rights Movement came to pass, highlighted by a cycle of action/reaction large-scale mili-tant black rebellion in the face of large-scale, violent white hatred, fear and anger. The images are indelibly etched in the na-tional memory: who can forget power fists in the air, buildings burning, windows breaking, people running in the streets, stores looted, shots fired, limp bodies on the ground, frightened eyes, angry eyes, desperation, activist organizing? Who can forget swollen reddened necks come to a boil, threatening bloodied fists, National Guard rifles aimed and cocked; tear gas, fire hoses and police bullets gone wild; German Shepherds growling and ripping at black skin? This yin was all going on alongside of the yang of peaceful protest marches and the concerted efforts of black consciousness-raising. The end result? Black liberation fi-nally woke the sleeping white giant and tapped into his moral conscience enough to gain a foothold and ultimately a full inclu-sion in the spirit of the national culture-at-large.

Gaining that foothold didn't happen in an instant. A growing rumbling of minority complaints captured the imagination of the

intelligentsia and the younger generation; they were the first re-
sponders to the demands for equality that were loudly banging
against the older generation's longstanding closed door to minority liberation, the first to have their moral conscience tweaked by
the black complaint. As social ideological movements normally
go, the advocacy of these newly-minted white supporters of
black liberation, along with the continuing insistent demands of
the movement black people, began massaging the moral sensibilities of vast numbers of older whites out of their slumber. A
noble fever took hold of the national psyche. Social liberation
ideology had come to the forefront and grabbed the reins of the
culture-at-large and its norms. Along with it, the hard-fought-for
cause of black liberation had arrived as a real force within that
public culture. With the election to Congress of enough members sympathetic to the cause along with this new public pro-
black liberation sentiment, there followed the passage of the Civil
Rights Act of 1964 and the Voting Rights Act of 1965. The openly
anti-black racist forces that had always owned the levers of political and judicial power and the cultural norms now were
rendered subculture status. Or so it seemed.

With this change of the culture-at-large's public conscience
and political and judicial power, there had been a change of the
guard. The racists fumed at being replaced by black liberationists
and their white advocates. Even though, as I alluded to earlier,
they would impatiently paw at the ground and champ at the bit
for the next 50 years in an effort to regain their former status,
with the constant threat of censure, political sanction and judicial
punishment, they no longer were entitled to openly voice their racist impulses as straightforwardly and unapologetically as they had
before. But *that*—spewing their anti-black hatred openly—*was all*
that was proscribed by the culture-at-large. Watching one's tongue
was one thing, but ceasing unspoken racist behavior was quite

another; it continued unabated. Yes, laws were passed to deseg-regate our society and to make some movement toward reparations (in the form of various kinds of affirmative action programs) for our historical national sins against black people. And, yes, the more horrific forms of intentional violent hate crimes against blacks were no longer tolerated. But the culture-at-large embrace of black liberation only went so far; it had left the rest of racist behavior out of the equation. Black people con-tinued to be treated as second-class citizens, still funneled into low-wage service jobs, their communities therefore inundated with the temptation and easy availability of street drugs. Easy ac-cess to voting was still a challenge in black communities. Discriminatory housing practices continued. Racist behavior continued to flourish.

Yet the white conscience was spared much of this reality and thus was able to be in *denial* about it—all the while focusing on our proud, sometimes sanctimonious, cultural commitment to black liberation. The mechanism was simple: don't *call* racist be-havior "racist behavior." Instead, give it some seemingly benign designation—something inoffensive sounding, maybe even praiseworthy. So, systemic police violence against black people was called "public servants doing their duty." A court system and prison industry that made systemic incarceration of the black man a busy and lucrative default social option was called "fighting the war on drugs," "cleaning up the streets," "making America safe" and today, "Making America Great Again." Con-servative opposition to all law-of-the-land social programs aimed at redressing past and continuing discrimination against black people was called "taking a reasonable political stance against out-of-control government spending." In this regard, the racists were emboldened to fight tooth and nail against all the accomplish-ments that black liberation had been making in government policies and law. They opposed welfare, food assistance and after-school programs. They criticized employment quotas aimed at levelling the playing field for the underemployed black community. They complained about the desegregation of schools that had insured black kids the same quality educational opportunities as white kids. Conservatives challenged all of these settled laws and policies without any fear of material censure by the culture-at-large, because, as they insisted, all they were really trying to do was to keep government spending under control (ugh!).

This linguistic trick of simply re-describing racist behavior in ways that, to many, *sounded* nothing like racism was a very effective tool for the anti-black racist's mission. This awful truth must be faced: no doubt, part of what aided the effectiveness of this linguistic tool was the fact that many whites who embraced black liberation *unconsciously* still harbored their own white-privileged, racist feelings. Unable to face their own racism, they remained in denial about the aforementioned forms of racist behavior. This was true back in the day and it's just as true today. Many liberal whites still don't acknowledge institutional racism. And, of course, there's no easy fix for making conscious the unconscious.

Let's return to our history, though. With the election of one of their own to the presidency in 1980, racist Reagan Republicans felt even more emboldened to call a final halt to any more *incursions* by black liberation into the culture-at-large. Reaganites would do all in their power to stop black "progress" and actually would begin to reverse many behavior gains that had been won in law and policy. This rearguard action was taken in the name of innocuous-sounding "fiscal responsibility," covering their tracks of guilt and doing their best (worst) work with this sanitized language. So, too, many white liberals were in denial about that language, but if it looks like a duck and quacks like a duck....

This is how slippery racist behavior regained a firm foothold during the Reagan years.

Of course, the seeds of this racist conservative anti-black liberation backlash had already been sown a decade and a half earlier. Angry conservative racists who could no longer freely voice their feelings found a political ally in the person of President Richard Nixon; they constituted what Mr. Nixon proudly called the "silent majority." A gentlemen's agreement was struck between Nixon and his new silent majority base: "You guys keep your racist language to yourself and give me your votes; I'll turn a blind eye to your less egregious kinds of racist behavior." Nixon didn't feel he had the cultural license or political capital to allow *all* forms of racist behavior. He understood the liberation *zeitgeist*. Whatever his failings as a person, Nixon was a smart political actor. In hindsight, it appears that in making his political calculations, he factored in the strong pro black-liberation bias of the culture-at-large along with his need to lock down the racist silent majority. He struck a deal with himself of turning a blind eye to less egregious racist behavior on the one hand, while disingenuously praising black liberation on the other.[13]

Nixon's Silent Majority base was continually fed red meat about how they were being "left behind" by the culture that now championed the rights of people of color, the rights of blacks especially—how his hands were tied by previously passed liberal laws that "forced" him to support welfare programs that were being paid for by whites; how other laws on the books "forced" him to guarantee there would be no anti-black racial discrimination in employment hiring and that there would actually be quotas

---

[13] "Disingenuous," because it's well documented that he saw the black liberation movement as a proxy for communist infiltration into our social fabric; a definite evil. To Mr. Nixon, Dr. King was bad enough; you wouldn't want to get him (Nixon) started on his feelings about the more militant black activists.

that sometimes led to the hiring of a black person over a white person; and so on. And the Silent Majority ate it up. Over the years, they were fed an ever-increasing diet of it that reinforced and even intensified their feeling of being *left behind.* One consequence was that their electoral support for conservatives kept increasing as well. And the more their conservative advocates were elected to public office, the more empowered those advocates felt in opposing the now culturally-entrenched pro-black liberation policies.

The so-called Reagan Revolution was a logical extension of this marriage between the Silent Majority and conservatism. Where President Nixon was at least publicly sensitive (probably for political reasons) to the message of the pro black-liberation *zeitgeist,* President Reagan—not so much. Or if he was sensitive to what black people were saying, he didn't seem to care. He drank his own Kool Aid—he sincerely believed that the Silent Majority had just cause in their complaint against black liberation. He thought that blacks (remember the "Welfare Queen"?) had been coddled and given "free stuff" by "guilty" white liberals at the expense of hard-working white American taxpayers. Skilled at getting this message across to the citizenry, Reagan successfully grew the size of the Silent Majority, adding to their number the "Reagan Democrats"— the white working-class Democrats who also felt abandoned by liberalism's love affair with minority liberation ideology. With Reagan's affirmation, many of his followers who had stayed relatively quiet before began coming out of hiding to openly voice the bigotry they had been feeling all along, regaining their footing as an effective cultural subgroup.

With the passage of time, the white working class of today has added new particulars to their litany of complaint, much of which has nothing to do with anti-black liberation sentiment. However, as these things quite often go, the new complaints have gotten folded in with that sentiment, further intensifying their racist feelings. Over the past 30 years, many from the white working-class have not only felt culturally left behind by our "rainbow" nation, but *they have in fact* been abandoned economically by the government, with no effective governmental actions taken to relieve their plight. Of course, this lack of action was unintentional, but that hardly matters to the white working class...and it shouldn't. There have not even been many sincere efforts by our leaders to *talk* about that plight in a meaningful way. Bernie Sanders and Mr. Trump have been the only recent voices in the dark, but neither has any detailed solutions that fit with the reality of the globally integrated world we live in. Despite Mr. Trump's feckless policy efforts to support his white working-class base, they remain out on a ledge.[14] International trade deals, the fast pace of changing technology and the wholesale movement of jobs overseas have left many of them out in the cold to join the ranks of the unemployed poor; they are fast becoming the *unemployed* poor white working-class and the *soon-to-be unemployed* poor white working-class. Their sense of despair is deflected away from themselves and transformed into an added layer of hateful racist rage toward black people; it's easier to blame a black person than it is to wake up each day so focused on their own sense of hopelessness. This is a variation on the kind of strong bias we've looked at where fear gets turned into hate, in order to avoid the discomfort of feeling fear. More specifically, the *dread of one's hopeless-seeming future* is transformed into a bigoted hatred of the black person in the service of toning down one's *feelings of abject hopelessness*.

In addition, many of these same people pass their hopelessness

---

[14] Commenting on Mr. Trump's successful efforts to remove us from international trade deals and rewrite others would take us too far afield. I'll simply say that obviously, these efforts haven't been of much value for the working-class poor, while they have been a fairly good deal for many of the big business players. See Chapter 14.

through the filter of their unconscious or non-reflected-upon di-minished white privilege; the exception being the unapologetically open racists among them whose hopelessness quite consciously passes through that filter. When white privilege is severely threatened, this has the consequence of stimulating the racist's anger at those he thinks have co-opted his privilege. Indeed, he's angry with both his privileged-group replacement and the cul-ture-at-large that he feels has unfairly moved him off his perch of white entitlement, the last symbolic vestige of any power this economically stressed white person had been holding onto. Un-der these circumstances, the run-of-the-mill racist turns his ire toward the black community that he sees as the main transgres-sor against his formerly favored privileged status. In his eyes, all that the culture has been focused on and talking about for the past 50 years has been the "the poor downtrodden black people," bending over backwards to atone for its past sins of slavery and the thoroughgoing marginalization of black people that fol-lowed. Agreeing with the previous generation's Reaganites, today's working-class racists think that black people have been given too much. The more virulent among them believe that *anything* that's been done for the black community is already too much because, as inferiors who have always sapped the strength of our white Christian nation, black people are deserving only of scorn, or worse.

While this phenomenon of white privilege inciting working-class racism is especially noticeable today, the plain truth is that the general phenomenon has always been around and especially advocated by the American white underclass (to be distinguished from the white working class). What I mean is that in addition to today's newly coined poor white working class, there has always been a white underclass that has used its white privilege to lord over black slaves and then over black people since slavery in order to bolster their compromised sense of self. The lineage of these people can be traced back to the very beginning of colonial America, when the British were intent on sending off their criminals, malcontents, intellectually deficient and mentally ill to the New World. Seen by the British as irretrievably worthless, these people became the first white underclass to inhabit our nation, scavenging to survive. They mostly settled in the South, where they became an enduring underclass living near black slaves and resenting them as the only thing that stood between their minimally-privileged selves and the bottom rungs of society. They've gone by different epithets—ruffians, ramblers, hillbillies, poor white trash, rednecks. From the beginning, they never had a sense of being part of civil society, nor were they much beyond being low-functioning, fractured selves. A 400-plus year lineage has kept these white people fixed in place, unable and/or unwilling to compete in the larger community, the only thing giving them a sense of any value at all being minimally privileged superiority over the black race.

The issue of white privilege and racism isn't limited to marginalized whites. "White flight" from America's cities to the suburbs—beginning 60 years ago and picking up steam during the racial/social "unrest" of the 1960s and again in the 1990's—is also a symptom of the social disease of white privilege. These middle- and upper-class people often are of a *socially liberal* persuasion; regardless of their political party affiliation, many of them actually champion black liberation and other liberal causes. They don't realize that they also walk around with an unconscious or non-reflected-upon sense of white privilege, unaware of this double-consciousness. The mental mechanics of this phenomenon work much the same way as in white privilege anti-Latino racism, with the same unintended but nevertheless racist consequence of demeaning black people. Still other suburbanites harbor a sense of white privilege, often quite consciously; unapologetically racist whites who happen to live in the suburbs. They range from the middle-class on up and are not only aware of their white privilege, but they wear the badge proudly. Unlike the liberal suburbanites, they are intentional racists, unhappy that their former playgrounds have been "stolen" from them and transformed into "rotting ghettos." Designating themselves as *different from* "those people" is an honorific as far as they're concerned.

There's one more community of white-privilege racists. It should come as no surprise that there are black people who, like certain Latinos, identify with the enemy and in the process unintentionally help white racists do the job of demeaning and dehumanizing black people. As such, they internalize the same sense of white privilege that white racists use to fuel their own black bigotry against other blacks. The psychological defense mechanism generally works in the same way it does for Latinos; to unconsciously advantage themselves and disadvantage other blacks. And indeed, this has gone on since the days of slavery. There are countless examples, but I'll just mention two. Consider that most plantations had *black slave drivers* doing the straw boss bidding of the white overseers. The drivers were in charge of seeing that the other slaves did their appointed jobs, all the while unconsciously assuming white privilege. These were black men who identified with the white enemy, unconsciously internalizing the notion that white is good and powerful, they used this second-hand sense of privilege to terrorize fellow slaves, identifying them as bad, powerless. Fast forward beyond the days of slavery, there have always been less horrifying examples where the idea of white privilege (white is good, black is bad) has played a role in black people's image of themselves, unintentionally playing into the white racist's project of demeaning and dehumanizing them. The case I'm thinking of is the notorious "brown bag" test that black people used in the not-so-distant past in order to gauge skin tone. How close in hue one came to the supermarket paper bag graded how close one came to being like the preferred white person.

These two examples are good reminders of the destructive effectiveness of white racism; so effective that it has enlisted the unconscious aid of some black people to accomplish the mission of racist anti-black bigotry to demean, devalue and dehumanize the black psyche if not to remove the very existence of black people. Thankfully, slave-driving and the brown bag test are no longer part of the culture. Nevertheless, identifying with the enemy and his white privilege most certainly still exists in the black community. We'll say more about this in a different context in Chapters 10–13.

The various types of people I've just described are the face of the large anti-black subculture. They all have to confront the culture-at-large that opposes them. Some are more than willing and able to engage the liberationist in angry hateful debate, or worse; some are still too shy, though they would dearly love to be more vocal; and some, such as the white liberals and black racists with an unconscious sense of white privilege, would never even think to undermine the forces of liberation, even though in fact, in their double-consciousness stance, they do. With the exception of unintentional white-privileged racists, these people are a cancer looking to destroy black liberation ideology, wholly opposed to any form of letting go of their privilege.

Bigotry—Exhibit 3: Racist Hatred of Native American Peoples (Genocide and White Privilege)

Let's shift our attention to the American hate affair with Native Americans. White people have always demeaned, devalued and

dehumanized Native Americans, American Indians.[15] This has
undoubtedly been the vilest of all our racisms. Along with the killing work done by imported diseases (we've all heard about the
mass deaths that purportedly came from gifted blankets infected
with smallpox), white racism led to the intentional *extermination*
of whole nations of American Indians. Accomplished at torturing
and slaughtering enslaved black people, racist white America at
the same time executed a full-on genocide of American Indians.[16]

From the earliest days of European settlements in the "New
World," racism has been aimed at the continent's indigenous peoples. We were in fact the immigrants to *their* land, but we didn't
petition them for "immigrant" status. Instead, making the assumption of white privilege, we felt empowered to do as we wished, even
to view ourselves as colonialists who could justifiably assume power
over the indigenous inhabitants.[17]

---

[15] Unlike brown and black peoples, Native Americans despise being called "the red
man" or "redskins." That terminology was wholly a Hollywood invention—the movies being the primary vehicle for spreading a demeaning, infantilizing, utter contempt
for various tribal nations of Native Americans, a.k.a. American Indians (these two terminologies being the more acceptable terminologies of choice).

[16] In no way do I mean the following as a mitigating factor, but, clearly, we are not
alone in our genocidal impulses. We have joined the legions of people of all colors
who have done the same throughout history. We don't have to go back to the Crusades
to find examples. There have been far too many genocides in the recent past, right up
to the present. We need only look at the Turkish genocide of Armenians, the Soviet
genocide of Ukrainians, the Holocaust of Jews in Nazi-occupied Europe, the Pol
Pot/Khmer Rouge Cambodian genocide, the Ba'athist genocide of Kurds, the Indone-
sian genocide in East Timorese, the Croatian genocide of Serbs, the Burundi genocide
of Hutus and Tutsis, the Rwandan genocide of pygmies, the ISIL genocide of Yazidis,
Shias and Christians, the Darfur genocide in the Sudan that continues to this day. And
there are far too many more examples. People of all races seem to be capable of anything when it comes to savagely aggressing one another.

[17] An interesting side note: this trick of language around the issue of "privilege" and
"immigrant" has a variation that Americans are fond of purveying today when they
live in other nations. Instead of making the assumption of *white* privilege, when we
go abroad, we make the assumption of *American* privilege when talking about our

Initially looking to avoid bloodshed, Europeans paternalistically said they were only trying to improve life for these "savages"; their conquest began via thrusting upon them the white religion of Christianity. Of course, the actual underlying motive was to grab the indigenous peoples' land in order to expand the *white* population and steal its natural resources. When the American Indian responded appropriately by defending himself against this unwanted invasion, the European carpetbaggers went to war, time and again. A countless number of philosophers, theologians and generals had for millennia talked about their "just wars," pursued in the name of their God, their state pride, their "need" for expansion. The settlers, too, defined theirs as a just war. But the white British and European invaders used a more recent form of justification—John Locke's idea that a people were justified in forcibly taking ownership of lands that weren't being used for economic profit in the way that white people would use them. The special character of the kind of war they would engage in—genocide—would require something more. And so, designating the indigenous as "heathens" was the beginning of the white person's internalizing a kind of rabid racist bigotry which has remained white America's unacknowledged self-justification for all means of abuse in our just war; the kind of strong bias characterized by a wholehearted disapproval of a race or

---

status as inhabitants of our new country. When Americans of any race move to another country, we don't define ourselves as new "immigrants" to that country. Rather, we become American "ex-pats." That's a term of empowerment. It tells the people of the "host country" (this itself being a loaded term that further empowers the Americans who must be the honored "guests") that we Americans are a group of equal importance (or perhaps superior?) to the citizens of that country. The ex-pat isn't to be seen as an un-empowered immigrant currying favor and acceptance by the empowered citizenry of that country. Instead, assuming American privilege, we are to be seen as a particular kind of American—with all the privileged power that being *any* American citizen brings with it—alongside of, but not absorbed by, the other country's citizenry.

ethnic group, with the effect of distorting one's beliefs about them. In justifying the use of raw, unhinged power in stealing the Native American continent and the genocidal slaughter of much of the American Indian population, whites came to wholeheartedly hate and disapprove of everything about these "others" who would oppose them: white privilege at its worst. This shutting down of the normal cognitive processing of reality continues in America to this day; white people had to develop a strong, reality-distorting bias—seeing the indigenous tribes as savage beasts that needed to be put down; a hatred that would drill deep into the core of their identity so as not to acknowledge the loathsomeness of the brutality they perpetrated.

Once the blood lust had been satisfied and the genocide had done its worst, white people returned their attention to civil society and to taming the land. For those Native Americans who had survived, white "Americans" added insult to injury viewing them as unwanted immigrants in their own land. They furthered the insult by robbing the natives of their sacred homelands. As victors, white Americans moved tribal peoples around the country as casually as one might move chess pieces on a board. Isolating the indigenous peoples to reservations and taking no responsibility for their subsequent well-being became part of the white American culture-at-large self-justifying *given*.

In time, white Americans played a little psychological trick on themselves, transforming the bigoted hateful feelings toward the Native American into something more palatable: the feared American Indian enemy—the dangerous savage beast—became a silly cartoon character; think of the Lone Ranger and Tonto, or the Disney version of Pocahontas and John Smith. The only time whites would allow the former kind of hateful bigotry to rear its ugly head would be when they wanted to tout white heroism—to be "the good guys"—in the face of the murderous savages, "cowboys and Indians."

155

The result has been not simply the decimation of the Native American population and the continuing appropriation of their lands (most recently the revocation of the Mashpee Wampanoag tribe's land trust in Massachusetts), but also the effective destruction of their mental health and self-esteem. White America's bigoted behavior has been so thorough as to break the spirit of an overwhelming portion of the Native American nations, making them the most brutalized and marginalized of any American minorities. Beyond the ongoing assault on their mental health, there have been multi-generational problems of abject poverty, the scourge of alcoholism, the plague of drug use, epidemic suicide, rampant unemployment, unequal educational opportunities, and the crushing psychological weight of historical, *openly* racist and thoroughgoing *disrespect* for them; a viewpoint currently gone into hiding from public view, but remaining a constant presence nevertheless.

Thankfully, many Native Americans have responded to the culture-at-large's general embrace of social liberation and have tried to establish a place for their peoples under that umbrella. In fact, the vocal demands they've made for their rights have forced the formerly open anti-Native American racists to recede to the shadows. Because the culture-at-large says that disrespecting minority rights is taboo, the rest of us at least pay cursory attention to the Native American's complaints. We've shelved the "savage Indian" talk and most of the cartoon allusions (with the exception of certain remaining, offensive sports team names, logos and mascots). Obviously, though, we haven't done nearly enough; while the U.S. government has tried to make some degree of reparation in the form of programs to fight poverty, alcoholism and drug use, as well as endowing University scholarships for Native Americans, these have been half measures at best.

And so, the vocal demands for Native American rights have,

by necessity, continued. Much effort has gone into promoting a public awareness of the various Native American cultures, including displays of fine arts—music, dance, painting, textiles, pottery and sculpture, as well as jewelry—that find their way into concert halls, performance spaces, galleries and museums throughout the country. This is all very important consciousness-raising for getting the culture-at-large to finally pay attention to the human beings who live on the reservations who have proud traditions worthy of respect. But fine art alone won't make a significant dent in the consciousness of the rest of the country. For example, there haven't been nearly enough popular movies starring Native Americans in serious roles that deal with everyday drama—love stories, detective stories. Relatively few (self-identifying) Native American musicians appear on the popular music scene. And although popular literature by and about American Indians has a niche in our bookstores (law enforcement stories about intrigue on the reservation, for example), most of these popular novels are written by Anglos. It's these three modalities specifically—popular film, music and literature—that most condition "mainstream" American taste and that will get its attention. (Notable exceptions: the novels of M. Scott Momaday, Leslie Marmon Silko and Louise Erdrich; the poems of Joy Harjo; and the short stories of Sherman Alexie.)

While consciousness-raising hasn't been effective enough, there has been somewhat effective political action. Numerous groups promote the cause of Native American rights—the American Indian Movement, the National Congress of American Indians, the Native American Rights Fund, the Association of American Indian Affairs, and a myriad of Native American tribal organizations lobbying the U.S. Congress among them—as well as political protests that have grabbed the headlines. In the recent past, the most public of these have been the demonstrations against the proposed laying of an oil pipeline through the sacred burial grounds and cultural sites of the Standing Rock Sioux Indian Reservation of North Dakota; the 1973 Wounded Knee murder incident that sparked years of protests by the Oglala Lakota Indians on the Pine Ridge Reservation; and more protests over the non-enforcement of treaty obligations by the U.S. government to improve tribal living conditions and honor the sovereignty of the Lakota nation.

The common thread tying such groups and protests together is the relatively blind response the government has had to the utter desperation of Native American citizens—once again, adding the crushing psychological weight of racism to their self-esteem, abject poverty, and generations-old battles with alcoholism. The unhappy truth is that the protests in the name of exposing these desperate conditions don't stay in the news; the public consciousness of the Native American cause moves to the background.

In sum, Native American efforts at consciousness-raising have done some good. And so have their efforts at political action. But the sad truth remains that anti-Native American racism is still winning the day and the rest of America simply returns to business as usual. While the general *idea* of liberation for Native Americans is part of the culture-at-large, it pretty much remains only an idea, one that has yet to see any meaningful concretization. Beyond paying lip service, the culture-at-large has not yet offered effective national support for American Indian liberation. Who knows what will become of the Native American liberation cause in Trump World? I'm waiting for the time at one of his rallies where he points to a Native American planted in the crowd and proudly crows, "Look at my American Indian; *look* at him!"

Bigotry—Exhibit 4: Anti-White Sentiment (Reactive Bigotry)

I want to briefly discuss another area of bigotry that's also very much with us: the hatred that some people of color have for white people. Let me make a few pertinent distinctions.

The kind of hateful bigotry spouted by American white people against people of color is virtually *intrinsic* to white racists, meaning that white racists have always spouted their bigotry out of the sense of white privilege that's virtually at the core of how white racists define themselves. I suspect it showed its face the first time a white person on our continent first saw a person of color. I want to distinguish this virtually *intrinsic* racism from what I call *reactive* bigotry; what is expressed by, say, some brown or black or yellow or Native American people when they rant against whites. Understand that this kind of bigotry doesn't come from an assumed place of power as it does for the white racist. So too, it doesn't normally amount to an expression of the person of color (POC) feeling superior to the inferior white person around the issue of *power*. Rather, it's a hateful reaction to—a consequence of— having been the victim of systematic disempowering abuse. It's a rational, self-protective response to the minority person's life experience of living in a world of angry, often violent white racists.

I should point out that, while there's typically not a person of color with an assumed sense of *power* superiority, there *is* quite often an assumed sense of *moral* superiority, relative to white racists' historical moral bankruptcy of their mistreatment of people of color. This sense of moral superiority would be the softer side of the person of color's bigoted feelings, in the sense that it's not necessarily a hate-fueled opinion. Indeed, it's the more emotionally raw side of the person of color's bigotry that white people complain about—"Why do they have to hate us so much? They're just as bigoted as any white racist."

The white person's response of feeling victimized by a person of color's bigotry is problematic; it's clear who has historically been the *aggressor*—the *victimizer*. To then whine about the victim (the POC) victimizing white people strains credulity. But while the whining white racist doesn't have a leg to stand on, what about white people who genuinely don't harbor racist feelings against people of color? Are they deserving of this hatred because of the "sins of the fathers"? The plain answer is, no, they're not. So, while anti-white hatred by people of color is understandable, this is not to say that it doesn't sometimes go overboard and spatter all white people, racist or not. There's a very rational explanation[18] for the genesis of POC bigotry towards white people due to the need for people to defend themselves from violent aggressors, even while it doesn't make sense to take aim at people who haven't been aggressors.

While this rational explanation does to a degree mitigate the reactive bigotry of people of color, it ultimately is not to be excused. Defending oneself is a good thing; however, that doesn't mean that all possible defense mechanisms are acceptable. Bringing a nuclear bomb to a fistfight would be out of bounds, for example. I don't mean to equate reactive bigotry to a nuclear weapon, but I do want to say that, in the final analysis, using hatred to defend oneself is ultimately a poor choice. The bigotry of any group, acted upon for any underlying motives, never does the body politic any good. Listening to one another and meaningfully empathizing with one another's complaints becomes impossible. Civility and good citizenship flee the scene. So, while reactive

---

[18] I can imagine someone not sympathetic with what I'm saying in this section complaining that I'm ultimately trying to mitigate the person of color's reactive bigotry by citing the fact that it can be *explained*. This critic points out that we can also find some explanations for why the white racist harbors his racism. (Indeed, I discussed a few explanations of white racism in Chapter 3.) So, shouldn't this mitigate for the white person's racism as well? (What's good for the goose is good for the gander.) The simple answer to this objection is that the explanations for a person of color's anti-white reactive bigotry are *rational* explanations—i.e. they make common sense—and the explanations for white racism are not—they are irrational and don't make common sense (again, see Chapter 3).

bigotry is understandable, it doesn't trump the overriding need for people in a society to aim for social harmony. And just as vile white racism rules out the possibility of that harmony, so too does the person of color's intolerance or prejudice towards white people.

Bigotry—Exhibit 5: Intramural People of Color's Racism and Displacement

This next kind of racism is a variation of reactive bigotry. Once again, it's a reaction to white racism, but it's not really aimed at the white racist. Instead, it's people of color holding racist judgments against other people of color. That could be black-on-black, brown-on-brown, black-on-brown, brown-on-black, brown-on-yellow, black on Native American—you get the idea. This phenomenon is historically very well-entrenched in America. The root cause is plain: the racism of people of color is motivated by a desire (a need?) to find a group that they perceive—or that they want to perceive—as being "less than." A time-honored way of defending against feeling worthless or inferior is to form a hateful bias against another. So racism against other nonwhite people arises in people of color in order to give them a sense of power over others who they perceive as being close to them on the hierarchy of power. Put another way, it's a person of color's defense against the feeling of inferiority that white racism has so effectively hammered into the psyches of most people of color.[19] Sorry to say, hatred feels empowering. To the degree that a POC hates another POC, she may feel that much more powerful and superior than she would were she not hating.

---

[19] Other peoples of color—the wide variety of nonwhite American ethnics (e.g. South Asian Indians or Polynesians)—haven't been *quite* so hatefully focused on by whites. So, I'll leave them out of the equation.

The POC's *true* target for her hateful bias is white people; the people who have made her feel unempowered. And, as we've just seen, many POC feel that hatred and express it. However, the hatred of white people can be so intense and overwhelming to experience in consciousness, she defends herself against this feeling by *displacing* some of that hatred onto other POC as a safety valve, as it were. Sometimes this gets expressed in the form of one black person calling another the n-word.[20] Sometimes it leads to gang warfare between gangs of the same race or gangs of different races. Sometimes a person of color negatively stereotypes a person of another race or ethnicity: "dirty" this or "money-hungry" that. Additionally, this racist displacement feels relatively "safe" to the transgressor. Since the other POC she has targeted is close to her on the hierarchy of power, in her fantasy, she doesn't worry about the other's response to her display of racism as much as she thinks she would have to worry were she to similarly target a white person; in her fantasy, she has more power than the other people of color.

Bigotry—Exhibit 6: Misogyny and Male Privilege

To begin unpeeling this particular offensive onion, we first need to distinguish between the misogynist and the sexist. Broadly speaking, the sexist is biased toward men over women in the sense that in his behaviors, beliefs and attitudes, he shows a consistent favoring of men over women. The misogynist is the sexist who also disparages, demeans, possibly hates and, through sexual objectification, dehumanizes women. While dealing with both misogyny and sexism is important for us as a culture to do, I am only going to address the more egregious of the two, misogyny.

---

[20] Obviously, language is always a complex matter. So, we all know that a black person's using the n-word against another black person isn't always intended as a hateful slur. Sometimes it's a term of affection, as in "I love you, my n___".

There seems to me to be a menu of four general stances of misogyny from which people in America may choose. The first is our publicly stated cultural bias against all forms of misogyny. The second is what I'll call "the underground view," referring to a biased, sympathetic misogyny that many in the culture-at-large hold tightly in the deepest recesses of their souls, but would never admit to because of cultural censure. This misogyny is normally an unconscious or non-reflected-upon bias that people in the public culture unhesitatingly display in their behavior, even though it is condemned by the culture-at-large and even though they would deny advocating it. This is the sort of double-consciousness we saw earlier regarding unexamined white liberal anti-Latino and anti-black racism. Here, though, it happens to pro-female liberationist anti-misogynists who are in fact also secret misogynists. In their conscious minds, these people are four-square against misogyny. In their unconscious or non-reflected-upon thinking, they are in agreement with the misogynists. The third choice on the menu is the stance of the unapologetic subculture of bigots who have no truck with the culture-at-large that sees women as equal to men. This third group consciously believes that women are inferior to men and deserve to be disparaged. And then, there's the fourth item on the menu, the person is confused about his own misogyny. *At the same time* that he *consciously opposes* any kind of misogyny (especially regarding his loved ones), he also *consciously exhibits* it himself. It's the idea that he is *conscious* of the fact that he behaves misogynistically that distinguishes him from the second variety of misogynist, the double-consciousness kind. This individual lives out a *conscious* inconsistency and fails to see the problem. Let's look at each of these four kinds of misogyny and see what we can make of them.

Mr. Trump is once again the poster child for bigotry—this time, for misogyny. His misogynistic exploits are well known, so

I won't recount them here. In his own way, he has a foot in the second, third and perhaps even the fourth camp as well. So, on the one hand, he is as good a standard bearer as any for today's proud unapologetic misogynist member of the third camp who thinks very little of women—dehumanizing them as sex objects and belittling them if they dare speak up to him. (Of course, he belittles anybody—man or woman—who speaks up against him.) On the other hand, when he behaves as a misogynist, he refuses to take his lumps from the culture-at-large about it, instead insisting that "No man respects women as much as I do." If he were sincere about this claim, he would be in the second camp of people who harbor unconscious or nonreflected- upon misogyny. One suspects, though, that he's very much aware of his disparaging thoughts and feelings about women. That would put him in the fourth camp, someone who is a conscious intentional misogynist while at the same time he consciously cares about women (his eldest daughter or some of his female employees, for example). He lives with this conscious inconsistency, never bringing the two together in a moment of reflection.

In any event, many well-intentioned, loving men—men who are well-intentioned and loving toward the women in their lives—are precisely like Mr. Trump; they are of the second and fourth camp variety. There are many men who don't behave as egregiously as he has, but who certainly exhibit the same misogynistic attitudes and beliefs that they express on a daily basis, while at the same time are unable to admit to it. Of course, some men are like this because it's *all* unconscious or they're not self-reflective enough about this particular subject matter to realize they are from the second camp of people who misperceive who they are. But so many others are from the fourth camp; confused in the sense that they maintain a conscious inconsistency about the matter. They both intentionally disparage women and care about them, never bringing the two ideas together at any given moment of reflection. They jump from one position to the other, suffering no cognitive dissonance.

The points of view described in the second, third and fourth camps all amount to another kind of bigotry that puts undue stress on the nation's social fabric. The consequences of this bigotry are at least as devastating for women as the racism is devastating for people of color. With this in mind, then, I'd like to take a look at the more recent history of misogynistic social stress as it has unfolded in the American setting, as well as how it gets played out on a daily basis.

A paradigm of unapologetic hateful misogyny—the third camp—is easily demonstrable by looking at the events of Hillary Rodham Clinton's life for the past 30 years, as well as what transpired during her unsuccessful bid for the presidency. Her lifelong involvement in all forms of liberation rights advocacy dates back to the 1970s when, serving as Wellesley College's student body president, she actively lobbied for the hire of more black professors. Upon graduation, she began her lifelong crusade of advocating for children's rights. For example, as a 24-year old law student and civil rights activist working for Marian Wright Edelman's Children's Defense Fund, she went undercover to Dothan, Alabama to chronicle the Nixon Administration's non-enforcement of the legal ban on granting tax-exempt status to "segregated academies."

Later, as the First Lady of Arkansas, she would continue to advocate—on the national stage—for the rights of children and equal education. Her resume as a social liberationist would only grow from there. It wasn't until 1993, when President Clinton made the first lady the point person chairing a task force on National Health Care Reform, that the misogynists came crawling out of the woodwork. "Hillarycare" was damned by Republicans as the government's attempt to take over the ordinary citizen's healthcare decisions. I won't comment on the reform efforts the Clinton Administration made; suffice it to say that there were many mistakes made in crafting the legislation. I'm only concerned with how conservatives, in their opposition to any kind of reform legislation, used Hillary Clinton as a piñata, and how, in the midst of their political furor, many of them carelessly allowed their misogynistic beliefs and attitudes to show. "Presumptuous," they called her, "power-hungry," "not intellectually up to the task"—barely-disguised code words for "She's *just* a woman. What gives her the right to try to wield power?"

The central issue for most of these misogynists was about raw male power. HRC was seen as an emasculator who needed to be stopped in her tracks. An assumption of privilege was at the center of the Hillary-hatred. But instead of white privilege, it was *male* privilege; more precisely, *male power* privilege. That quality was and still is—for not only the anti-Hillary Republican bigots, but for most men—a central defining component of what it is to be a man. Like the racist who defines himself as superior to the "inferior" black or brown person, so too do most men assume themselves to be *powerful* and superior in the context of a woman being essentially *powerless* and inferior. So when it came to "Hillarycare," not only were conservative Republicans disdainful, but also many Democrats who were otherwise supportive of the idea of healthcare reform were all too often willing to wink at their Republican colleagues' misogyny. Once more, some of these responses were intentional—they were the product of fully embraced male supremacist misogyny—and some were unintentional. In the latter case, there was again a kind of double-consciousness on the part of these men (the second camp, the underground view). Whether Mrs. Clinton's Republican critics, her Democratic allies, or the man-on-the-street—many men made the unconscious or non-reflected-upon assumption of male power privilege while at the same time publicly and consciously frowning upon any form of misogyny.

This wasn't only true of men. Women, too, made the assumption of male power privilege. And like some men, they too were intentional male supremacy misogynists, while others were double-consciousness unintentional misogynists. For the latter group, although modern feminism had for three decades already been advocating for women's rights for external material equality—for example, that women should have the same opportunity as men to work outside of the home, be considered as candidates for the same kinds of jobs men traditionally held—advocacy for effecting a woman's internal psychological sense of herself hadn't made much progress. For most women living during the Hillarycare era, assuming male privileged superiority was part of *their* self-image—they were used to being relatively powerless and subservient. Who was Hillary to rock the boat? As one might expect, when a lot of people—both men and women—felt their sense of self threatened by a powerful woman, a strong misogynistic bias backlash took precedence over anything they might have otherwise thought about healthcare reform. Even if they ended up supporting the proposal, many were nevertheless internally disposed against Mrs. Clinton the person—the presumptuous woman.

Anti-Hillary misogyny hasn't changed much since. Between then and now, there has been a veritable cottage industry of conservative critics who have made their anti-Hillary misogynistic bones with their movies, books, conservative think tank white papers, volumes of fake news reports and Congressional investigations (Benghazi, the missing emails, the Clinton Foundation) that have all been aimed at promoting conspiracy theories about Hillary Clinton as the devil incarnate who would collude with international bankers to overthrow the government of the United States; who would use her political power to have her political opponents murdered; who would enrich herself from the coffers of government and her various campaign war chests; who would be a sexual deviant pleasuring herself through her many lesbian sexual affairs and by trafficking in children and child pornography....The level of hatred for this woman has been nothing short of hysterical. The strongly biased, wholehearted disapproval of her for daring to challenge the male power status quo is so intense for so many conservatives (and for far too many liberal Democrats) that they can't accurately assess the facts about her life and work. The assumption of male power privilege is so deep that these people end up practicing a misogyny so insidious, they can only thrive in a social media echo chamber where they and their fellows can pump one another up in reaffirming their shared, cognitively distorted views. Had it been a man exerting political power in promoting the very same policies as Hillary Clinton, there never would have been these sorts of deeply disturbing biases set against him.

Matters only got worse during her 2016 presidential campaign. While Hillary-the-presidential-candidate clearly had her flaws and while there certainly were people who opposed her solely for reasons of policy, I, like many others, believe that the root cause of the treatment she received during the campaign and since (e.g. the "lock her up" crowd) has been primarily motivated by an abiding misogyny. All the same variations of it that she suffered through the previous two-plus decades are again on full display. Some people whose self-definition at its core has involved male power privilege and, so, have felt emasculated by her assumption of female power (the presidency being emblematic of "ultimate male power") have formed very strong, hateful bigoted biases against her. Others for whom male power privilege has not been quite so central to their self-definition have reacted initially by merely demeaning her. For those of the latter bias variety who in time might become open to hearing and finally believing that they have all along harbored an unconscious or non-reflected-upon sense of male power privilege, with the proper absorbing of consciousness-raising around this issue, their form of bigoted bias could conceivably dissolve. For those of the former variety whose strong bias will never be shaken, some are unapologetic intentional misogynists, some are unintentional double-consciousness misogynists, and some are the confused misogynists whose conscious behavior is inconsistent. Those from the unintentional double-consciousness camp genuinely champion the culture-at-large condemnation of misogyny and they harbor unconscious or non-reflected-upon misogynistic bias against Mrs. Clinton. Their level of bias ranges from the demeaning variety to the hateful demeaning and dehumanizing kind.

Then there are the misogynists from the confused inconsistent group who are conscious misogynists and conscious anti-misogynists. We saw plenty of these confused Hillary-bashers during the campaign. We heard them interviewed at Trump rallies. They bounced back and forth from one position to the other, embracing two conscious contradictory biases without realizing their inconsistency because they apparently never experienced any sense of cognitive dissonance about the matter. Odd, to say the least. And finally, there's the case of Mr. Trump himself. As I've said, he's the dissembling kind of individual who on the one hand disingenuously swears his allegiance to the cause of female liberation, while on the other, he's certainly shown his misogyny toward Mrs. Clinton on a daily basis for the past five years. All these types capture the kinds of misogyny that Hillary Clinton has had to endure in her public life over the past 30 years.

Now we will take her case as a jumping off place to make some more general observations about the nature of misogyny. To begin, two quick points that come directly from the Hillary case: first, there are a fair number of openly misogynistic people today, many of them proud supporters of Mr. Trump and his hateful behavior against women; second, the assumption of male power privilege always entails an attitude of misogyny, even when it's unintentional, which always has the effect of demeaning a woman, sending the message that she is powerless and inferior.

Here are some more general thoughts about misogyny that are loosely inspired by the Hillary case. I believe that the assumption of male power privilege is not only unconsciously held by individuals; it's also *an unconscious norm of the culture-at-large* alongside the culture-at-large norm of condemning misogyny. It's part of the collective unconscious, part of our ancestral memory. While condemnation of open, intentional misogyny is embraced by our culture-at-large, so is the unintentional—unconscious or non-reflected-upon—assumption of male power privilege, which inevitably breeds misogyny. We have a culture-at-large double-consciousness. And because it's extremely difficult for a culture-at-large and the people who inhabit it to change what's in its unconscious, it's at least equally difficult to tame our culture-at-large double-consciousness about misogyny.

In a better world than the one we live in now, it's the unconscious or non-reflected-upon misogynistic side of the culture-at-large equation that will need serious psychological work. It won't be easy; the assumption of male power privilege is buried in the deepest subterranean bowels of our culture as a change-resistant bias that, although we obviously are aware that it's there—hey, we're talking about it right now, aren't we—eradicating it would seem to require changing the very definition of that culture. Many temporary defining aspects of the culture-at-large—not the least of which are the prevailing ideologies at different points in time—have come and gone throughout our nation's history. But one defining and unchanging aspect of The American Culture has been the ideology of male privilege—of America as a *patriarchy*. That's a reflection of how very central to our culture's self-definition—indeed, how very central to all of Western civilization—that ideology has been. For perspective, patriarchy and the misogyny that it engenders are even more a part of us as a nation than the racist bigotries we've discussed have been—and heaven knows that racist bigotries are deep and have been virtually impossible to finally eradicate. Male privilege runs even more deeply. How do we excise that historically core notion from the culture without losing the patient? There are no easy answers; but defeating misogyny will require that we find some.

From a different angle: male power privilege stays rooted in the culture and virtually untouchable because it has to do with the very definition that men, women and the culture-at-large they comprise have held from time immemorial about what it is to be a male and what it is to be a female. Again, historically, "male" equals "powerful" and "female" equals "powerless," and to imagine otherwise is tantamount to stripping males and females of a central aspect of their respective self-images. And just because many women have succeeded in rearranging in their own eyes their self-image to counter this historical image, this doesn't speak to the women who have no interest in such a project and it also doesn't speak to the men who have no interest in redefining their own self-identity. Certainly, *talking* about changing one's sense of self is easy; but doing anything effective beyond talk—actually succeeding in such a change—is always fought against tooth and nail. Even for those with a genuine interest in such change, success is far from automatic. It's one thing to want to change to a different fundamental way of being yourself; it's quite another to rip away a fundamental way of being that has been at the heart of who you've been since birth and has been reinforced by the deepest (unconscious) and most powerful of cultural norms as long as you've drawn breath. So much the worse, then, for our chances of ridding the individual and the culture of misogyny. By the same token, so much the better for dedicating ourselves to embark on this difficult, though not impossible, endeavor, knowing full well that the effort is more than worthy of our commitment.

Shifting gears, another observation about misogyny has to do with recognizing an interesting sociological truth: *some of the very same people who oppose white privilege are people who favor the assumption of male power privilege.* I'm thinking primarily about certain men of color who are openly misogynistic. Many factors aside from cultural ones condition toxic masculinity and spousal abuse, not the least of which include poverty, being the historical victims of violence, mental health vulnerabilities and substance abuse. (Of course, this also happens in white communities.) But another factor has to do with seeing women as easy pickin's for abuse; violence towards and mistreatment of women is an effective way of displacing the anger with white racist victimizers onto someone beneath them, "weaker" or "inferior." There is nothing acceptable or mitigating about this behavior and it needs to change.

Yet another observation about misogyny: while the "issue" of misogyny has certainly been at the center of feminist academic discourse and women's liberation activism, it hasn't until quite recently been so central to the general public discourse. Since the 1960s right up to the Age of Trump, the average person didn't think or talk much about misogyny in the same way that we have approached racism, religious discrimination or homophobia. Of course, if asked pointedly about their feelings about misogyny, most people would have a ready answer—they would condemn it. They've known what the politically correct position is as promoted by the culture-at-large and they've genuinely held that politically correct view. But B.T. (Before Trump), simply stating their agreement would have been the end of the matter. It's my contention that this once again has to do with the underlying cause of misogyny—male power privilege buried so deep inside both the culture-at-large and the individual as to be effectively hidden from view and certainly something that would be very uncomfortable to discuss were it brought to the surface.

I want to add something I haven't said much about beyond my earlier brief mention of it; along with the male and female bias that favors male power privilege for males is the attendant biased belief that the powerless female is *inferior*. The idea of female inferiority is just as deeply buried inside both the culture-at-large and the individual—and is just as hidden from public view—as is the assumption of male power privilege, because people don't want to talk or think about either. It has once more to do with the anxieties swirling inside people concerning the maintenance of a secure sense of identity. As long as the male identity feels threatened, a full public discussion of misogyny will be consigned to the back burner of genuine public consideration. Thus, we will continue to need both female and male advocates for the feminist cause to repeatedly and forcefully insist that serious reflection on this very fundamental matter occur, reoccur and continue to reoccur into the indefinite future.

My final general observation about misogyny will bring us full circle back to racism. The racist not only acts from an assumption of white privilege, he does so in tandem with his assumption of male power privilege. Men and women who are *already* bigoted against black or brown or Native American peoples or other people of color feel that part of their entitlement to spew hateful rhetoric and commit vile actions against minorities comes from a sense of superiority, conditioned by their assumption of *white* privilege; it also flows from that perception of superiority conditioned by their assumption of *male power* privilege. If there's a group of "others" to whom a person is already negatively disposed for any of a combination of the kinds of reasons we talked about in Chapter 3, then both of these kinds of privilege are the icing on the cake of self-justification. Privilege is the bigot's psychological shield that defends *to himself* why it's okay to feel as hateful as he does. He's internally protected. If, as he thinks, certain minority peoples are inferior, then of course he's entitled to do with them what he will. These powerful backstop assumptions of privilege wall off most objections to his bigotry; more factors in maintaining the intense change-resistant nature of his bigoted biases and certainly part of the armament he brings to the knife fight when he decides to tussle with the liberationist ideologue.

Bigotry—Exhibit 7: Religious Discrimination

Because I will have more to say about it in the next few chapters, I will only make brief mention here of the bigoted forces of religious discrimination in our country, centering around a preference for and implied superiority of the Christian religion. Many bigoted Christians see our country as "a Christian nation" that entitles them to reign supreme and demean other religions, regardless of the religious freedom guaranteed by the Constitution. Religious bigots have especially had a field day demeaning Jews.[21] Think, for example, the KKK and their rabid feelings toward everything Jewish, or more moderate Christian bigots who through the years excluded Jews from membership in social clubs, universities, participation in higher political office and in certain professions. Or think the conspiracy theorists who feared *The Jews* because they are devious,

---

[21] Although I comment specifically on some of the same following examples elsewhere in the text, it bears repeating here.

scheming , evil Christ killers who care for nothing but money and power and have made it their mission to become the wealthy power brokers of Hollywood, the media and the major international banks. The Christian bigot has all along feared—indeed, he's been convinced—that the Jews use their cleverness, wealth and power to try to politically undermine the very fate of the world and ascend to world dominance over the forces of Christianity and its institutions. The Christian bigot sees himself as a noble warrior defending his religion. Today, jokes about big-nosed, cheap, conniving Jews are very much in the social winds. For a Jew to complain about this results in the bigot claiming that the Jew is just being *overly PC* about mere words— "Can't you take a joke?" But if only that were the worst of anti-Semitic matters today. The drumbeat of contemporary anti-Semitism has gotten louder and louder. More and more alt-right anti-Semites have come out of hiding to make bomb threats to Jewish Community Centers, vandalize Jewish cemeteries and tag swastikas on the entrances to Jewish places of worship. And then, there was Charlottesville—"Blood and soil. Jews will not replace us."

Because of this movement of rising bigotry and the mixed messages we hear from Mr. Trump regarding the anti-Semitic alt-right (which in fact is also anti-*everything* that's not white and Christian), one can't help but wonder if we are at the beginning of a new fascist era where in time, the forces of anti-Semitism might insist that "extreme measures" be taken to rid the Jewish cancer from the American body. Luckily, at this moment, Jews on the contemporary American scene have enough political voice and are enough a part of the fabric of American culture that the rest of the country seems willing to sit up and take notice of recent events. At this juncture, it seems that the forces of non-bigoted America are totally attuned to what's been going on and side with the Jewish community, reacting with horror to these dangerous assaults. Hope springs eternal.

The other religious group that has recently been most noticeably victimized by Christian bigotry is Islam. The bigoted onslaught has been even more ferocious than the national strain of anti-Semitism. Since I've said quite a lot about anti-Islamic bias by Christians in Chapter 3 and will have more to say about it in time, right now I'll just comment about the most recent national instance: Mr. Trump's Muslim ban. In the early days of the Trump administration, the courts repeatedly thwarted his efforts to keep Muslims from immigrating to this country. But Mr. Trump is nothing if he is not persistent; after some tweaks in the language of the proposed ban, the Supreme Court finally weighed in and sided with Mr. Trump. So now anti-Islamism has been inscribed into law. Of course, our president doesn't speak for all Christians regarding the ban, but certainly many of his evangelical supporters agree with him. They think that Islam is simply too alien a religion to be allowed to take root on our shores. At the extremes, there are those on the alt-right (e.g. David Duke) who flat-out proclaim that our Christian nation is at war with Islam.

Christian bigotry doesn't only pick on Jews and Muslims, though. All non-Christian religions are seen by these bigots as heretical. There is only the Christian *Word*; all else is an affront to the One True God. But not only non-Christian religions get the back of the hand from Christian bigoted zealots; there has also always been a fair amount of infighting about which brand of Christianity is the truest, a kind of Christian anti-Christianism. Throughout American history, Catholicism—the sole Christian religion for 1500 years—has always taken a back seat to the claimed primacy of Protestantism. It has gotten to the point where, today, it is commonplace for Protestants to make a distinction between "Christians" and "Catholics," as though the two were mutually exclusive and clearly relegating Catholicism to a cult status.

Obviously, other kinds of religious discrimination exist in our country and across the world. Jewish, Muslim, Hindu, Taoist and even Buddhist zealots have had their day oppressing members of other religions. But in our country, Christian bigotry has been responsible for more than its share of hateful discrimination.

So where does this leave us? My discussion in this chapter has been about the conservative bigot and his out-in-the-open, in-your-face challenges to the rights of minorities and, more recently, to the liberation ideologies that champion those rights. However, there's one more challenge to minority liberation we need to look at: the challenge to the rights of the LGBTQ community. In the next chapter, I will devote the discussion to how the principled conservative attempts to engage with that community about some of their claimed rights. We will see how in the process of promoting his anti-LGBTQ rights principles, the conservative challenger often enough devolves into the kind of bigoted argument against the LGBTQ community that would make the bigots we've discussed in this chapter proud.

CHAPTER 9

The Principled Conservative
and Liberation Ideology

In contrast to how the unapologetic conservative bigot confronts minorities and minority liberation ideology, in this chapter I will look at the ways in which the principled conservative directly confronts both. I will limit his confrontations with minorities and liberation ideologies to one context: his challenge to the LGBTQ community and the ideology that champions rights for its members, using it as a model for how principled conservatives typically confront most minorities and their supporting ideologies. We will see how the principled conservative begins to challenge his opponent through a direct dispassionate appeal to principles, and then, if his argument falls apart, the way he sometimes settles into the bigot's modalities.[1]

The issue of transgender rights will be our focus. A *cause célèbre* of the recent past[2] was the trans community's claim that their members have the right to use the restroom facilities appropriate to their self-identified gender. Transgender people and their allies embrace this rights claim as the politically correct position. To the principled critic, though, this seems like a bridge too far. He says

---

[1] Not all principled conservatives devolve in this way. There are those who genuinely oppose LGBTQ liberation for reasons of principle alone; bigotry plays no part in their thinking or behavior.

[2] The restroom debacle continues in the news and in the courts; however, without the same notoriety as it did four or five years ago.

that, while transgender people have the right to live out of their gender preference under the law, he insists that they and their supporters are attempting to add a *new unfounded right* that in fact infringes on the rights of other citizens. So, as the argument goes, the transgender movement doesn't in reality have the particular right that its members and their advocates claim. And as all rights debates on the liberation frontier normally play out, this one too will finally be decided by what the culture-at-large and the concerted liberation efforts at consciousness-raising and persuasive arguing decide—whether the practice in question is to become a social norm absorbed in society or not—and by whether or not the courts codify the practice in question into law. For the time being, the culture-at-large along with what I frankly consider to be relatively weak liberation efforts at consciousness-raising and argument still seem to side with the critic; and the law, only in certain states, sides with the transgender community. If this were to remain the case, then the critic's views wouldn't be considered an oppressing principle bias against liberation ideology, but rather an accurate culture-at-large take on who is entitled to use which bathrooms. If, in time, both the culture-at-large and the courts were to move their allegiance to favor the issue, then the critic's views would be considered an oppressing, politically incorrect stance.

The principled conservative generally tries to avoid talking about where the culture-at-large stands on most issues about minority rights. That's because in that arena, one ends up arguing about things like social forces and the current norms of society— whether the culture-at-large favors transgender rights demands or not—and to the principled conservative, the court of public opinion is too open-ended. Instead, the principled conservative throws his hat into the ring of legality, for the courts adjudicate who has the proper standing in a given rights debate. In deciding to fight in that arena, the principled conservative does his best to present considerations that the courts will find favorable in determining questions of minority rights claims.

Getting down to brass tacks, how specifically do the principled conservative and the advocate for transgender rights do battle in the judicial arena? Regarding the question of who should have standing in the transgender "restroom rights" debate, the principled conservative typically appeals to the Constitution. In that context, he asks the court to decide whose rights claims are most consistent with a person's freedom of expression. Are the trans community's demands most consistent with the freedom of expression, where those who identify as other than the gender on their birth certificates should be able to carry out their very personal and ordinary restroom functions in the restroom where they feel psychologically most at home? Or do the needs of the community the principled conservative claims to speak for, where that community's members are able to carry out their own restroom functions and not feel invaded or threatened by members of the "other" gender? Aye, there's the rub: the "other" gender. Leaving this aside for the moment, let's acknowledge that answering these questions determines which community is deemed to have the higher standing, and thus whose rights claims are infringing on whom.

Now, although the principled conservative wants to keep the public's focus squarely on these legal questions of principle and standing, and although he tries mightily to avoid talking about gray areas like social forces and cultural norms, it's those fuzzy areas that tend to matter most to us. It's the efforts of transgender liberation consciousness-raising programs, together with the *social forces* that are put in play as a result of the *emotionally charged public drama* over transgender behavior, that will finally determine which *social norms* and mores will settle approvingly into public consciousness, into the culture-at-large. And the courts take these kinds of considerations into account as relevant factors in adjudicating the above questions about basic principles of rights and rights infringements.

Using the direct argument over principle and the emotionally charged public drama about the fuzzy considerations as context, what's the current state of the "bathroom debate"? Truthfully, nothing much has been settled yet. That being the case, this is where we might begin to see some principled conservatives begin to display anti-LGBTQ bigoted attitudes[3] that up to this point have been layered over by their normally overriding concern for principles. Now they will change their focus away from principles, moving the discussion from a civil and rational debate to an attack on LGBTQ *political correctness*. Although he hasn't lost the debate yet, having failed to actually win it with all of his best principle arguments, many principled conservatives leave behind their rational challenge to minority liberation ideology and opt for the old *ad hominem* take-down strategy in an effort to *poison the well*, influence the court away from the concerns the transgender community and, by extension to finally adjudicate the issue of whose rights of free expression infringe on whom. We're all familiar with this strategy: convince the court that PC is bad. Have it associate the negative quality of PC with transgender people and their claims for restroom rights as being a prime example of transgender people overstepping the bounds of what's reasonable, opening up the culture to sexually deviant behavior in girls' bathrooms by predatory biological males. Have this newly-created poor opinion about transgender people and their rights claims infect the court's deliberations. In playing his

---

[3] Again, I'm not claiming that this is what most principled conservatives are like. I know that there are many principled conservatives who are motivated solely by principles, with not a smidgeon of bigotry. Nevertheless, in the context of the transgender bathroom debates specifically, these purists are frankly hard to find. The mix of principles and bigoted animus are much more prevalent.

"*too* PC" trump card, the principled conservative now pulls out all of the emotionally pejorative stops at his disposal, mostly appealing to his own and others' *fear* that LGBTQ gains will inevitably lead to problems a society shouldn't have to deal with in the first place.

Breathless, the conservative critic continues his diatribe. He advances his case of complaint with a raised voice, a sneer, a narrowing of the eyes, an unmitigated sarcasm and, at the same time, a thoroughgoing sense of joyfulness over being able to finally slam his opponent. The conservative critic exclaims, "You're being *just so politically correct* and you expect everybody to go along with your agenda." He complains that the transgender advocate is nothing more than a PC ideologue, out of the same mold as the old 1950s communist ideological purists. Addressing the transgender rights advocate, the critic mockingly exclaims, "Yes, comrade. Anything you say, comrade." What he really means is "No way, 'comrade.' You can take your sanctimonious, dangerous political correctness and claims about transgender rights and shove...." Then, continuing his Soviet analogy, he complains that the PC ideologue has been whining incessantly to the public about how conservatives are "not giving them their (bathroom) rights," about how conservatives are purveyors of transgender (bathroom) rights oppression, and that this PC whining is nothing more than the transgender advocate's attempt to send the critic off to a metaphorical gulag of shame for not being PC enough. The critic concludes his harangue with an emotion-laden observation that such PC advocacy is nothing more than heavy-handed psychological warfare.

That's quite a barrage. It's extremely difficult for anyone under such an *ad hominem* onslaught to know how to get out from under it. Sometimes fighting fire with fire is effective—i.e. the transgender rights advocate lobbing his own *ad hominem* grenades at the conservative critic. But that's not the path chosen by most minority liberationists. Instead, they try to pull the discussion away from the conservative critic's emotionally-charged focus on political correctness and back to the relatively civil and rational head-on liberation rights debate. They try to find any real factual content buried in all the emotional noise. They might, for example, focus on the last part of the diatribe, where the conservative critic charges that the advocate is trying to shame him. That's a factual claim that can be addressed rationally. Indeed, the liberation advocate would probably respond that the conservative critic is right that she (the rights advocate) does believe that the critic should be ashamed of himself, since the critic's prejudices and the oppressive limitations he would put on a transgender person's freedom of expression are clear. The transgender rights advocate is making what she would argue is a reasonable assumption: that the legitimate opposition to any rights infringement should certainly lead the "infringer" to feel shame in his role as a citizen and moral actor. Of course, it would come as no surprise if the principled conservative critic then countered that instead, it is the rights advocates who should be feeling ashamed, because the principled conservative critics genuinely believe *they* are being oppressed by the transgender rights advocates' attitude and the limitations those advocates would put on the critics' freedom of expression. If matters ended here, there wouldn't seem to be any way to settle the argument between the two parties: a rational stalemate. However, this is *not* where these matters end.

Here's where "the rub" I noted a little while ago becomes important for this now rekindled, relatively rational discussion about liberation claims. The transgender rights advocate would acknowledge that the principled critic feels oppressed by the transgender advocate's willingness to have a person born a male "invade" a bathroom expressly meant for biological women.[4] The

---

[4] Presumably, the conservative critic would feel the same outrage were a person born a woman to "invade" a bathroom expressly meant for men. Or maybe not. If not, what would that indicate about what's really going on here?

advocate would then go on to point out that if (as was stipulated earlier in this discussion) the conservative critic has already accepted that the transgender person by law has the right to live out his gender preference and if he (the conservative critic) thinks that it's just this new rights claim about bathrooms that's the sticking point for him, then surely he must see that he's being inconsistent; if, as postulated, he truly accepts the right to gender expression claimed by transgender persons, then he must acknowledge this right *means* having the right to identify themselves as they prefer. That, in fact, is at the very heart of the *definition* of "transgender." If the conservative critic nevertheless continues to maintain his objection to "bathroom rights," then, finally, if he's at all concerned with being a logically consistent, dispassionate and honest broker, he *has* to acknowledge that he hasn't really accepted *any* transgender rights at all in the first place. If he says once again that he is trying simply to protect little girls from being violated by biologically male transgender predators, then he's failing to accept the fact that transgender women who were born biological males are actually females *by definition*, not pretenders…and that when they enter the girl's or women's bathroom, they don't do so as men, predatory or otherwise. Failure to accept this fundamental truth is failure to accept that the transgender person has any of the rights that are important to a transgender person, among those the right to live out one's gender preference. This takes the debate about transgender rights to a whole other level of full-on denying the most fundamental transgender right that's already been inscribed into law.

Clearly, the conservative critic doesn't want to carry the debate to this level, where he would have to call into question the very *being* of the transgender person and would have to acknowledge that he doesn't believe the transgender person has *any* "protected class" civil rights, even though that particular ship has already sailed. He doesn't want to publicly acknowledge that he harbors these beliefs. This would not make the principled conservative look good in the eyes of the general public, nor in the eyes of the court.

This may be too charitable, but I believe that at this juncture, the more pure principled conservative who is motivated *solely* by his liberty principle—who would have no truck with the *ad hominem* antics of the kind of principled conservative we've just been describing—would probably fully withdraw from the debate. For one thing, arguing about the *being* of transgender people isn't in his wheelhouse; it has nothing to do with the principle of liberty. Second and more importantly, he doesn't want to be seen as having the view that transgender people have no rights at all. He has in fact accepted legally established transgender rights claims; it's this new, not-yet-established bathroom rights claim that rankles him. But if continuing the present fight would unavoidably commit him to this view that he doesn't hold, there wouldn't be any sense to participate further.

This is not necessarily true for the other, less pure kind of principled conservative. At this point, she would have no reason to turn back. She has already shown who she really is and how she really feels about transgender people. She does in fact challenge the very nature of the transgender person and doesn't accept any "special" rights claims at all, new or established, for the transgender community.

I'd now like to move the discussion away from focusing solely on how the transgender debate typically proceeds. I think what we've seen is enough to appreciate how this and so many of the other debates about minority liberation on the rights frontier normally proceed. Yes, there are "pure" principled conservatives who advance their case solely with principles. But we can't hide from the fact that there often enough are the impure conservatives who will forego their principles for the less rational route and challenge minority liberation ideology. Now I will offer some thoughts about what I consider the inherently troubled nature of the latter group's behavior, both in the context of the anti-transgender debate and in the broader context of many other anti-minority liberation debates.

My first comment is a brief one, concerning the less pure principled conservative just as she's running out of argumentative gas about principles and getting ready to level a bigoted *ad hominem* anti-liberation attack; the point at which she begins to sense that she might be losing the debate to the minority rights advocate—for instance, in the transgender bathroom case, where his principle of liberty that she marshals in defense of the rights of innocents (little girls) comes up against and is defeated by the principle of a transgender person's right to fully express her gender identity in her choice of which bathroom she wants to use. This mixed version of the principled conservative is now experiencing herself as a member of a minority group whose rights are being trampled by the minority rights advocates. Her impulse is to strike out. She feels that she shouldn't have to succumb to the liberationist ideology, it's unfair for her now to be in the minority.

There's a troubling irony about the conservative critic's situation. One would think that someone who doesn't appreciate being a minority whose rights are "under attack" would be sensitive to the rights claims of historically recognized minorities (in this case, transgender people) and who likewise haven't had their rights claims honored. One would think that consistency and empathy would move her to appreciate the plight of the minority she opposes, but there's not even a hint of any such impulse to appreciate the rights claims of "the other side" coming from the "impure" principled conservative. She would rather go for the throat. And doubtless she would respond here that the transgender minority is no less guilty than she (or, as far as the critic is concerned, "he") is; that the transwoman, too, has no impulse to appreciate the conservative's liberty rights claims. But this is a troublesome position for any principled person to be in. Pointing out that "the other side" is just as bad in lacking an impulse for consistency and empathy doesn't mitigate the fact that one is in error oneself.

There is a second point that I find particularly troublesome about the transgender rights debate. We find ourselves again with an elephant in the room. It's obvious that a fair amount of critique aimed specifically against transgender liberation—and it's certainly the case in the bathroom rights debate—is motivated by a kind of homophobia, normally defined as a fear and hatred of homosexuals. But transgendered people can be straight, lesbian, gay or bisexual. Conservative critics miss this idea, lumping all the factions of the LGBTQ community together and confusedly seeing them *all* as homosexuals. Add to this the fact that some of the more strident of these conservative critics have identity issues themselves[5] and you end up with an extremely pernicious kind of homophobic, anti-transgender aggressor. That is to say, for many of these critics, the very consideration of a person's being transgender—and the confused assumption that a transperson must also be homosexual—triggers the critics' own unconscious homosexual impulses[6], which in turn threatens their own sense of gender identity and sexuality. The weaker their own sense of self, the more forceful and threatening their unconscious (or conscious but closeted) impulses become. This goes for both male and female critics: in general, the male critic is just as concerned about

---

[5] I haven't offered any evidence for this claim. It is merely my clinical observation from afar.

[6] Of course, psychoanalytically speaking, all people have unconscious homosexual impulses. Most, though, are not as conflicted about these impulses as the conservative critics I'm speaking of.

his male identity being threatened as he is about a perceived threat to his male power privilege identity; the female conservative critic is equally concerned about any threats to her gender identity in her encounter with a transgender person as she is about her sense of identity as a "powerless" woman (relative to men) feeling threatened in the presence of a powerful woman (e.g. Hillary Clinton). What I'm saying, then, is that a fair number—not *all*—of conservative critics of transgender rights are in fact transphobes responding to their own threatened sense of gender identity.

My third point has to do with anti-transgender PC-bashing. With all of the lashing out and noise from the anti-transgender critics aimed squarely at political correctness, there is layered on top of the whole spectacle: an air of desperation, a hysterical affect attached to all their words and gesticulations. I think that this is an indication of just how much they have on the line psychologically in opposing the transgender rights advocate. Many of the kinds of strong biases that we looked at in Chapter 3 play a role in defining exactly what's on the line for any of these actors. I'm certain, for example, that strongly biased anti-PC theatrics are an attempt to soothe what is undoubtedly their overwhelming fear of transgender people, and probably their fear of people of color, feminists, Jews and Muslims as well. For others, their actions defend their intense and wholehearted disapproval of the minority group in question along with the belief system that would justify this disapproval. For some, their strong anti-transgender bias is simply a mirroring of what other important people in their lives feel about the transgender population, or about people of color, etc. For others, forcefully opposing the given minority group's rights and sharing this stance with their fellow conservative critics has the effect of solidifying their bonds and sense of kinship with their fellow critics. Sometimes, too, in displaying their shared anti-liberation bonds, these people work each other up into a lather of increasingly strong anti-transgender rights feelings. For this last bunch especially, the anti-PC *ad hominem* diatribe becomes quite fierce. There is so much on the line for them that they take on a mob mentality. Once again, perhaps the anti-PC critic who has the most at stake—and therefore has no qualms about forcefully savaging transgender people and their ideology—is the person whose bigoted feelings centrally anchor his sense of self. His self-justifying runs wild. He may point to what he thinks God intended human sexuality and gender to look like—men are men and women are women and never a crossing of these categories shall meet. But more often, I think his anti-transgender behavior is tied up with his own strong views on sexuality and his own gender identification; the confusions about sexual preference and a threatened sense of gender identity that I was just talking about above. Either way, the hysterical affect of many an anti-liberation principled conservative (with an underbelly of bigoted attitude) reveals just how important his opposition to liberation rights claims is in order for him to maintain his own sense of self.

Moving away from psychologizing about why principled conservatives might oppose transgender rights claims; in a more general arena, I've heard some principled people talk about their concern for the integrity of our society in the face of transgender behavior. That is, they focus on the principle that, above all else, we must not allow behavior that will shatter the cohesion of the social fabric. I've heard such critics claim that allowing much of what the various minority rights liberationists insist are their rights is actually responsible for many of the ills of society: that crime, decaying sexual morality, loss of respect for life (of fetuses), etc. are the result of too many new PC rights battles being waged and won by advocates of the various kinds of minority liberation. The critics see the transgender bathroom debate as the latest of such assaults— "Men sharing bathrooms with little girls? It's moral degradation. What's America coming to? Not on my watch." These people see themselves as principled critics, saving the nation from liberationist destruction and from the fifth column attempts to compromise what they believe America to be. Usually they are sincere in seeing themselves as principled patriots and their behavior is quite consistent with their claimed principles. They really do view liberation as a national enemy of conscious, evil intent. So, they take strong exception to anyone claiming that although *they* (the critics) might *view* themselves and their actions in this way, they are nothing more than bigots in patriots' clothing. While I am certain that for some, their sincerity is borne out by the facts, many others are simply in denial; they don't realize that they're using patriotism as a front for their bigotry. In the public lexicon, the term "bigotry" is so lethal and so morally repugnant that principled conservatives, seeing themselves as moral and well-meaning, simply are unable to square their sense of themselves with the truth that, in at least a part of their souls, they are neither moral nor well-intentioned.

What about the underlying assumption made by these "patriots" that they are only trying to save the integrity of America from the societal ravaging that comes with liberation and political correctness? Regarding all minority rights claims, these liberation critics are of the mind that "if you give them an inch, they'll take a mile"; that minorities and their politically correct agendas will keep coming back for more and more and more—the consequence of which will be the erosion of the very foundations of our nation in the form of the aforementioned crime, moral decay and what-not. In other words, all of society's problems can be laid at the doorstep of liberation and political correctness.

It seems clear to me that this idea is off base. For one thing, these critics never provide the causal link between the establishment of new protected rights for minorities and the societal ills that they think inevitably flow from them. If that link is obvious to them, I have to say it's not to me. Simply to claim that since liberation ideology is popular in the culture at the same time that there has been what they see as societal erosion—that the two are *correlated*—doesn't prove that liberation ideology is the *cause* of that erosion. It's hard to imagine that removing minority liberation advocacy from the equation would go anywhere toward alleviating any societal problems. In fact, if we're looking for causal factors in what these critics see as our societal erosion, it seems much more plausible that it's our societal failure to acknowledge and enforce the rights of the various minority populations, as well as the rights of all American citizens (e.g. universal quality healthcare and affordable college tuition) that's been one of the major causal generators of our societal ills. Social erosion occurs when society doesn't pay *enough* attention to people's rights. Moreover, it's far more plausible that racism, misogyny, religious bigotry and homophobia are major causal generators of our problems. If none of this is enough to give one reason to pause and raise doubts about the bigoted critics' complaint, then one should also consider the question of whether all of the social ills at which the critics level their liberation complaints are really ills at all. Not everyone agrees that matters such as a woman's right to choose, freedom of sexual expression and who can use which bathrooms are societal ills. In the final analysis, then, the principled "patriot" who is out to save America by defeating our cultural liberation ideology is at best standing on very shaky ground.

There's one final problem with the principled critic's way of thinking—specifically, his complaint that if you give them an inch in terms of new protected rights, they'll take a mile in never-ending rights claims. As I pointed out in Chapter 8, this complaint quite often is code for the patronizing idea that minorities who have been given so many protected rights have been so coddled (there's that Reaganesque idea again) that, like spoiled children, they will never be satisfied. Therefore, it's up to the adults (the critics) to tell them when they've had enough. Metaphorically, if you let them eat too much, they'll get sick and the society will end up getting sick as well. And to top matters off, the patronizing critic takes it as a *given* that the rest of us (i.e. straight white Christian men) are the power brokers who "give" rights to minorities, as though rights are not a person's genuine entitlement but rather expressions of white Christian generosity. This kind of thinking strikes me as being so jaw-droppingly outrageous that at this point, in what's clearly become the downward spiral in the debate with the principled conservative, I must throw up my hands and acknowledge that there probably isn't any reasonable way to respond to such self-absorbed thinking.

PART IV

In Defense of Political Correctness

CHAPTER 10

PC and the Word Police

As I said in the Introduction, I am an unapologetic proponent of political correctness. To me, it's precisely the condition a person wants to be in as a supporter of the prevailing ideologies of his culture. One would hope that anyone would want his behavior, attitudes and beliefs to be consistent with those prevailing cultural ideologies if he's in agreement with them. Therefore, he should be respectful and proud to be on point in this way—the more politically correct he is, the better the citizen he is. Indeed, what critics of those ideologies and the advocate's supporting behaviors, attitudes and beliefs call people being "*too* PC," the advocate calls "not PC enough"—one can never be the *perfect* citizen. In light of the critics' incessant carping, it's hard for the politically correct individual not to become annoyed. The critics' basic stance is that they (the critics) are the anti-PC challengers against whom those PCers had better defend themselves.

But why should the PCers *have* to defend themselves for being good citizens? Well, the sad truth is that the critics have been so successful in sabotaging the meaning and former laudatory connotation of the term "politically correct" that many from the liberal PC camp have (wrongly) been convinced that there truly *is* something wrong—something unsavory, perhaps—with the idea of political correctness; that they must be embarrassed and apologetic about their leanings and avoid sounding "*too* PC" at all costs.[1] Sadly,

---

[1] A few years ago, I read online ("Obama on political correctness: Don't go around

these liberals have capitulated to the skillful rhetorical tricks of conservatism. They have been sold a bill of goods. Others, however—and I count myself among them—haven't gone over to the Dark Side about PC, continuing to celebrate its cause as the champion of minority liberation and good citizenship. That said, most of us have felt the lethal blows of conservative anti-PC attacks and have taken the defensive posture that conservatives insist upon…but if PC advocates are to continue to be consistent with our preferred prevailing ideologies, we must defend ourselves. It's with this in mind that I will mount my defense in a more sustained way in the next five chapters, getting much more into the weeds of the specific, popular anti-PC anti-minority liberation complaints today for the typical conservative and what a responsible detailed pro-PC liberationist response to those specific complaints looks like.

Attacks on political correctness and liberation ideology are all about undermining the PC checklist. The action of these attacks occurs on different fronts. Some critics berate a person's PC behavior—his ideologically consistent behavior. Some berate his PC attitudes. Others berate his PC beliefs. So many fertile targets. That said, behavior seems to be the favorite target these days. So, for example, the critic thinks that if he has to disturb the norms

---

just looking for insults." *The Hill,* 12/19/2016) about President Obama reflecting that liberals were too PC, which he equated with being too sensitive—especially about social issues having to do with race and gender identity—and that political correctness is a device many liberals use to try to shut down debate. He took solace in knowing that there were issues about which conservatives, too, are "too PC"—e.g. their over-wrought concern with the liberals' "war on Christmas." It seems that our own normally insightful former President has fallen victim to the successful conservative sabotage of the entire PC concept. Of course, he's right that some liberals use their demands for political correctness *extravagantly* (recall my Chapter 1 discussion of PC extravagance)—being "overly sensitive" when it isn't warranted—but that doesn't justify apologizing for political correctness *per se.* I hope that Mr. Obama will someday reconsider his mistake.

of politically correct behavior by cracking a few minority heads as a means of bringing some semblance of order to the country, then so be it; PC be damned. Trump and his people have said exactly this on numerous occasions. I recall, for example, Republican Representative Peter King floating the idea of a federal Muslim surveillance program:

> "The main issues I discussed were what we have to do to have the Justice Department and the FBI be more leaning-forward when it comes to investigating Islamic terrorism…. I suggested a program similar to what Commissioner Kelly did here in New York, and that we can't worry about political correctness." (*Politico*, 12/15/16)

What's a little un-PC offensive behavior when there's so much on the line? We can't worry about stepping on some Muslim toes if we surveil their mosques. The American public is afraid, so we've got to do something to protect them, even if that means we use politically incorrect behavior against Muslims.

It turns out that the absolute favorite kind of PC behavior the critics most like to complain about is linguistic behavior; politically correct language. It's great sport to pounce on the PC liberationist's insistence that everyone—especially during encounters with or about people from minority populations—use only a vocabulary that is perfectly matched with minority rights and has passed muster with the minority populations in question. The critics jump all over this demand for absolute preferred *linguistic precision*. They find such a demand outrageous because it forces people to walk on eggshells. So unfair. Liberationists, they charge, are nothing more than "thought Nazis" and "word police," with a hair-trigger desire to send offenders off to the "thought concentration camps" or to write up a "word ticket" for them. With all their preferred linguistic precision, liberationists are like Nero fiddling while our country burns, and we don't have time for that. So, if some Native Americans have their feelings hurt because Washington area football fans cheer on their hometown "Redskins" and simulate a cartoonish Indian war cry when the team is close to the goal line, that's just too bad. Our nation has been on edge about so many things, so we need to be able to freely express our innocent enthusiasms. "Hey, Washington's been the Redskins forever, well before the PC police arrived. So, leave us alone. We've got enough to worry about. Those Indians will just have to suck it up. And as for the word police? Get real!"

This kind of thing—hollering "Word police!!"—is standard fare for the anti-PC critic and will be my focus in the next four chapters. I would like to look more carefully at the charge and show why I think the preferred linguistic precision demands of political correctness are perfectly fine. In fact, they are necessary supports for the cause of minority liberation. Before arguing for the case, however, I'll say a few words about the typical minority liberationists who make such demands and what the typical indignant critics responses are like.

Most people would acknowledge negative stereotyping of any group (e.g., as "Redskins") runs a very strong risk of offending the members of the stereotyped group. People want to be known for who they are as individuals, not for offensive caricatures or generalizations about their group. The practice of negative stereotyping is especially egregious when it's leveraged against minorities who are already fighting for inclusion, acceptance and respect. In a world where the majority routinely insists upon its strong, natural bias in favor of itself in any situations involving itself versus minority populations, this puts minorities at an even greater disadvantage as they try to navigate their lives within the broad culture. Moreover, this stereotyping goes against our national ideology of egalitarianism—meaning, among other things, that no one should start life at a disadvantage when it comes to competing in the daily activities of the culture-at-large. Clearly, the natural tendency of a majority group to favor itself doesn't square well with this ideology. And it is even more insidious when a majority group intentionally (consciously or not) disadvantages minorities through the deployment of demeaning stereotypes. That kind of behavior completely makes a mockery of the egalitarian ideology.[2]

No minority group appreciates offensive stereotyping speech or imagery. Not all male Latinos and Hispanics are named José and Chico, while the racist may use those designators with demeaning intention when addressing any Spanish-speaking male. No American Indian[3] likes being called "Indian," "red man," "chief," or hearing the term "Indian-giver." No gay man appreciates being called "faggot" or "sweetie" by a straight person; no lesbian likes being referred to as a "dyke" by a straight person.[4] Most women don't like being called "honey" or "sweetheart" or even "Beautiful" by complete strangers. The fact is, all minority

---

[2] Were a person from the majority to try to mount a defense for such behavior by saying, "Just as it's human nature for the majority to favor itself over minorities, so, too, is stereotyping minorities part of human nature and therefore it needs to be accepted," he would be guilty of promoting a paper-thin excuse for flouting an important cultural norm (egalitarianism). Stereotyping or not is a matter of choice for a person. And so, when a person from the majority chooses *not* to make the effort to *stop* stereotyping, he chooses to offend both the minorities he stereotypes and the culture-at-large that condemns this behavior. Assuming that our culture-at-large really does embrace egalitarianism, such stereotyping, whether a person thinks it's "natural" or not and whether or not he's willing to make the effort to fight such a tendency in himself, is unacceptable and needs to be challenged.

[3] As noted in Chapter 8, many Native Americans are fine with being called American Indians or, typically, with the tribal designation preceding the "Indian" designator—so there are Shawnee American Indians, Sioux Indians, and so on.

[4] Interestingly, when people of their own group use such terms, the designation may be seen as being in jest or affectionate, e.g. black people sometimes using the n-word as a term of endearment (Chapter 8, footnote 20)).

groups have their sensibilities about how they want to be addressed. Demeaning stereotyping designators are most definitely out of bounds and only the designators they prefer are in bounds. Women have their taboo designations ("chick," "ma'am") and their preferred terminologies. Latinos, Asian-Americans, Native Americans and people of other ethnicities have theirs. Gay men, lesbians and bisexuals have theirs. Transgender and nonbinary people have their own preferences (and choose their own pronouns). Individuals who are "differently abled" either physically or mentally (e.g. it's no longer PC to say "retarded" or "handicapped") have theirs. And so on.

Historically, perhaps the most vocal among the minorities who hate verbal designator stereotypes and insist on their preferred terminologies have been African Americans. Black people have always been offended by the n-word, the coo_ word, and the German/Yiddish *schv*___ word. Moreover, being referred to as "coloreds" and "colored people" (and told that they have to use the bathroom facilities for "coloreds only" or that they can only enter a building through the "colored" entrance or that they need to go to the "all coloreds to the back" bus entrance) has never sat well with them, either. For the past 60 years or so, black Americans have claimed the right to expect that their wishes about the use of such denigrating terminologies be honored. At some point in the 1950s, for example, they insisted that although the term "Negro" had been in use since the 18th century as the polite English term for black people of African descent, now it would be the *only* acceptable group designator. However, while civil rights leaders such as Dr. King embraced the term, by the mid 1960s, more militant leaders such as Malcolm X criticized "Negro" as harkening back to the days of slavery. With this critique capturing the imagination of a critical mass of black people, "Negro" was now seen as a disrespectful "Uncle Tom" terminology, while "black" or "black people" became the preferred designators of choice. "Black" became a point of pride. It ultimately captured who they were as a race and how they were recognized as political actors in the minority rights-liberation debates of the time. That is, it referred to people who had black skin and people who had certain political interests that they were pursuing on the national stage.

Then, sometime in the 1980s, a new critical mass of black people felt that they didn't want to be defined *solely* by their race and political action. The self-definition problem they saw was that "black" didn't capture who they were as an *ethnic* people; it neither captured the fullness and richness of who they were as a culturally identifiable group with a cultural ancestry, nor did it capture their pride in their geographical roots. So they insisted that *in addition to* the "black" designator, they also be called "African Americans," where "African" implied their geographical and historical origins and a complex cluster of traditions—their cultural heritage—that they brought with them to this country from various African tribal areas when they arrived here as slaves. Now "black American" and "African American" were both the acceptable designators— "black American" being the accepted race and political designator, "African American" being the accepted ethno-cultural-geographical origins designator. Just as, say, Polish Americans or Italian Americans are at once white Americans and people of Polish or Italian descent, so too are African Americans both black Americans and people whose ancestors and cultural heritage come from Africa.[5]

---

[5] I hope it's obvious that a parallel dual designation applies to brown Americans/Mexican-Americans (as well as to other brown/ethnic American Latino groups—brown/Salvadoran-Americans, brown/Nicaraguan-Americans and so on) and to Asian-Americans/Chinese-Americans (as well as to other ethnic Asian-American groups—Vietnamese-Americans, Laotian-Americans and so on). For the reasons I spoke of in Chapter 8, Native Americans eschew the color term "red man" as an acceptable race designator and prefer instead the cultural designators "Native

Since the '80s, which designator is favored over the other in public discourse has fluctuated, usually depending on whether or not race issues are front and center in the national conversation. When they are, then "black American" seems to take precedence. "African American" seems to be used in contexts of black Americans wanting to highlight pride or respect, as when referring to "the African-American community" or to African Americans as American citizens, or to African Americans as celebrities, or to African Americans as political leaders. It's also the term that most in the "white liberal establishment" (for example, most arms of the liberal-leaning media, the white liberal political class and the ordinary white liberal citizen) use. And many (though clearly not all—see below), in the non-bigoted white conservative community as well (for example, most arms of the conservative-leaning media, the white conservative political class and the ordinary non-bigoted white conservative citizen) do likewise.

In sum, whether it's "African American" or "black American," people are entitled to be addressed as they prefer. Furthermore, when it's part of the nation's history that the nation has *systematically victimized* minority groups in as *thoroughgoing* and *traumatizing* a fashion as we have in this country,[6] then not only are minority groups entitled not to be demeaned by negative stereotypes, but they are also entitled to having their linguistic sensibilities honored— these entitlements being the most minor of conceivable "reparations" for past sins. Part of the unspoken cultural landscape around the victimization of minorities is the assumption that formerly

---

American" or "American Indian." Interestingly, they collapse the distinction that some other groups make between their color and their culture and refer to themselves as the "Native American race."

[6] Here's another situation where the United States is certainly not alone. Displaying this kind of behavior happens seemingly everywhere

disempowered minorities are entitled to be called what they want to be called. This has already been ingrained in the mores of our culture-at-large and in some instances, it's been codified into law. Minorities certainly have the right not to be re-traumatized by anyone's poor choice of words. And rest assured, whether consciously intended or not, some words can in fact re-traumatize members of groups that have a long history of being bigotedly attacked both in word and deed. No amount of complaining about a minority group's being *too PC* can erase this fact.

The moral of this story and of the many other similar stories that all minority peoples can tell about their histories in this country: *words matter*. Most importantly, it's through words that the civil life of a society ebbs and flows. We all use certain "hot" terms to praise or demean one another. So sometimes we celebrate our positive bonds with one another through words that describe our caring emotions. At other times, we use words to describe our disdain for those with whom we decidedly have no feelings of kinship. So, yes, words matter. Using hot stereotyping terms to disparage minorities is anything but a virtue, while using preferred respectful designators is precisely just that.

Of course, many anti-PC conservatives completely disagree with this view of the world. They would like to do away with the PC focus on linguistic precision because, they claim, bigotry doesn't exist anymore. Times have changed, they say; overt racism, misogyny and homophobia have been defeated. And because of this new reality, they believe that minorities shouldn't be so sensitive about so many words. They might agree that the deplorable bigots among them need to be censored, but this is as far as conservatives will go. They don't want to walk on eggshells in referencing minorities. They don't want to have to worry about being automatically deemed racist, stereotyping purveyors of intentional politically incorrect designations whenever they let slip any non-preferred speech. Of course, they say, the n-word is unacceptable, but to demand that they always be completely up to date with all other new minority group designators that come down the pike is *too* PC: the African American needs to "man up" and adopt an attitude of "sticks and stones." They think that as conservatives, their not using the n-word is proof positive that they are not racists, and so if they use the wrong terminology once in a while, they shouldn't have to look over their shoulders to see if the PC police are coming for them. If there's a new usage of terms, it's only to be expected that mistakes will be made once in a while, at least in the beginning. They've got to be cut some slack; it's just an innocent mistake—old habits, a slip of the tongue, that's all.

Of course, if "innocent mistakes" *were* all that was going on, then I think there would be something to their complaint. However, so many who raise the "*too* PC" objection about linguistic precision are not in fact people who have only recently been introduced to the new terminology and use the wrong terminology only once in a while. Many of them *go out of their way* to misuse it, thumbing their noses at the minority victim group without having to take responsibility for such an obvious sign of disrespect. These "mistakes" are racist when aimed at misusing designations for African Americans. It's misogynistic when misusing designations for women. It's homophobic when misusing designations for homosexuals or anyone else in the LGBTQ communities. In short, the bigots come out of the shadows when it comes to intentional word imprecision that they disingenuously claim is not intentional.

Certainly not all bigotry is so blatant. For example, there are many bigots who don't think of themselves as bigots but instead as principled conservatives who simply can't abide by liberationists' controlling the very words they use in talking about minorities. With these principled conservatives in mind, in the next three chapters I will offer an in-depth commentary on the following emails I received a few years ago from a very principled conservative friend, illustrating that he is unaware of a clear underbelly of bigotry beneath his principles:

As a philosopher, you know far better than I the importance of defining terms. So what is it that we mean by PC? I am not in favor, nor would any reasonable person be, of behavior and verbiage that is calculated to insult or inflame or demean. While there is much hypocrisy in the black community about the "n" word (they can say it, you can't), to be sure a deliberate use of that term is calculated to offend—there is little if any subjectivity about that. What I am objecting to is the recently evolving cultural norm, brought on by the rampant relativism of your deconstructionists, that places little or no value in opinions and beliefs that contradict those of the offended. It's ironic, of course, that the offended himself is the product of the same genetic and cultural forces that he believes shape all viewpoints, but these guys usually aren't that rational. As a result, the offended ignores, belittles, marginalizes, even reacts violently, against the alleged offender and wants to shut him up and move him out. I cite the dispute between ALL lives matter and BLACK lives matter and the resulting outrage against people who didn't want to make racial distinctions. The campus boycotts and protests against reasonable people like Condi Rice, *et al.* the rampages against "white privilege," the failure to distinguish Islamophobia from a genuine concern about the teachings of Islam that in fact do encourage violence against infidels (i.e. non-Muslims), the reluctance to criticize antisocial behavior for fear of being called a racist, the outrage against silly, horny men who make unwanted but non-physical advances to women (not the hypocrisy here as well in that

Clinton and JFK's infidelities are okay), and the like. I could go on for hours. These are all examples of PC run riot. But…. If all you are saying is that there are some instances where what we call PC serve positive purposes, I can't disagree with that. But I think the term has now been so overused that it has come to stand for all of the insulting and demeaning behavior that is carried out in the name of PC. I think the white people who supported Trump were reacting to it in that manner….

…. I detest those aspects of PC which shut down honest debate in the name of microaggressions and all the restraints on free speech that are now rampant on college campuses. I understand the initial impetus of the early "movement," but it has gotten out of hand and actually contributed in part to Trump's victory. Be careful what you wish for….

…. That is now what PC has come to—it's now a form of McCarthyism and strict conformity to prescribed ideas, some of which are counter-productive. I guess what you like about it—but the issue now is that it is entirely subjective in terms of what is genuinely offensive behavior and what just seems to be based on the individual's feelings. Like, calling Hillary "nasty" is not sexist or gender driven, however impolitic and stupid.

Great stuff! This is an exquisitely compact yet detailed, thoughtful version of the "*too* PC" rant and a perfect foil for someone like me who wants to defend against the anti-PC, anti-liberation critic. We certainly get the idea that my friend has no patience with politically correct *behavior*. So, he thinks PC has gone amok when it takes the form of students boycotting and protesting campus speeches by reasonable people like Condi Rice, or when it insists that criticizing minority antisocial behavior is tantamount to racism. No doubt, he would have agreed with the ominous inquiries that the Trump EPA team made a couple of years ago about which individuals in the Energy Department had over the years advocated for politically correct programs to slow down global warming and about what the State Department policies and programs have been regarding PC gender equality and asylum-seeking. And surely, given what he says in his rant about Islam and terrorism, he would have agreed with Peter King's suggestions about surveilling American Muslims. In other words, my friend and like-minded people are out to put an end to all politically correct minority rights-based *behavior*.

Since, as I pointed out in Chapter 1, I would agree that there are some situations where practical concerns about the facts on the ground really do trump concern for behaving in politically correct ways (i.e. trump the letter of the reigning ideology), I wouldn't dismiss out of hand any and all behaviors that are, all else being equal, politically incorrect. All things aren't always equal, though; and I also wouldn't be as trigger-happy as people like my conservative friend and Peter King to assess so many behavior-situations as trumping concerns for political correctness because "we don't have time to be worrying about being politically correct." Perhaps we *do* have time. However, that's certainly something that reasonable minds can always argue about.

In any event, it's not these sorts of PC *behaviors* on my friend's list that I am *most* interested in looking at. Rather, I'd like to focus my attention on what he says about PC *speech*; what he says about *the PC word police*. And what I think about this divides into two separate discussions: one having to do with his direct and implied objections to particular *examples* of politically correct speech, the other more generally about his criticism of basic PC-speech *methodology*. Accordingly, in the next three chapters I will discuss each of these. Chapter 11 will discuss methodological issues. Chapter 12 will cover the critic's concerns about a set of specific word-policing examples. And Chapter 13 will deal with one special word-policing example that has received so much notoriety over the past seven years that it deserves special attention in a chapter of its own: the PC word police's insistence that one correctly understand and respect the tenets of the motto "Black Lives Matter."

CHAPTER 11

Defending PC Word Police Methodology

W e begin by characterizing the PC speech methodological problems drawn from my friend's email complaints from the previous chapter. Here's a list:

- PC serves some purpose when it condemns blatant racists for using the n-word, but its word policing has been overused and gotten out of hand in condemning language that it shouldn't be condemning.
- PC has come to stand for insulting and demeaning behavior toward anyone who commits a PC language infraction.
- The PC word police are intent on shutting up and moving out all conservative opponents.
- PC has placed restraints on free speech on college campuses.
- Black people have always claimed that they don't want to make racial distinctions or for race to be a factor in interpersonal relations with non-minority persons—yet the excesses of linguistic PC only serve to bring racial differences front and center.
- Linguistic PC is in league with a recently evolving cultural norm that stems from a kind of relativism placing little value on the opinions of non-minority persons.
- PC focuses unduly on linguistic micro-aggressions.
- PC word-policing is the new McCarthyism, insisting on strict conformity to prescribed ideas.

- What is assigned the label of being politically correct language by its advocates is entirely subjective in terms of what's *called* offensive language as opposed to what *is* objectively offensive language.

I will now discuss and offer defenses against each of these complaints.

Micro-aggressions:

In fact, my friend's concern about these amounts to four related anti-PC complaints: that minorities focus too much on micro-aggressions; that word-policing has been overused and gotten out of hand in condemning the linguistic infractions of nonminority persons; that the PC micro-aggression stance is aimed at shutting up all conservatives by demeaning those who commit linguistic infractions; and that black people especially have always claimed that they don't want race to be a factor in interpersonal relations with nonminority persons, yet the micro-aggression excesses of linguistic PC only serve to bring racial differences front and center.

The complaint about micro-aggressions is the idea that politically correct liberationists as individuals or as groups (i.e. the black community, the gay community) are obsessed with finding minor infractions by the politically incorrect conservatives and then beating them over the head about it, as though micro-aggressions were major aggressions. The liberationist overuses his word-policing in order to shame the non-minority perpetrator. To the conservative critic, however, this obsession only serves to alienate and anger the supposed perpetrators, heightening their sensitivity to racial differences rather than eliminating race as a factor in their thinking when they socially interact with minority persons. To the critic, PC minorities these days *always* seem to be *looking* for comments made by people (especially by white men) that might be construed as being the least bit off from preferred terminology. So if, for example, some white man tries to get the attention of a black man by saying "Hey fella," and the black man becomes infuriated because in his eyes calling him "fella" comes dangerously close to calling him "boy" (a pejorative slave-era terminology), the critic complains that the black man is being unreasonable about the infraction, if it really can be considered an infraction at all. Or take the case of the woman who becomes righteously indignant when a man refers to her as "a lady" instead of "a woman." In both cases, to the critic's ear, the difference between the preferred terminology and the terminology used is so slight as to make no difference. The critic suspects other motives, none of which are mitigating as far as he is concerned. Perhaps, for example, the person (or minority group) feeling offended was, for psychological reasons specific to him (them), overly sensitive. Or perhaps he or she was disposed to interpreting what goes on in the world in a way that always allows them to assume a "victim" position. Or perhaps this person or group was merely itching for a fight with the non-minority offender. Or maybe he or she is always prepped to using any such supposed infraction as a pretext for guilt-tripping the offender. Whenever any of these motives are in play, the critic charges, it's clear that the linguistically-sensitive minority person has gone beyond reason and is in no way deserving of anyone's serious attention regarding his or her complaint. Why should he, the critic, have to feel constrained in the words he uses simply because someone who "has psychological problems" or is "too sensitive" feels offended?

I will address these concerns by first saying that there is much to the complaint that I agree with, although in the final analysis it goes overboard in its conclusions about politically correct, preferred linguistic precision. Recall in Chapter 1 that I said I agreed that sometimes, advocates of PC are excessive in their use of PC as a rhetorical tool. I gave the example of the individual who was overly sensitive whenever anyone would comment that it was a nice day outside today. Such talk hurt his feelings. But he insisted that because one should never hurt anyone's feelings, the linguistic perpetrator should repent and refrain in the future from speaking in this way. In other words, the PC word police insist that hurting anyone's feelings is *always* politically incorrect and that using any terminology that hurts anyone's feelings is always politically incorrect as well. It would be ludicrous to honor such linguistic PC extravagance. We shouldn't have to hold our tongues simply because this person, who obviously has psychological problems, becomes agitated from our comments on the weather. His expectations of the world are beyond the psychological norms of what's acceptable. In short, he's neurotic about the issue of "weather words" and the general population shouldn't have to suffer on account of his neurosis.

In a similar vein, when the anti-PC critic complains that the micro-aggression focus by minority groups amounts to the same thing, he often has a point. The minority individual who enjoys guilt-tripping or seeing himself as a victim, for example, is someone with his own special psychological problems. Why, then, should anyone have to feel constrained in their use of language simply because the minority individual "has problems"? The clear answer is that no one should have to suffer for any undue extravagances of PC word policing. I can appreciate the critic— or anyone else for that matter—not wanting to feel forced to micro-manage her every word having to do with minorities. I'm very familiar with this impulse to not have one's speech censored; there really is such a thing as freedom of speech that all Americans are supposed to have. And I certainly can agree with the critic that when someone wants to curb everyone's speech behavior to satisfy some idiosyncratic psychological difficulties they're going through, that should be more their issue to deal with than everyone else's. Unfortunately, the critics of linguistic PC often use the objection to the unacceptable extravagances of the *psychologically disqualifying micro-aggressions* as justification for their more general condemnation of *all* linguistic PC concerns about micro-aggressions. This is where I part ways with the critics.

Not all micro-aggressions are about psychologically disqualifying matters. To assume otherwise is to throw the baby out with the bathwater. There are in fact far too many linguistic micro-aggressions committed against minorities to allow that mistaken idea to stand. I'm not talking about obvious infractions such as using the n-word. There are plenty of not-so-obvious micro-aggressions committed daily at which minority persons rightly take umbrage. For the reasons I spoke of earlier, minority persons in this country are very much entitled to their PC linguistic sensitivity, no matter how overly sensitive it seems to others. People who historically have been systematically traumatized by overt racism, misogyny, religious discrimination or homophobia do have the right to be addressed precisely in accordance with what the norms of their group's preferred self-designators dictate. If they are linguistically sensitive to micro-aggressions, that sensitivity is a wholly rational response to the legacy of bigotry. If honoring their preference entails a psychological inconvenience for some people in the majority population, then even though they specifically might not have been the perpetrators of that historical intentional bigotry, the legacy of its effects certainly linger on. Therefore, the majority is morally bound to acknowledge that legacy and to understand that what might seem like a minor linguistic infraction on their part isn't minor at all in the eyes of minority populations.

If the anti-PC critic is unable to truly understand and appreciate the power that the historical legacy of generationally repeated bigoted trauma has over a minority group and he is instead intent on focusing only on the objectionable cases of extravagant, psychologically disqualifying linguistic micro-aggressions, remaining blind to the *genuine* cases when they are staring him right in the face, then I have to ask myself why he misses the obvious while others don't? If, say, a conservative, Jewish anti-PC critic (I'm imagining Mr. Kushner) is able in his own case to fully appreciate and acknowledge why Jews—given the miserable history and legacy of the world's ubiquitous rabid anti-Semitism—might be offended by certain linguistic micro-aggressions aimed at them—and, indeed, feel that they have a right to feel offended—then why can't he wrap his head around the linguistic sensitivities of other minority groups? I'm at a loss to provide a good explanation for this lack of empathy. Certainly, there are well-known social factors that can dull moral sensibilities about such matters. But, frankly, my bias toward the psychology of things has me surmise that this inability to appreciate and acknowledge the linguistic sensitivities of most minorities has more to do with some version of the unconscious or non-reflected-upon kinds of bigotry that I've referenced in earlier chapters. Among the unconscious factors relevant to this particular example, a person might have unconscious bigoted feelings,[1] but it might also be true that unconscious wealth- and power-privilege play a role. The truth about such critics of linguistic political correctness is the same as the truth that I've argued pervades the critics of political correctness in

---

[1] I am mindful of the fact that, similarly, some members of minority groups are insensitive to the PC linguistic preferences of Jews. The Rev. Jesse Jackson's notorious 1984 anti-Semitic slur, referring to NYC as "Hymietown," comes to mind. I am just as disheartened and suspicious about the unconscious reasons for their insensitivity as I am about those of the conservative Jew—Mr. Kushner—in my example here. I discussed some of these reasons in Chapter 8, where I talked about intra-mural minority racism.

general, of PC *per se*. That's the inconvenient truth: that in opposing linguistic political correctness, these critics are in fact creating a *smokescreen* for what they believe about their real target—the entire enterprise of minority liberation rights-claiming.

I have other problems with the critic's micro-aggression issue. He says that the minority person's hyper-focus on micro-aggressions amounts to an obsessive overuse of word-policing specifically aimed at shaming the non-minority perpetrator, but which in fact only serves to alienate and anger the supposed perpetrators, heightening their sensitivity to racial differences rather than eliminating race as a factor when they socially interact with minority persons. I have to question the critic's focus on this point. Obviously, when the word police are motivated by any of the extravagant disqualifying psychological factors and they insist on linguistic acquiescence with the intent of shaming all of the non-minority so-called perpetrators, that will lead to alienating and angering the so-called perpetrators. And I would agree that the shamed non-minority critic is justifiably angry; a rational response to being abused by these particular PC police. Once again, however, not *all* word police are bad apples. For the critic to believe otherwise and then focus on the differences between himself and people of color, for example, and then blame all PC linguistic police for his going there—well, I just have to wonder why. He could just as easily have limited his anger to certain minority persons who, because of their pre-existing, extravagant, disqualifying psychological difficulties, had abused him with intent. To go beyond that population, however, and feel alienated and angry at all minorities who insist on preferred linguistic precision suggests to me once again that there is unconscious bigotry at work. When a person—say, the conservative critic—is shown to be wrong about matters of linguistic precision, there's no good reason to be angry. And even if anger were an individual's initial response to being corrected (after all, no one *prima facie* likes to be corrected), only a moment's reflection on his part should allow him to regroup and see the error of his ways and clean up his language usage. Not to do so is irrational. Of course, people can be irrational from time to time...but in the very public discussion of the relations between minorities and the rest of the population, and the issue of linguistic political correctness factoring into those relations, one would think that all participants would be more than motivated to respond rationally to any considerations brought to light. One would think that someone who has failed to use a preferred terminology of a minority group would want to be shown his error and not irrationally confuse the case of unwarranted extravagant linguistic shaming with the warranted case of pointing out a linguistic mistake. If he chooses to be irrational instead, then his sense of alienation and anger is on him and has nothing to do with the purportedly evil intentions of the linguistic PC police.

There's another problem the critics have with PC micro-aggression sensitivity about which I have mixed feelings. My friend's parting shot, "Be careful what you wish for," was made in the context of what he sees as PC's having *exhausted* the public's *tolerance* for all the seemingly endless micro-aggression-related demands made by the PC word police; what my friend experiences as their guilt-tripping tactics.[2] People can take only so much, he infers. Enough is enough.[3] Part of me agrees with elements of this

---

[2] One wonders if sometimes those who see others as guilt-tripping them are in fact simply feeling guilty all on their own, and that they are having these feelings because somewhere in their psyche they realize that they are perpetrators of bigotry (probably of the non-reflected upon variety) instead of the defenders of free unencumbered (i.e. not to be restricted by the PC micro-aggression word police) speech they claim to be.
[3] I would point the reader's attention again to Chapter 10, footnote 1, where even President Obama seems to have had enough. This is proof that even some liberationists have been cowered by the anti-PC rhetoric about micro-aggression.

lament and part of me chafes at the whole objection. I agree that many in the public do seem to have lost their tolerance for minority demands for word precision. On the one hand, I generally have empathy for most people. And so, in the case of these specific people, I can see that they truly have reached their limit. On the other hand, speaking of tolerance—frankly, I find myself losing any empathic tolerance *I* might otherwise have had for their situation because as an academic philosopher, I see them failing to make distinctions between unacceptable extravagant cases of micro-aggressions and acceptable ones; distinctions any honest broker needs to make. Then again, not everybody is interested in being an honest broker, especially if there are unconscious or non-reflected-upon factors motivating them not to make distinctions. The point is, were the anti-PC anti-liberation critics to make the proper distinctions here, they and the general public wouldn't have gotten to the point of exhaustion.

That said, however, the public *is* exhausted and we can't depend upon the anti-PC critics to begin making the proper distinctions that might relieve them and the public of some of that exhaustion. If one wants to continue insisting that minorities are quite often in the right when they complain about linguistic micro-aggressions, then measures need to be taken by the PC advocates themselves to relieve the public's exhaustion. In the case where a minority person unjustifiably sabotages the whole PC cause by extravagantly insisting that, for any of the disqualifying psychological reasons, people ought to speak only in the way that suits his idiosyncratic fancy—it requires that this saboteur be called out by the PC advocates for his behavior. Failing to do so does not do the cause of legitimate micro-aggression PC complaint any favors. If they don't call out a minority person's micro-aggression complaint misstep when he makes one, it only serves to convince the general public that there's no objective

evaluation of the worth of anyone's micro-aggression complaints—i.e. about whether they really are politically correct
complaints or not. And so, the micro-aggression-related exhaustion will just continue. In the name of relieving the public from
this exhaustion, PC advocates simply must enforce a kind of
tough love and be willing to criticize false claims of linguistic micro-aggression.

A final problem I have with the micro-aggression objection
has to do with the *particular way* in which the critics use their
complaints about PC linguistic micro-aggressions to further attack
any and all attempts to keep language politically correct. By now,
their technique should be clear: focus on the obvious objectionable,
disqualifying linguistic micro-aggression cases only when you talk
about linguistic PC; hope that the rest of the public will agree that
the deficient intentions in these extravagant micro-aggression cases
represent the intentions of *all* cases of linguistic PC; and have the
public thus conclude that all advocates of any and all linguistic
PC are empty suits. The main rhetorical tool the critics use to
achieve this goal is to inveigh against micro-aggression sensitive
"word police" and all of the pejoratively associated meanings that
go along with the term "police." Ironically,[4] the critics claim that
the word police are trying to silence them, demean them and label them as bigots, when (from where I'm standing) it's the critics
doing the silencing and demeaning in their fierce campaign to
trivialize the PC concept (by repeatedly inveighing against the
word police and linguistic precision micro-aggressions) while at
the same time complaining that they have been victimized by the
powerful cultural force of political correctness. Once again and

---

[4] I say "ironically" because it is usually the minority population that complains about
heavy-handed police aggression toward minorities, while the anti-PC critic defends
the police against such accusations. In the anti- micro-aggression context, though, it's
the anti-PC critic complaining about the word police doing the same to them.

inconveniently, this attack on PC is really aimed (consciously or not) at silencing the advocates of the minority rights liberation project in toto.

It's difficult to escape yet another irony about what's going on here. The critics are clearly aimed at using their disparagement against PC micro-aggressions to destroy linguistic political correctness altogether, expunging the concept from the lexicon. The problem is, if they succeed, many of them will no longer have access to their favorite smokescreen, with their antipathy for all manner of rights liberation showing. And then the problems they have in this regard with the culture-at-large come to a head once more. That's why it's so interesting to me to observe how so many critics on the current scene have come out of hiding to rage against linguistic political correctness. With Trump as their leader, they feel empowered to go out of their way to tell liberals just how angry they are. And I'm absolutely certain that most of them have no idea what's in store for them if they succeed in taking down linguistic political correctness; many of them (the ones who don't want to admit to having bigoted intentions) will then be left exposed. "Be careful what you wish for," indeed.

There's yet another problem with the strategy of trying to trivialize linguistic PC by hammering away at PC micro-aggression complaints. If the critics can *successfully* convince us that word usage regarding minorities and their protected rights is a piddling little concern in the course of what they would call larger, more important human events…then that would indeed have the intended effect of trivializing linguistic political correctness. However, if they were successful, it would also present a slippery slope leading to the trivializing of all political discourse; what's good for the goose is good for the gander. If words really don't matter, then a similar strategy to trivializing the specific target of linguistic PC ("Oh, those micro-aggressions the liberationists complain about are *just words*. They can't possibly be so important to what actually happens in the world of concrete human affairs.") can be applied to *any* issue or ideology ("Oh, they're just words…"). That would be dangerous, especially were the conservative anti-PC crowd to attain powerful elected office, where presumably they would want their own ideological language respected. Oops.

Linguistic PC is an attempt to silence free speech:

Another point: while I think that it's the critics of linguistic PC—not its advocates—who are trying to silence their opponents, once again I am of a mixed mind about the anti-PC charge regarding college campus debates—that the forces of PC are trying to shut down honest, open debate among students and professors. I understand what the critics of linguistic PC are responding to, but I am only sympathetic with them up to a point. I agree that there has been much done on college campuses in the name of political correctness that makes honest, open debate more difficult than it should be. I'm referring here to the cultural forces on campus that people like philosopher Allan Bloom and New York Times reporter Richard Bernstein famously worried about. They and a slew of others—mostly conservatives, but many liberals, too—were distressed over what they saw as the creeping power of PC and its troublesome influence over campus debates concerning various issues of the day.[5] A current-day example would be politically correct "safe zones" for minority students—mostly race and gender minorities—to speak their minds and know that they are safe in this environment against proscribed counter-speech. The critic points out

---

[5] They worry about more than PC's influence over free speech. The content of academic curricula; the favoring of social policies such as multi-culturalism and affirmative action and a bias toward postmodern relativistic philosophies are also examples of what conservatives would see as PC on campus run amok.

that safe zones have resulted in defeating the very thing that liberals used to brag about: that college campuses were bastions of free speech and incubators of new ideas, where anybody could say anything and invite open debate. Now, however, with all the PC safe zone linguistic policing going on, open debate has been shut down in favor of protecting liberals to speak their minds in feedback loop echo chambers almost as insidious as the conservative versions I referenced in Chapter 6. In this regard, safe zones definitely have had a chilling effect on genuine, open debate.

The same can be said about the PC phenomenon of "trigger warnings." This idea entails that authors, film producers, schoolteachers and college professors announce to their respective audiences that they will be discussing certain issues that may be potentially distressing to some of the audience. Once warned, then buyer beware. Warning or no, though, the idea of trigger warnings has had a similar chilling effect on free, open discussion.

I can understand that anybody looking at these examples of constrained free speech would respond with horror. However, when conservatives lay all the blame at the feet of political correctness *per se*, we part ways. Once again, they have failed to make important distinctions. I think the critics suspect that the very idea of political correctness inevitably has led to the campus free speech problems that they rightly bemoan; that somehow the very nature of political correctness inevitably and always makes its influence rise to excess. I disagree with this sentiment. Excesses of ideologies and principled ideals have occurred throughout history. People get carried away with perfectly good ideas and, in the extreme, sometimes turn matters into shambles. So, for example, there's nothing wrong with getting the trains to run on time. But look what happened in Mussolini's Italy: the excess—and the general fascist ideology that it was an expression of—was bad, but the principle (of trains running on time) was still good. We shouldn't lose sight of that distinction. Better yet, consider this example: Plato, in his damning and dismissive critique of democracy as a form of government, envisioned that any democracy would eventually lead to a situation where the majority of the citizenry would vote an incompetent into power (someone decidedly not a philosopher-king). Plato had little faith in the ability of the masses to know what's in their best interests. That's why he railed against democracy as defective; from the unintelligent majority, incompetent leadership must inevitably arise. I'm sure that, were Plato alive today, he would point to the election of Mr. Trump as Exhibit A.[6]

We wouldn't all agree with Plato regarding his condemnation of the concept of democracy. Most of us would say that the concept is just fine, but that people can sometimes use good concepts to do foolish things. Similarly, I think that the concept of political correctness is just fine, but once in a while people use it foolishly—or "extravagantly"—in ways that create unnecessary problems. That's precisely what's happened with some liberals using PC to create objectionable excesses about speech on college campuses. We shouldn't close down the concept of political correctness *per se*, though, just because there have been extravagant excesses. We must distinguish between the offending excessive use of the concept and other, quite acceptable uses.

But instead of looking at more examples of linguistic PC as it pertains to social issues, I want to change up the discussion to comment on how it pertains to political issues. Specifically, let me refresh our memories and then elaborate about a particular

---

[6] No one expresses this Platonic idea better than H.L. Mencken did 100 years ago when he mused, "As democracy is perfected, the office of the president represents, more and more closely, the inner soul of the people. On some great and glorious day, the plain folks of the land will reach their heart's desire at last, and the White House will be occupied by a downright fool and a complete narcissistic moron." —H.L. Mencken, *The Baltimore Evening Sun*, July 26, 1920.

linguistic PC political issue I mentioned in Chapter 1: the student debate over the Israeli/Palestinian conflict. You may remember that I talked about the pro-Israel student who took exception to what a pro-Palestine student said in passing when he mentioned what he called "the occupied lands." The pro-Israel student said that those lands were part of greater Israel, territory *justly won and appropriated* after the '48 Jewish war of independence and the defensive '67 and '73 wars against the aggression of Palestinians and neighboring Arab states. In the case of the lands won in 1948, they no longer in fact belonged to the Palestinians who had formerly lived there. Regarding the lands appropriated in the '67 and '73, aggressions carried out by the Palestinians living in Gaza and the West Bank as well as the state actors of neighboring Arab countries, they also no longer belonged to the Palestinians and those neighboring Arab countries. The disputed lands consist of the nation of Israel that was formerly the territory of Palestine, along with the Golan Heights and parts of the West Bank. The pro-Israel student insisted that the current-day debate isn't about "*occupied* lands," but about lands won in just wars of independence and defense. The pro-Palestine student insisted the debate *is* about "*occupied* lands," but about lands taken in unjust wars of Jewish invasion, aggression and occupation. Both the pro-Israel student and the pro-Palestine student understood themselves to be using precise politically correct language. To the pro-Israel student, it was politically correct to refer to these geographical areas as part of greater Israel, while the pro-Palestinian student believed it was politically correct to refer to them as occupied territories.

I would argue that this is a case of where political correctness is *not* trying to shut down free speech as the PC's critics claim it always inevitably does, but is actually promoting free, open debate. In other words, the principle of political correctness *per se* isn't doing anything untoward at all. Rather, both sides of the debate are appealing to political correctness to further their respective claims in the debate. So, the pro-Israel student insists upon politically correct linguistic precision when he demands the discussion be about "the lands won in just wars," and the pro-Palestine student does the same when he demands that the debate be about "occupied lands" instead. This difference of opinion has nothing to do with the anti-PC critic's contention that the word police on college campuses are running riot and attempting to shut down free discussion. Of course, it's most likely that neither student will finally sway the other's opinion; each is probably more interested in swaying the general public to their side; for most people to agree, after evidence and argument from each side is laid out in detail, that their respective version of the politically correct locution and underlying political ideology is better thought-out than the other side's.

The upshot is, I think the anti-PC critic is right when he says there's been a chilling effect on free speech on college campuses by some of the forces of political correctness. But that has to do with what I consider a mistaken use of linguistic PC advocacy (Chapter 1). Just as we've seen that there are advocates of linguistic political correctness who misuse PC in pursuing their own personal agendas stemming from extravagant disqualifying psychological factors (personal problems) around their claims of micro-aggression, so too are there advocates who misuse linguistic PC in pursuing their own personal social and political agendas, sometimes in unacceptable, heavy-handed ways. Just as those minorities arguing from extravagant disqualifying psychological factors should be sanctioned, so too should the people misusing political correctness to shut down free social or political debate be sanctioned. None of this means that we should eradicate the entire linguistic PC project. The distinction needs to be appreciated, respected and left in place to be properly used by the proponents of various social and political views. You don't abandon respecting people's rights—neither those of minorities nor of the general public—altogether. You don't abandon political correctness solely because it's difficult to be surgical with the public's use of that terminology. You don't chop off a person's arm to get rid of a mole on his elbow.

PC is all hopelessly subjective:

My email friend from the previous chapter believes that all college campus political correctness amounts to "McCarthyistic" censorship of open debate and that it stems from the dreaded philosophy of postmodern subjectivity. As he says:

> ...but the issue now is that it is entirely subjective in terms of what is legitimate offensive behavior and what just seems to be based on the individual's feelings. Like, calling Hillary "nasty" is not sexist or gender driven, however impolitic and stupid.

My friend is saying that there's no way of adjudicating linguistic precision claims about what should or shouldn't be called offensive language (aimed at a minority person). If a minority member says in the name of linguistic political correctness that someone has used an offensive term in addressing him (for example, a black person's saying, "Don't call me 'Negro,' I'm 'African American'" or Hillary says, "Don't call me 'nasty,' what I am is 'a woman who speaks up for herself'"), my friend believes that this is really just a case of the minority person's feelings being hurt or offended; we can't make decisions about what's right or wrong language usage based on feelings. Feelings are *entirely subjective,* he says; therefore, there are no *objective* standards that linguistic PC advocates can point to in deciding if the minority claimant has objectively been the victim of an actual offense.

My friend is mistaken. Knowing where to draw the line of where linguistic PC is legitimate and where it is McCarthyistically extravagant is clearly the rub. As I've said repeatedly, I do understand and am sympathetic with the view that there are cases of illicit linguistic PC excesses. Now we can characterize some of those excesses in terms of their sometimes being based solely on a minority complainant's subjective hurt feelings of being offended, where those subjective feelings are idiosyncratically extravagant. However, I beg to differ with my friend's complaint that the minority person's feeling offended "is *entirely* subjective" (my emphasis). Again, while there indeed are instances where a minority claimant bases his linguistic objections on his hurt feelings (which may be irrelevant because they might be related to any of the dreaded idiosyncratic psychological disqualifying factors we've just been talking about), naturally we can't honor these objections. There's simply no reasonable person who would hold to the principle that *all* hurt feelings are *always* to be honored. Okay, fine. But surely, sometimes a person's subjective feelings must be honored. Surely some emotional responses to certain politically incorrect word usages are *clear cases* of *rational responses* to genuine (objective) linguistic offenses; moreover, the *rationally* linguistically PC-attuned person should feel obligated to respect and honor this. I'm ruling out overt bigots from the realm of the reasonable; we wouldn't expect them to respond to a minority person's subjective feelings as we would the rest of the population. I also have to rule out the unconsciously motivated and the non-reflectively aware bigots who don't know that they're bigots in the first place and so don't have the opportunity to self-correct. These people aside, subjectivity in the form of hurt feelings or being offended can sometimes be a good indicator that an infraction really has (objectively) occurred. It's the job of any good citizen not to conflate the two but rather to be appropriately sensitive; sometimes subjective feeling states do need to be objectively honored.

For what it's worth, I don't see the Hillary "nasty" comment as being a clear case of either side. That comment seems to be on the border of what is or isn't a legitimate subjectivity claim of linguistic PC; and that's okay. Reasonable people can disagree and then argue it out. In this case, they would each argue for their psychological views about what Trump "really" means when he uses such a designator, what motivates him. Is it "sexist or gender driven, or just impolitic and stupid"? Minimally, it would be nice if, as rational people, we could all say enough about our respective views so that we could at least come to understand where each of us is coming from. We probably won't change one another's mind, but at least we can come to appreciate that we're on the same planet with different interpretations of people's motives. Anyway, this is what I would hope people could accomplish when they debate borderline cases of subjectivity.

A second corollary has to do with the idea that there's something McCarthyesque about the linguistic PC tactic. Allow me to mix historical political metaphors: the charge amounts to the claim that the word police have attained the social power to enforce Gestapo tactics with a McCarthy overlay. "Gestapo tactics" refers to a political entity having absolute political power to accuse and charge someone of any infraction it wishes and subject her to withering questioning, where the political entity also has the power to draw any preconceived conclusions about evil intent that it wants to. The "McCarthy" part of the word-police tactic refers to PC's being a powerful demagogic entity, in league with the Gestapo wing, that has taken possession of the spirit of the general culture-at-large. It has its metaphorical hands around the public spirit's throat, threatening terrible violence if there's not complete cooperation. Through its demagoguery, it creates a public air of fear that the demagogue will use Gestapo-like questioning tactics to falsely accuse an innocent victim of some terrible transgression (e.g. being in league with Communists), not giving her a realistic chance to defend herself and finally bringing a strong public reprimand against her, resulting in her being severely shamed in the public's eye. The only carrot thrown by the political entity is that things will go easier for her if she rolls over on any friends who might conceivably be guilty (or not) of a similar transgression to what she's been accused of. With this idea as background, the McCarthy-like political entity creates a sense of fear, panic and helplessness in the general population, as though anybody could fall prey to its whims at any given time.

I find this Gestapo/McCarthy charge against linguistic PC not only insulting (intentionally, I think), but also bordering on the hysterical. To even imagine likening linguistic PC—the "word police"—to a political entity wantonly enforcing its wishes on the public—strikes me as being beyond belief; the anti-PC critics here must be kidding. But then, when they say they are not, I have to take them at their word. So, we have to look at exactly what they see in the minority linguistic word-policing actions that makes them liken those actions to the Gestapo/McCarthy-like tactics.

Adapting that metaphor to political correctness, I think the critics are saying that the word police have become powerful McCarthy-like forces who have a strong grip on the public's throat, threatening terrible retribution for the slightest linguistic infractions that politically correct minorities imagine have been committed against them. According to the conservative critics, people supposedly live in fear of PC's making any such charge against them; they feel helpless because they think the charges, for the most part, are preconceived by the word police. They are terrified that they might slip up linguistically when the police are monitoring them. However, according to the critics, any preconceived accusation that the word police might make will be based on their subjective mood. This brings an added layer of panic to the people charged by the word police, because there's no predicting the moods and feelings of the word police.

Set against all of this is my friend's contention that no one should have to honor the demands of the linguistic PC police and worry about reprimand, just because a minority person takes offense without any objectively solid proof that an offense actually has occurred. In other words, we can't equate someone's feeling offended with an actual offense having been committed. So, the critique goes, the power of linguistic PC is defanged and people needn't pay attention to it.

My response is that if it's so easy to defang the word police, then it's difficult to believe that the critics really see linguistic PC as McCarthy-like in the first place, because a political entity that is truly McCarthy-like can't be dismantled that easily. Again, for this reason, it's hard to imagine that the critics are sincere in likening the PC tactics to McCarthyism. It's more likely just another *ad hominem* smear against the forces of minority linguistic PC. But that's just a small problem with the critique when compared to another problem, that of the pot calling the kettle black. Where the critics say that people needn't listen to the charges of the word police because those charges are preconceived, based solely on the subjective feelings of offense on the part of minority persons…so, too, are the critics' feelings of being threatened and offended by the PC police charges of word infraction "entirely" subjective. Well…if subjective feelings are no arbiters for questions about whether an offensive infraction has occurred against a minority, then the critics' feelings can't be an arbiter of their view that the word police, in the form of their PC behavior, have committed an infraction against them.

If I'm wrong about the insincerity of their claims that they fear the enormous power of linguistic PC in the culture, then I wonder what real basis they have for being so frightened. I myself over the years have committed a few linguistic infractions against minorities that I wasn't aware of at the time; I didn't know any better and I was called out on it by minority persons. My reaction, after some initial defensive denial, was to self-reflect; recognize my error for what it was; sincerely apologize; and finally dust myself off and go about my business, being a little wiser about my language use. There was no McCarthy-like campaign on the part of the liberal community or the minority person I offended to publicly censor and humiliate me and make my life a living hell, as my friend's critique here implies. My world didn't in fact collapse. And the truth is, I hadn't experienced the minority insistence that I use preferred designators as an oppressive, damning McCarthyism in the first place. As I've argued, other than the extravagant psychologically disqualifying cases where minority persons make linguistic infraction charges, linguistic PC isn't, in my experience, willfully trying to make people fearful of their words when they are referencing minority persons.

Why the critics of the word police feel different than I do about the matter intrigues me. My clinical thinking is that they appear to be caught in a paranoid delusion about the intent of linguistic political correctness. That delusion is probably motivated by their underlying grievance with the very idea of minority liberation and the need to pay special attention to the rights (linguistic or otherwise) of minority populations. They are tone-deaf to minority persons' claims to feeling insulted, demeaned and re-traumatized by unfettered, poor designators coming their way. The anti-PC critics don't understand that the minority individual has the right not to suffer any of this. Since the critics don't share the same minority social liberation ideology that the culture-at-large embraces, they can only imagine that (i.e. the paranoid delusion is that) any requirement that they at least behave *as though* they are sensitive to minority persons' complaints is a terrible, offensive force. And that would explain their antipathy both toward the forces of linguistic political correctness and the culture-at-large that embraces it.

This then, completes my comments about my friend's critique of linguistic PC's methodological problems. Now I will turn to his list of concrete examples of certain supposed politically correct terms that he finds problematic. In each of these cases, I suggest he is far off base.

CHAPTER 12

Defending Specific Examples of PC Speech

Let's recall the examples of objectionable PC speech found in my friend's email (Chapter 10). They include the following:

- The PC word police are wrong to rail against the politically incorrect, foolish things said by silly, horny men like Trump.
- They are wrong when they complain vehemently against the use of "Islamic terrorism"—they fail to distinguish Islamophobia from a genuine concern about the teachings of Islam that in fact do encourage violence against the Western infidels.
- They are wrong when they insist upon the sanctity of the term "white privilege" and the underlying phenomenon that the term expresses.
- They are wrong when they complain about Trump having derisively called Hillary Clinton "nasty."
- They are wrong when, in the form of the Black Lives Matter movement, they take offense to the conservative critic's insistence that *all* lives matter

Let me begin with what my friend says about Islamic terrorism.

Violence, Islamic terrorism and Islamophobia:

I will start with my friend's claim that the linguistic PCers fail to distinguish between Islamophobia and "a genuine concern about the teachings of Islam that in fact do encourage violence against infidels (i.e. non-Muslims)." There is a virulent strain of Islamophobia in our country that is largely a consequence of the violence that Muslim terrorists justify in the name of Islam. The Islamophobe jumps to the conclusion that Islam, therefore, is "inherently violent" and promotes "Islamic terrorism." According to the anti-PC critic, the word police would censor us from using these two descriptors, designating them as being politically incorrect. And the critic will have none of that.

Let's consider the first idea, that Islam is inherently violent. My friend says that PCers are incorrect to think that if someone has a legitimate concern for the textual references in the Quran about slaying infidels that they are also Islamophobic. I don't really see the distinction here. Whenever I've heard anyone pull out this old trope of Islam being "inherently violent," they have always, to a person, been making the point that Islam is a vile religion. This amounts to a fear and hatred of Islam, psychologically stemming from seeing Islamic terrorists committing violence in the United States and threatening our civil order. The critic would have us take at face value this idea that textual references to slaying infidels proves that Islam is a violent religion (that it's inherently violent), when in fact we shouldn't take it at face value at all. By now, everyone has heard the argument that, if finding scriptural references is the measure of assigning the quality of inherent violence to a whole religion, then both Judaism and Christianity are at least as violent, if not more so, as Islam. Famously, in the first Book of Samuel, we hear about God's commandment to the Jews to practice *harem*. This is the idea that the believers in the one true God should slay all the Amalekites. Current critics of the Israeli government's treatment of Palestinians cite this passage in condemning what they call the slaughter of the Palestinians of Gaza—inferring that Israelis are bloodthirsty purveyors of *harem* and that the text proves that Judaism is an inherently violent religion. As for Christians, throughout history, whenever they wanted to justify their violence against other people, they would typically refer to those people as that era's version of Amalekites. Referencing the Book of Samuel has always been part of the Christian warring tradition; whereas in Islam, the Quranic exhortation to commit violence is defensive in nature—defending one's self, one's property, or one's God. The history of Christianity is littered with examples of full-on genocides, from the various religious wars during the first millennium, to the Crusades, right up through the slaughter of native peoples that the colonizing and missionizing European Christian nations committed over the past 500 years. The Amalekites have been quite busy dying. So, if we're really interested in calling out religions that are inherently violent, perhaps Christianity should be first on the list.

My point is that the kind of violence we see today coming from Muslims has nothing to do with the defensive violence attributed to the Quran. Yes, terrorism is about violent acts and, yes, it is committed today predominantly by Muslims, but that's no testament to Islam's being an inherently violent religion. In fact, the Quran explicitly distinguishes between two kinds of violence: *jihad*, referring to lawful (i.e. condoned by Islamic teaching), defensive warfare that never allows for the killing of innocent civilians (the latter being the precise targets of terrorists); and *irjaf*, a wanton kind of violence that the Quran explicitly condemns. Today's terrorism is a prime example of *irjaf*. The well-regarded 20th century Ayatollah Mutahhari clearly points to this distinction in his *Fundamentals of Islamic Thought*,[1] assuring both the faithful and the curious outsider that,

---

[1] Ayatullah Murtaza Mutahhari, *Fundamentals of Islamic Thought: God, Man, and the Universe*. Mizan Press, 1985.

while terrorism might sometimes be an effective political strategy, it is in no way consistent with Islamic teachings. In fact, *irjaf* in any form is explicitly forbidden.

So, when the linguistic PCers rail against the critic's assertion that Islam is inherently violent, they are not just whistling in the wind. Rather, they are insisting that an important distinction (between *jihad* and *irjaf*) needs to be made and understood by all. Alas, that distinction is not made in the minds of many Westerners, and so some see Islam through phobic eyes only. The very thing the Quran forbids—*irjaf* as terrorism—is what these Westerners believe to be at the heart of Islamic tradition. I don't say any of this to mitigate in any way the violence that radical Muslims rain down on the West. Moreover, we have to acknowledge that these terrorists always justify their actions by wrapping themselves in the robe of devout Islamic faith. Truly though, these are religious fanatics who refuse to interpret their behavior as *irjaf*. They insist they are always performing *jihad*; that their behavior is a pious, defensive response to what they see as a history of Western oppression of Muslim Arab peoples. But even if one were to accept that the *"jihadis"* want to defend themselves against what they see as Western oppression, there is no way for them to get around the fact that their terrorism is aimed at civilians, something decidedly un-*jihad* like.

Linguistic PC is correct, then, in challenging the idea that Islam is inherently violent. Let me make a slight shift now in the discussion. My friend thinks that the PC word police are unreasonably focused on condemning anyone who uses the locution "Islamic terrorism" and would have the term removed from the lexicon altogether. I disagree with my friend about this, while I agree with my friend's insistence that we ought to be able to talk openly about the phenomenon that gets called Islamic terrorism. However, talking about the ideas underlying this phenomenon is one thing; using the expression "Islamic terrorism" to describe an entire religion is something else. We shouldn't give voice to the locution "Islamic terrorism" in our everyday political discourse. There is undeniably such a thing as terrorism. People who happen to be Muslim commit some of it and many of those Muslims claim they commit their terrorist acts in the name of Islam. That said, we need to be clear that, as in the previous distinction I was talking about, the expression "Islamic terrorism" does not in fact say anything about the inherent nature of the Muslim religion. Islam is not inherently terroristic; Islam does not condone terrorism, it condemns it. Nothing about terrorism in any way resembles the fundamental teachings of Islam (as opposed to where the Quran condones the defensive slaying of infidels). Terrorism is no more fundamental to Islam than genocide is fundamental to the tenets of "love thy neighbor" Christianity. And just as there have been Christian religious fanatics who have justified their wanton slaughter of innocents in the name of Jesus Christ (where most would argue that there was absolutely nothing in their justification or behavior that resembled Christianity), so, too, are there Muslim religious fanatics who commit acts of terrorism in the name of Allah.

Unfortunately, people don't make the necessary distinction between Muslims and terrorists. And it's with this in mind that I will challenge my friend's complaint about linguistic political correctness wanting us to exorcise the expression "Islamic terrorism" from public usage. My view is that the expression has nothing at all to do with political correctness. No liberal argues against using this expression simply because it sounds politically incorrect. When President Obama, for example, repeatedly warned against our using the locution "Islamic terrorism," he wasn't saying this in defense of the PC word police, but in defense of our national political strategy for dealing with our enemies.

He warned that our use of the expression allows America's political enemies (most pointedly, Iran and ISIS) to confuse the "Arab street" into thinking that all Americans conflate the ideas of Islam and terrorism and consider all Muslims to be terrorists who need to be destroyed. Using the expression is not bad PC; it's bad political strategy. Censoring ourselves from using it is not bowing to the forces of linguistic political correctness; it's appreciating sound political thinking. We can and should still voice our disapproval of those Muslims who are terrorists, but we shouldn't voice our disapproval of what, to the Muslim ear, sounds like a disapproval of Islam *per se*.[2]

One might think of it this way: as uncomfortable as some liberals are about hearing talk of "Islamic terrorism" because doing so is bad political strategy, I can well imagine some conservatives being similarly uncomfortable were we to start using the expression "white domestic terrorism" in the context of the widespread racism that terrorizes much of the civilian black and brown populations in our country. I'm sure the initial response of most conservatives to hearing this expression would be to howl at the very suggestion that there is anything approaching terrorism in the context of how racial minorities are treated in this country. Many are not only to a large extent blind to continuing widespread racism, but even if they could admit to such a thing, they would be loath to call it "white domestic terrorism." Actually, it *is* terrorism when civilians are systematically targeted with messages and acts of racial hatred and harm. They are the civilian victims of the unannounced war on black and brown people,

---

[2] I think the same kind of reasoning applies to what is going on as of this writing with how some people refer to COVID-19, the novel coronavirus. President Trump insists on calling it "the Chinese virus," the implication being that just as the disease is a bad thing, so too is the country where the virus originated, as well as the Chinese people and their government. This kind of talk may play well with his base, but on the broader world stage, it isn't a particularly smart political strategy.

carried out by unapologetic racists and by the legions of other white people who simply are not aware of the racist attitudes and behavior they unswervingly endorse and rain down on minorities. So, yes, there is such a thing as white domestic terrorism. But even if the conservative could be convinced of this, I'm sure she would then point out that "not *all* white people are racist," so one shouldn't confuse the issue of racism by using such an expression which has the practical political effect of running together two ideas ("being white" and "terrorism") and thereby antagonizing far more white people than those who are racist. I can even imagine this conservative acknowledging that the problem with the expression doesn't really have anything to do with political incorrectness; rather, the problem is that it inflames many white people who in fact totally condemn racist activity of any sort. ("How dare you imply that we're all racist terrorists?!") Of course, the conservative would be right here. That said, though, one would hope that if for no other reason than consistency's sake, the conservative could then understand that the problem with "Islamic terrorism" is not that it's politically incorrect, but that it's a dangerously inflammatory expression that isn't appreciated by the broader Muslim public and, therefore, at least for practical reasons, its usage should be avoided.

It's maddening to witness people who are otherwise quite savvy about making distinctions seemingly unable or unwilling to make the required distinction here. Instead, they join those in the public debate who equate Islam with terrorism; Rush Limbaugh, Alex Jones, the "Fox and Friends" cast, and Sean Hannity immediately spring to mind. It's easier for such public figures to defend their repeated mention of "Islamic terrorism" if they can make it an issue of political correctness rather than political strategy. If they can defend their mention of "Islamic terrorism" by insisting they are fighting the forces of political correctness, then since there is already a powerful litany of complaint against political correctness *per se*, this is one more item they can add to the list of sins of the PC establishment. PC is a convenient whipping boy for all manner of complaints that have nothing to do with political correctness. It's part of the conservative mob mentality intent on throwing everything they've got at the hated idea, no matter that some of the litany is misdirected. The conservative mob takes *all* views they disagree with and tars them with the brush of political correctness. And it turns out that it's not a bad strategy for convincing the public that it's perfectly fine to talk about "Islamic terrorism" if that public is already convinced that there is something unsavory about all things PC.

The reality is that people will continue to use the term "Islamic terrorism." Issues of political correctness aside, it's clear that we need to find ways to educate Muslims worldwide as well as Americans about the distinction in question—that the expression "Islamic terrorism" isn't a claim about any faults inherent in Islam; rather it points to the reality that there are Muslim fanatics who justify their terrorism in the name of Islam, even though acts of terrorism are forbidden by their religion. Many of us already understand this. But until the wider public absorbs the distinction—if peace and a non-escalation of violence are ultimately a nation's goals—it's politically prudent to avoid using the expression.

Peace and non-escalation of violence isn't a goal shared by everybody. There are those who understand the distinction in question but who insist on using the expression "Islamic terrorism" in order to trigger more violence from and toward Muslims. They aren't interested in peace with the Muslim world. Some are bigoted religious fanatics who harbor a preexisting hatred for the Muslim religion, not because it is inherently violent, but because they see it as alien and blasphemous—i.e. non-Christian. These

Islamophobes actually want to invite more terrorism, so they can use it as pretext for waging war against all of Islam—e.g. Christians wishing to bring about "The Rapture" by having a great religious battle to the death with the hated alien Islam, leading to the great conflagration and finally, to the Second Coming of Christ.

There's also a secular wing of this group who invite terrorism: some of the people who celebrate America as the ultimate world power, the jingoistic "America First" and "bring it on" crowd that doesn't want to have to put up with the troublesome behavior of Third World countries.[3] Their sense of identity is largely wrapped up in an all-encompassing idea of self-power, borrowed from America's position as the world's preeminent all-powerful nation. This self-power ideal convinces them that they are superior to all others in the world. And so, they are spoiling for a fight to the death with Third World Islam, their goal being a total destruction of those who would dare challenge the rightful place of America as Supreme. Of course, they relish the idea of insulting all of Islam by running together the ideas of Islam and terrorism. So much anger and confusion around this terminology, this lack of distinction between "Islam" and "terrorism." How our political future will play out vis-à-vis effecting peace in the world will have a lot to do with how we decide to talk about these two terms and deal with the locution in public discourse that runs the two together.

I want to return now to some of the other specific example complaints from my friend's list of grievances against the PC word police and offer a few brief comments about them.

---

[3] Obviously, many people in the "America First" movement are *not* aware of the distinction between Islam and terrorism. But here, I'm talking about those who *do* have this awareness and use the term provocatively.

White privilege (again!):

The linguistic politically correct class (obviously, I include myself here) has made the phenomenon of white privilege and, therefore, the expression "white privilege" a favorite object of complaint, and the conservative backlash has been considerable; they've had enough of what they consider insulting and demeaning PC name-calling. I've already talked about what the concept means and how it has manifested itself consciously in the actions of proud, unapologetic racists as well as in the unconscious or non-reflectively bigoted actions of white people who don't harbor racist beliefs consciously but who nevertheless hold a sense of racial superiority. Because I've already said most of my piece about white privilege, I'll simply make one additional comment concerning the oft-made anti-PC charge that the linguistic PC slam against the white privilege phenomenon is nothing more than an *ad hominem* attack against all white people. This is yet another instance of the anti-PC pot calling the kettle black. Linguistic political correctness is correct in its critique of white privilege. The white person's assumption of privilege is real, not a made-up contrivance used solely to disparage anti-PC critics. Granted, "white privilege" does not paint a flattering image of white people; but it's one more of those inconvenient truths we must acknowledge and deal with if we are ever to reach a point of racial understanding and harmony in our country.

Silly, horny men:

Another concrete example in my friend's list of grievances is his complaint about the PC word police's "outrage against silly, horny men who make unwanted but nonphysical advances to women (not the hypocrisy here as well in that Clinton and JFK's infidelities are okay)." I think we can all agree that, yes, silly, horny men do sometimes make unwanted but non-physical advances at women. But calling them "silly," where the implication of this term is that they were cute innocents who are "just talking" ("boys will be boys") and not ever doing anything about that talk, misses the point. Misogyny is about disrespecting and demeaning women as a gender. It's about getting away with certain behavior because women are *only* women. Men who repeatedly make unwanted remarks to women they find attractive are behaving disrespectfully and are demeaning them; their verbal advances are aimed at particular women *as women*, particular women as members of that gender. Any woman perceived as attractive is fair game. That's misogyny; and the excuse of "it's just words" is in no way mitigating. We can be charitable and allow that many such misogynists don't mean to hurt a woman's feelings when they make a particular non-physical advance. However, these verbal advances by men do nevertheless have the effect of demeaning women as individuals and quite often do hurt their feelings, whether this was a man's intent or not. Equally offensive is the way these verbal advances demean women as a group. When a man thinks that he's entitled to say whatever he wants ("I'm only complimenting her on her attractiveness when I whistle at her; she should feel flattered"), he comes from an assumption of "male power privilege" over women as a gender. As I pointed out in Chapter 8, this idea is buried deep within the collective unconscious of the culture-at-large and has the profound impact of effecting misogynist behavior.

Men who would feel aggrieved by these ideas complain that the PCers make no distinction between "mere" *words* and overt disrespectful and demeaning *actions* toward women. Surely, they think, there's a difference between innocent salacious talk and unwanted physical advances. Well, of course there is a difference. The misogyny of men who make actual unwanted physical advances is worse than the misogyny implied by men who make unwanted nonphysical verbal advances; however, they are both still misogyny. To say, "Well, at least I didn't actually do anything" is in no way mitigating.

The anti-PC critics will still try desperately to find another way to dismiss the complaint of linguistic misogyny. My conservative friend, for example, brings into the discussion the illicit sexual behavior of Presidents Kennedy and Clinton. The intent here is to imply that the liberal PCers would condemn the verbal sins of some "silly, horny men" for simply *saying* "stupid" things while at the same time defending liberal presidents over real, un-PC-like sexual encounters with women. The liberal who would defend such people, the antic-PC critics charge, are hypocritical. And, the anti-PC critics go on to say, if they (the PCers) want to claim that the overt acts of these presidents don't imply misogyny, then they surely have to admit that the innocent "mere" talk of silly, horny men doesn't either. Unfortunately for the anti-PC critics, this argument doesn't work. In the case of these presidents—and let's throw in Presidents Franklin Roosevelt and Dwight Eisenhower while we're at it—their behavior was *not* unwanted by the women involved. The anti-PC critics are comparing apples to oranges. It's the uninvited comments from silly, horny men's that makes that talk misogynistic. Since there's no good evidence indicating that the presidents' overt behaviors were non-consensual—we're talking, after all, about mature women who knew what they were doing—there's no reason to call the presidents' behavior misogynistic.

That said, I will make the case for the anti-PC critics' argument using a politically correct notion they most likely wouldn't approve of otherwise. If the anti-PC critics are saying that these presidents might have been unconsciously or non-reflectively using their positions of power—of their enhanced version of "male power privilege"—to lure women into affairs who were, relatively speaking, less powerful, then I could see the makings of a case that these presidents were assuming male entitlement regarding women.[4] Such an assumption (whether held consciously, unconsciously, or non-reflectively) would be disrespectful and demeaning toward women. If that were indeed the case, then I would agree that this was indefensible, misogynistic behavior on the part of these presidents. Thankfully, we would have been made aware of this misbehavior by advocates of political correctness; they would be the ones to point out the "male power privilege" that might have been at work here.

The n-word hypocrisy of black people:

My friend complains that the word police are all over racists for using the n-word but are completely silent when it comes to black people using the term themselves. He doesn't like what he sees as the hypocrisy at work here. In fact, there is nothing hypocritical about this. When racists use the n-word, it's intended as a hateful slur against the minority black population. But there are different contexts where black people use the term with one another, none

---

[4] Whether these women are rightly described as having been "lured" into affairs is another matter. "Being lured" has an element of coercion about it. It's not clear that we can attribute coercion to the actions of these presidents. Certainly, their sexual partners were *fully aware* of the power differential existing between them; that awareness would tend to argue against their experiencing their situations as coercive. By the same token, this matter is a lot dodgier in the case of President Clinton and Monica Lewinsky. We can't know if there was subtle or unconscious coercion going on; she continues to argue to this day that the relationship was consensual. If there was coercion, then clearly President Clinton was and is a misogynist who used his power as an entitlement over women, that being both disrespectful and demeaning. In any case, whether or not there was coercion in the instances of any of these presidents, I'm still of the view that there could have been "male power privilege" at play for all of them. On that count alone, I would argue their behavior was misogynistic.

of which have a connotation of hateful race bigotry. A black person's using the n-word in addressing another black person does so sometimes as a kind of defense mechanism, where the intent in using the term is to diminish the hateful sting it normally has when a racist uses it. It has the effect, at least in fantasy, both of robbing the racist of his position of power (the black person who says to the fantasized white bigot, "You see, I'm using the term myself and taking the venom out of it, much to your chagrin.") and allowing the black person to utter the word herself and experience no negative feelings. It's a means of changing the connotation of the n-word from a way for white people to provoke both tremendous fear and anger—both of these being extremely unsettling emotions for any black person to hold in consciousness—to new connotations that rob the racist of this kind of psychic victory.

In a slightly different context, sometimes the n-word is used by a black person to descriptively capture the idea that she's annoyed—sometimes even angry or hateful toward—another black person. This is intramural annoyance or anger or hate toward an individual, not an extramural "us versus them" slur. She's not saying she hates black people as a race, which is always the implied intent of any racist when he slurs any black individual this way. The racist makes no distinction between "I hate you" and "I hate all of you." In contrast, there's no racial hatred in the black person's use of the term against another black person.

These two aren't the only connotations the n-term has taken on. Sometimes it's a term of endearment, a signal of affection. ("I love you, my n___").[5] Actually, this connotation is by far the main usage the term receives today in intramural black conversing, having nothing to do with any kind of racial hatred. Interestingly, it's

---

[5] I referenced this earlier, in Chapter 8, footnote 20 and then again in Chapter 10, footnote 4

not only black people who use the n-word in these ways. I've known plenty of Latinos to refer to one another as "my n___," where there's absolutely no intent to racially slur black people or one another with hate speech. They are borrowing the endearment intended by black people in addressing each other, using that connotation when addressing other Latinos.

Finally, I'll chalk up my conservative email friend's comment about African-American hypocrisy to his total unawareness of the different connotations of the n-word as used by people of color. I guess the test case would be if a white person were to address a black person as "my n___," having only the intramural, non-racist connotations in mind. I suspect most black people would not be ready to hear that word uttered by any white person, no matter his intent. The history of white racist abuse is still too raw, too present for that.

Now I would like to address my email friend's complaint about the politically correct Black Lives Matter (BLM) movement. Because there has been so much anger, confusion and hysteria swirling around both the actions of the Black Lives Matter movement and the conservative anti-PC word police response to those actions, I want to spend more time looking at this particular example of word- policing than I have on the rest of my friend's complaints. This discussion deserves its own chapter.

CHAPTER 13

Word-Policing "Black Lives Matter" (BLM)

Consider my friend's criticism that, surely, in our supposedly color-blind country for which the minority word police have advocated since the 1960s, we ought no longer give special consideration to black lives over any other lives. My friend thinks that as a matter of principle, it's wrong to emphasize that *black* lives matter when in fact the inspirational motto should be *All Lives Matter*, including the lives of the average white citizen and the members of our police departments (Blue Lives Matter), as well as the lives of all other people in the world. My friend and other anti-PC critics believe that linguistic political correctness has gone overboard in bowing to the loud minority voices giving preference to minority rights over the rights of the rest of us, a kind of reverse discrimination…which is exactly how my friend understands the behavior of the Black Lives Matter movement.

I know it's unintentional, but what my friend is saying is music to the racists' ears. Racist bigots immediately jumped on board with the anti-Black Lives Matter principled conservatives when the latter began championing the alternative principle of All Lives Matter. This is yet another occasion when the racists hang onto—or should I say, hide under—the coattails of their conservative principled brethren. But fair is fair; my friend and his All Lives Matter associates shouldn't be blamed for whoever else (racists) might want to follow their lead. As we well know, guilt by association (well-poisoning) is never a valid kind of reasoning. But while they shouldn't be seen as guilty by association, principled conservatives should be held accountable for another invalid argument known as the *fallacy of accent*; an error of logic in dire need of PC word-policing. The poor reasoning occurs when a person puts an inappropriate emphasis (accent) on a certain terminology used by another, resulting in a misunderstanding of what that other person was actually saying and then drawing illicit conclusions from that misunderstanding.[1] So my friend and his compatriots take the expression "Black Lives Matter" and mistakenly put the emphasis on the word "Black." In that rendering of the expression's meaning—that it is *black* lives that matter—they draw a conclusion that was unintended by the advocates of the BLM movement; that BLACK lives should be *favored* over white lives (and all other lives), that BLACK lives are more valuable. And if *that* were what BLM truly peddled, then clearly that *would* be offensive and worthy of condemnation. Indeed, an appropriate further response would then be that no, black lives aren't more valuable than the lives of others; ALL lives matter. This mistaken interpretation leading to faulty reasoning captures exactly where my conservative email friend is coming from.

---

[1] Here is a paradigm example of this kind of fallacious reasoning. Consider the locution, "Woman without her man would be lost." If one were to put the emphasis on "woman" and "would be lost," (as in a *woman*-without-her-man *would be lost*) then the implication would be that a woman without a man in her life is *lost*—that a woman simply needs to have a man to depend on in order for her life to be meaningful (this sentiment perhaps being construed as a misogynistic comment). In a second interpretation, one would change the emphasis to "Woman; without *her, man* would be lost." (Minus the semicolon and comma.) Here the implied conclusion would be that a man who doesn't have a woman in his life is lost—that a man simply needs to have a woman to depend on in order for his life to be meaningful, that sentiment perhaps being construed as misandristic. The point is, if a person, because of his mistaken emphasis on the wrong parts of a statement, misinterprets the intended meaning of that statement, then he will draw a conclusion that wasn't intended by the person who put forward the statement. So in this example, if someone puts forward the statement and he means the emphasis to be on the second interpretation, then if someone else reads it and puts the emphasis on the first interpretation, he will draw a mistaken conclusion.

But all of this is based on an *incorrect* rendering of the meaning of "Black Lives Matter." What BLM advocates are emphasizing in the expression, rather, is the term "Matter." The meaning of the expression "Black Lives Matter" is that black lives MATTER, *as opposed to not mattering*, in which the idea that their lives don't matter gets played out again and again in the form of an unending stream of daily racist violence. The appropriate conclusion of *this* rendering of the meaning of the motto is that, because black lives really do MATTER (they matter as much as all other lives), people need to pay attention to the unsavory forces in society that act as though black lives don't matter at all.

Therefore, in missing the intended meaning of the motto and drawing conclusions from this misunderstanding, the critics of the BLM movement have committed the fallacy of accent. I would like to be able to say that this is just a case of sloppy, unintentional thinking on their part. Unfortunately, I believe that often this is not the case. The critics' insistence on focusing on their conclusion that ALL lives matter suggests a tone-deafness to what the Black Lives Matter movement obviously is all about. And, in fact, that tone-deafness seems willful; a matter of incredible *chutzpah*. It should be clear to anyone with even an ounce of empathy and only a passing awareness of racial history in our country that the Black Lives Matter movement is the latest important iteration of the Civil Rights Movement, reminding people who might have gone to sleep over the past 30 years that the drumbeat of racism has never really let up. Even with all the progress that has been made in race relations, it's progress set against a backdrop of unrelenting racism. Black Lives Matter is a way of putting an *exclamation mark* on the need to bring the reality of this continuing racist war back into public consciousness— the need for the public to start paying attention to the unsavory forces in society that send the message to black people that their lives don't matter at all. That's what the principled conservative needs to understand. And that's why the BLM word police are as adamant as they are that their motto should be understood *only as intended.*

Let me now flesh out in more detail exactly why I think BLM adamancy is a needed, righteous cause. The psychological face of racism that BLM is a reaction to and confronts head-on—the racist-induced psychological burden of being black in America—is indisputable. Black people wake up every day feeling that "white eyes" are upon them whenever there's a white person around. Even when they turn on the TV to watch the news, the white-dominated news tells black people how guilty they all should feel about the relatively few black people who commit criminal behavior. The media in general is quite persistent in this regard: to be black in America is to be wrong. And even when black people live, work or are portrayed in an environment where it's widely acknowledged by the culture-at-large that they are "safe" from overt racism—say, a liberal college campus or a TV documentary celebrating either the black middle class or the black individuals who have "overcome" their disadvantage—they still feel the "white eyes" judging them, now in the person of the well-intentioned, liberation-celebrating white man who nevertheless unconsciously or non-reflectively lords his sense of white privilege over them. To be sure, this happens in different degrees as perpetrated by different white liberals. But that it happens at all is the problem.

There's no let-up. Everything about "blackness" in a world where white people wield all the levers of power (former President Obama notwithstanding) requires that a black person remain on her guard. She can't predict when she might cross that invisible line of "infringing" on white privilege. It could be the tone of her voice, her Ebonics vernacular, the private vocabulary she shares with her friends, her *color*, her "uppity" behavior—who knows what subtle things about a black person offend and set off the anger of white-privileged people! A black person in this regard is always walking on eggshells, on her guard most every moment when in a white environment. One should hate that this is so, but it is. Even the well-intentioned white person cannot ever really say with certainty that some of his unconscious or non-reflected-upon bigotry-fueled white privilege won't rear its head in an encounter with his very best black friend. As I noted in Chapter 8, he no doubt would probably be horrified were this to happen and he were made aware of it. However, any black person knows that it's always a possibility, that true safety is impossible to come by.

That's the least of it. There are far worse ways in which a black person is not "safe" in America. As the Black Lives Matter movement points out, there is pervasive, systemic *violence* against black people, beginning with institutional racism. BLM is intent on bringing to full public consciousness institutional racist violence against the larger black community in the form of our discriminatory justice system (the courts), racial profiling, and governmental policies that invite black poverty, unemployment, health issues, homelessness and disproportionate incarceration. But while all of us should be concerned about this "soft" kind of racist violence, the central focus of the Black Lives Matter movement is on "hard" violence, violent *force*, which, in its most extreme expression, is violence aimed at bodily mortality. There simply is no safe place in America for the black body.[2]

One has only to review the long and ongoing history of police violence against black people dating back to the years of slavery

---

[2] Ta-Nehisi Coates spells this out in no uncertain terms in his *Between the World and Me*. The black *man's* body, especially, is mortally disposable, and Coates chronicles how he has fearfully and angrily gone through life being aware of this on a daily basis, hoping that his young son will be spared the same affliction as he grows into manhood.

to understand that the black body has always been at extreme risk. This has been brought into white public consciousness in recent years by news reports of police brutality against black people. Indeed, Black Lives Matter was founded out of the black outrage over the shooting death of Trayvon Martin and the acquittal of his killer, and since has become a modern-day social media venue for consciousness-raising about *all* of the race-related police shootings and killings of the recent past. All of the public marches and demonstrations, all the protest disruptions of political speeches and meetings, and all the social media sharing of cell phone photos and videos of this violence serve to educate the wider public. Average nonviolent black citizens formerly unknown to the wider public have, through the BLM reporting of their meaningless murderous deaths, become sad reminders that innocent black people are easily expendable; indistinguishable black faces among many black citizens who are seen by so many whites as a singular entity. "Those black people; you can't tell one from the other." Sadly, their lives have finally taken on more meaning to the wider public only because of their deaths. Because of the work of Black Lives Matter, many of us now know something more about the ordinary lives of Alton Stirling, Tamir Rice, Eric Garner, Sandra Bland, Michael Brown, Botham Jean, Ahmaud Aubery and Breonna Taylor; all people who for the most part were just walking down the street, living in their homes, asleep in bed or driving down the road minding their own business when they became victims. George Floyd, unarmed and not dangerous, was killed by Minneapolis police mere minutes after being arrested. Tragically, most black people not only go around with the constant awareness that there are always "white eyes" on them, but they also go around with a heightened awareness of their vulnerable reality when they put themselves in situations of WWB (walking while black) or DWB (driving while black). Black people live in fear when a police officer pulls them over while driving or when he stops them on the street while they are simply walking to their next destination.

In this regard, BLM recognizes that most average black people are equally at risk and they all go about their business in life knowing that at any moment they could become the latest tragedy, being in the wrong place at the wrong time. Because of this, BLM takes it as its overriding mission to expose the calamity of all this and to loudly demand the white public do something meaningful about it. Assuming we all embrace the culturally accepted ideology that everyone has a *prima facie* right to safety, BLM insisting on that right for black people is certainly the politically correct thing do to.

Of course, there are some exceptions to this black reality. Black celebrities are seemingly spared the everyday indignity of living in constant fear. Only black people with enormous wealth, high political status, or easily recognizable faces from TV or on the big screen are untouchables. They are easily identifiable; they are "special." Everybody knows who Kobe (Bryant) was; everyone recognizes Shaq (Shaquille O'Neal), MJ (Michael Jordan) Denzel (Washington), Spike, Reverend Al (Sharpton), Barack and Michelle (Obama) and Oprah (Winfrey). They are known by their first names and have risen to the status of cultural icons. Their reward is that they need not carry around the same weight of having to be on guard against imminent abuse or bodily harm.

These kinds of people, few and far between, are not really on the radar of BLM. But their situation is clearly the exception that proves the rule that the ordinary black person always has to be on guard against imminent abuse or bodily harm. BLM is there to sound the clarion call for action, to remind the larger public that black lives do matter. For my conservative friend and his compatriots to insist that this BLM reminder is tantamount to a PC favoring of black people over whites is ludicrous.

But to appreciate even more fully the *chutzpah* behind the conservative criticism of the politically correct "Black Lives Matter" motto, let's view a broader panorama of white racist violence; the historically relentless white bigotry aimed at violating the black mind and body. Our nation has a 400-plus-year-old cultural tradition of racist bigotry, where this hateful message of white racial supremacy coupled with white-on-black violence is continually drummed into the black person's mind. Slavery, lynching, Jim Crow laws, *de facto* segregation, jailhouse "suicides," hair-trigger policing all tell the black person that he is worthless, that his life has no meaning, that it's *insignificant*; and so, his very existence—his *mortality*—is *disposable.* A black person can't help but realize that his mortality has always been and continues to be on the line—disposable—in the white world; he's forever marginalized and inferior in that world. This knowledge is in every African American's DNA. Even in an America where the culture-at-large embraces minority rights and liberation, black people understand that they nevertheless must always be on their guard against the sizable racist subculture.

Miraculously, there are many in the black community who understand what the racist would have them believe about their insignificance and expendability but do not accept it and so are not defeated by it. In spite of the denigrating bigotry, they have a sense of themselves as being significant and they take precautions to be on the ready for the ever-present possibility of violent danger intruding. Some of these people are proud but don't want to make waves by *publicly* opposing the forces of racism. But there are many others in this group who, like their Black Lives Matter associates, are self-empowered and ready to fight the good fight against the threat of violence and the message of black insignificance.

Unfortunately, far too many other members of the black community end up buying as truth the racist onslaught. They internalize and self-identify as being insignificant and disposable; that's what 400-plus years of hellish racist tradition can do. They are victims twice over—first victimized by having to listen to the constant slurs of racist America and then by their own belief in the messages of those slurs. All too often, when a person comes to see himself and those around him as having no relative value—even as being unlovable—and therefore as expendable—violence becomes an *expectation* in his life, the normal way of things. That is, there's nothing about violence that really shocks him, whether it's the violence coming his way or, in some cases, the violence he decides to inflict on the world.[3] And so mere disputes between himself and others in his surround might quickly escalate into violent terror; a battle to the death is not uncommon.

This plays out nowhere as vividly as in inner city gang warfare. No one in our nation goes through life fearing for their safety, yet expecting that it will inevitably be violated, as much as young black youths living in the throes of gang violence. I've seen up close in my work at Homeboy Industries (a gang intervention program in the heart of LA) what brown and black youths' feeling both insignificant and mortally disposable looks like. Gang members typically don't expect to live into their 30s. I've seen how cheap their lives can be, having gone to my share of funerals, many resulting from gang violence. All this is the result of 400-plus years of bigotry's violent drumbeat; add to it the layers of ongoing social anomic forces these young black men especially[4] deal with—poverty, poor education, the constant threat of incarceration, broken families, childhood trauma in the form of repeated parental psychological and physical

---

[3] There is no doubt in my mind that this identity-sense of disposability and insignificance is the most important causal factor in the phenomenon of black-on-black violence.

[4] The lives of young black gang-member women are similarly vulnerable, though not nearly in the numbers that the lives of young black men are.

abuse, absent role models who have been swallowed up by the prison system, easy availability of drugs—and you end up with generations of people in existential despair and prone to violent explosion.

Black Lives Matters is particularly interested in reaching such people and letting them know that their lives are neither insignificant nor their bodies disposable. Contrary to how my conservative friend interprets the politically correct insistence that the lives of black people *do* matter, we're not saying that anti-social violent behavior is to be excused; when unlawful violence happens, the offenders should be held accountable. Rather, many of us are saying that along with holding them responsible, action must be taken to counter the devastating effects that racism has had on the psyches of violent offenders. It would be both prudent and moral to devise practical measures to help turn these lives around—prudent in the sense that such measures might stem the tide of violence; and moral in the sense that, if we don't do what we can to counter the effects of racism, we are complicit. Of course, the conservative critic counters that this kind of talk is bleeding heart, politically correct liberal noise, that we are looking past the fact that some of these violent people behave violently not because they are victims of racism but because they are simply evil, and are therefore deserving of no special treatment. To that I would reply that certainly, there is genuine evil in the world; truly bad people exist, no matter their color or social circumstance. Furthermore, some violent victims of racism might be counted among them; their tendency towards violence might be a pre-existing condition, as it were, that needs to be contained, maybe even punished. Perhaps such people can't be rehabilitated. But even if all that were true (a whole other discussion), pointing out that some of the violent victims of racism are evil and therefore undeserving of any special positive attention doesn't override the reality that the great preponderance of that population is not evil, but rather people responding in a way that one might expect when they've been fed a steady diet of hateful, dismissive and demeaning messages about their insignificance and disposability. No one in their situation should have to live with such a reality. And, yes, to allow it would undoubtedly be politically incorrect and the height of immorality.

In addition to Black Lives Matter, there is a plethora of gang intervention programs that were on the scene well before the BLM movement, championing the cause of these vulnerable black youths. The gang intervention program I just mentioned—Homeboy Industries—is a prime example. Detailing here the work done by such programs would take us too far afield. I will simply say that all of them face the same basic challenge: existential problems (regarding self-significance and self-disposability) piled onto an individual's psychological difficulties and soul-crushing social conditions are the toughest nuts to crack. The work is never easy. Indeed, even for the well-intentioned helper, it's often a matter of two steps forward, one step back. Sadly, even after doing incredibly meaningful work with people from this vulnerable group, well-intentioned helpers can sometimes unintentionally add to a young gang member's desperation, not necessarily having to do with his or her sense of disposability but definitely with his or her sense of insignificance. It's one thing to have the villainous, overt racists spewing their dehumanizing hatred at people of color, but you don't want to hear it from the "good guys" too. I've seen caring white social workers and therapists as well as empathetic mentors being patronizing and culturally insensitive to young POC. The message is clear: white behavior is right behavior; this from people who are four-square behind black and brown liberation, people who would give their right arm for many of their clients and who would be mortified to realize that these white bias-indicating messages are ingrained in their own psychological repertoire. Unfortunately, this just is the reality of unconscious and un-reflected-upon white privilege.

Certainly, most homeboys and homegirls are aware of this situation and many of them obviously feel conflicted about it. Finally, though, in my experience, most of them are forgiving because they are convinced of the overall good intentions of these helpers and the positive results of working with them. I've seen how providing meaningful jobs, family support, love, forgiveness and psychological understanding—all things that any gang intervention program worth its salt tries to effect—help bring about those results. I don't mean this list to be a platitudinal salve for the oppressed and their helpers. Rather, I'm talking about both racially vulnerable people and their helpers digging into these possibilities, daily doing the hard work it takes to bring them to fruition. Thankfully, there are forces in our society that, along with the Black Lives Matter movement, are aimed at remediating the terrible plight of vulnerable black youths. They and BLM are intent in their actions on driving the point home that black lives (as well as the lives of other people of color who are similarly vulnerable) really do matter.

This takes us back to where we began the present discussion. The BLM motto has nothing to do with a ranking of whose lives matter most. Being dim to this fact, the anti-PC critic often complains that BLM and all the other programs that focus on the well-being of black youths amount to purveyors of anti-white bigotry, purveyors of reverse discrimination. I hope it's obvious by now that this complaint is playing fast and loose with language. The BLM movement is solely about wanting white people to WAKE UP to the relentless BIGOTRY all around us and respond appropriately as moral beings. It's a call for the citizenry to pay attention to the historical and ongoing intentional and unintentional forces of bigotry that have rendered as acceptable the demeaning of and violence against black people. It's about realizing that ordinary black people—many simply minding their own business—are being psychologically brutalized and even murdered by police or other "open carry" citizens for no reason other than that they are black and their mere existence sets off the intense, change-resistant bigotry of both the fearful racist and the sympathetic white-privileged person; the black person is seen as guilty by virtue of being black.

Moreover, Black Lives Matter is about people coming to terms with the reality that all too many black youths have turned the racist and institutional message of their disposability and insignificance in on themselves, rendering them indifferent to violence, whether aimed at themselves or perpetrated by them. Black Lives Matter is telling all of white America that none of this is acceptable and that black lives must be respected as non-disposable and fully significant human lives.

One last point: I don't think BLM targets unapologetic, overt racists, trying to change their minds; racists couldn't care less about what black people want. Rather, I think the movement seeks the attention of the unthinking, insensitive non-racist conservative and the unintentional racist liberal, both of whom—in a perfect world—could conceivably influence the effecting of social policies that could overwhelm the destructive intentions of the overt racists. Unfortunately, we don't currently live in that perfect world and so this message doesn't always go down well with the target audience. More than a few white liberals and non-racist conservatives have made it abundantly clear that they don't like what they see as an angry, loud, theatrical display. Their common complaint is about the "impolite" approach of Black Lives Matter advocates. White complainers don't realize that their discomfort is their white privilege speaking. "I've been on your side for all these years," says the white liberal. "I've never opposed you in the past," says the unengaged, non-racist white conservative. "How dare you yell at me; I'm white and have always been in your corner," say both the liberal and conservative. Steeped in their sense of privilege, it becomes difficult for white people to see that the "strident" and "impolite" methods of the BLM movement are loud but not really impolite at all. One is naturally and appropriately LOUD when one is intent on striking an exclamation mark!!!

This, then, completes my treatment of the politically correct word-policed expression "Black Lives Matter." Obviously, any racial minority that has been the target of bigotry could challenge the remaining cultural norms of racism by encouraging their own "X Lives Matter" movement.[5] One would hope that if a person were sensitive enough to finally "get it" when they hear the angry challenge of "Black Lives Matter," they would also automatically extend the same insight to all other racial minorities, especially those with the most longstanding list of complaints, such as Native Americans. But that's a hope that, unfortunately, history doesn't bear out. People tend to be deaf and blind to the hardships of others unless the complaints are loud enough and right in their face. So, by all means, "Native American Lives Matter!", "Brown Lives Matter!", "Asian Lives Matter!".

This also completes my response to my conservative friend's list of grievances against word-policed political correctness. Words do matter, and people who are egregiously careless with them have to expect pushback. In fact, everyone ought to take pains to be politically correct when what we say and the way we say it has consequences for our fellow citizens. Sometimes the

---

[5] I hope it's obvious that alt-right white supremacists who champion the cry "White People Matter" don't count as a minority historically oppressed by racism and so don't fall into this category.

politically correct things we say have the effect of celebrating our lives with one another. At other times, the politically *incorrect* things we say have the effect of demeaning and devaluing others. And that's not something we ought to tolerate. This is precisely one very good reason why, rather than disparaging the cause of PC word-policing, we should nurture it.

With this idea as a springboard, I will now turn to Chapter 14, concluding my case for the virtue of political correctness and discussing the paramount role it plays at this moment in the life of our nation.

The Importance of Political Correctness

Chapters 10—13 constitute the first part of my defense of political correctness against the anti-PC forces of bigotry and principled conservatism. This involved defending against specific complaints about PC word-policing. In this, the final chapter, I will complete my defense of political correctness. But I'm going to approach the task from a wider perspective than I have up until now. First, I will point to what I see as some dangerous consequences to the world that flow from the degree of success the critics have had in assaulting the PC concept. After that, I will discuss why, given those successes, we need to redouble our efforts to protect the integrity of political correctness as a sacrosanct concept that undergirds the social ideological gains our nation has historically enjoyed. I'll also share some thoughts about what I think are some identifiable steps we must take in order to maintain the integrity of political correctness, along with the ideological gains that accrue from it. Moreover, I will suggest what I think we need to do to expand even further the PC concept's reach and applications, not only for minorities demanding both social liberation and an even greater absorption of that ideology into the culture-at-large, but also for the broader American citizenry and the rights and ideological horizons that are its due.

The Consequences of Degrading Political Correctness

The assaults against political correctness have been unrelenting, so of course, PC advocates need to stay on high alert. Failure to do so could lead to a public that eventually loses all respect for all things PC. If we haven't fully reached that point, we are coming close; and I believe that grave consequences are already starting to show. Unpacking these consequences will be the subject of this section.

Of course, we can already see that the cause of minority liberation has been severely strained by the weakening of the PC concept. But that's not all; an unfortunate reality is that the people looking to spread confusion about legitimate, serious PC with the aim of totally destroying it have aligned themselves—some intentionally (e.g. the Stephen Bannons, Michael Flynns and the Paul Manaforts of the world), some unintentionally (the liberal Bill Maher and a host of other conservatives, among them being my principled conservative email friend, as well as celebrity conservative Bill Kristol and even Sean Hannity)—with a larger, dangerous cast of characters both here and from abroad who would unleash forces that challenge the very foundations of our republic. These include domestic white supremacist terrorists as well as the foreign terrorists and their state supporters (Iran, for example), all who look to undermine the American citizens' confidence in our nation's institutions and ideologies as well as in our leaders' ability to protect them from wanton terrorist violence. The terrorists, sowing chaos and self-doubt, are clearly looking to undermine the very notion of democracy. There are other foreign political actors not directly aligned with foreign or domestic terrorists but who nevertheless are every bit as interested in undermining our nation. Most prominent among them are Russia's Vladimir Putin and his minions of computer hackers who would break into our voting systems—and thereby plant doubt in our minds about our election results—and who also create various sinister "bot" messaging on social media aimed at spreading false information about social issues and American institutions in order to pit one segment of American society against another. It becomes clearer by the day that, with his ultimate goal of cementing a decidedly undemocratic new world order, Mr. Putin is intent on unleashing what one political commentator has referred to as an international multipolar chaos of "all against all."[1]

Terrorists, their state supporters and Putin are our domestic and foreign enemies. As I've said, they are being aided in their attempts to sow division and self-doubt among our ranks by the witting and unwitting anti-PC critics. Again, in the unwitting camp, I place people like Bill Maher, Bill Kristol, etc. And I would add to this list the reinvigorated conservative warriors against liberalism in general who, in their most recent incarnation, celebrate Mr. Trump's anti-PC vision of "making America great again." But let's not forget the witting, anti-PC sowers of chaos. The Trumpist Stephen Bannon and the rest of his ilk (maybe even Mr. Trump himself, but who really knows) have as much as said that chaos is their friend and they would like to spread a healthy dose of it throughout the government, our institutions and the general citizenry. In their efforts to defeat political liberalism, derail the public's confidence in the idea of political correctness and destroy the primary social ideology it stands for—minority social liberation—they have (I believe, knowingly) made it that much easier for America's domestic and external enemies to succeed in their mission. In some cases (I'm thinking of President Trump as a central offender), they have even gone beyond tainting political correctness in order to degrade public confidence in the cause of minority liberation to planting seeds of doubt in anything that liberals advocate for, even our national liberal advocacy for the great freedoms promised by the Constitution—press, individual

---

[1] Molly K. McKew, "Putin's Real Long Game." *Politico*, Jan 1, 2017.

speech, religion. Almost daily, we hear complaints from the White House about the terribly dishonest politically correct press, the need to put a muzzle on some reporters, threats to jail political opponents, the ongoing war against Islam. And all of these pronouncements give aid and comfort to the likes of Mr. Putin.

Although the following observation is made specifically about the debilitating consequences of what might be called Putin's "new cold war" efforts to degrade America's confidence in its democratic institutions, I believe that these same consequences are also the result of the our own country's conservative war against PC:

> This war seeks, at home and abroad, to erode our values, our democracy, and our institutional strength; to dilute our ability to sort fact from fiction, or moral right from wrong; and to convince us to make decisions against our own best interests....[2]

While it's quite clear that his efforts have been rewarded—in that we now hear far too many American conservatives claiming that Putin is our friend, that global warming is a hoax created by a scientific community that can't be trusted, that immigrants in general (especially Mexicans and Muslims) are dangerous, that Jews are probably responsible for many of the "so-called" anti-Semitic threats to Jewish Community Centers and cemetery vandalism, that minorities are draining America of its resources, etc.—it's also true that many of these views were already in place in the conservatives' ongoing domestic attack against all manner of liberalism. Mr. Putin's efforts have merely thrown more fuel on the pre-existing fire.

Whether conservatives are wittingly or unwittingly showing aid and comfort to Mr. Putin by championing these views, it's clear to me that the central present-day means that conservatives

---

[2] *Ibid.*

use in carrying out their attack against all manner of liberalism is to cite the specter of political correctness. They charge that anyone who disagrees with their views only do so because these views are not politically correct. Any factual claims against Putin *et al.* that they dislike are put in the category of "just *PC nonsense*." The differences of opinion about what constitutes "the facts" have also been startling. There is no hiding from the truth that this now very sizable minority of conservative Americans has been making a concerted effort "to dilute our ability to sort fact from fiction, or moral right from wrong." In the process, they are trying "to convince us to make decisions against our own best interests." Obviously, from their view of reality, they don't think they're doing this. But from the reality that's determined by objective standards of empirical evidence, many of their views are merely paranoid fantasies to which they would respond, "just *too* PC" or worse yet, of "fake news." Sadly, the upshot of all these conservative moves has helped Mr. Putin in his efforts to plant chaos and self-doubt in the minds of far too many Americans.

Let me be a little more specific about the anti-PC conservatives' methods of sowing chaos and self-doubt and how they attempt to derail political correctness in the process. As we saw in Chapter 9, conservatives blame many societal ills on political correctness. They point to crime, decaying sexual morality, the loss of respect for life (of fetuses) and the fraying of our default rules of common curtesy, human decency and civility. They claim that PC doesn't allow us to be as tough as we need to be to clean up our societal mess. And then, with tongues firmly planted in cheeks, they claim that these social problems are natural expressions of the chaos and self-doubt all around us, and that in fact, it's PC that's responsible for the larger chaos and self-doubt.[3]

---

[3] A case of projection, plain and simple.

Disrespect for political correctness is done in the service of trying to throw everyone off the scent of the actual guilty party in these matters; more *chutzpah* on their part. In fact, the societal ills of crime, incivility and the like are not of PC's doing. Quite the opposite—the roots of crime and incivility and the rest are more likely the result of conservatives ginning up the forces of bigotry and turning a blind eye to poverty among society's most vulnerable, our minority citizens. But conservatives will confess to none of this; they continue to insist that day is night and night is day. When people are as intent about distorting reality as these conservative critics have been—when they are so single-minded in trying to destroy the integrity of the very idea of political correctness that would shield minorities from the aggressive impulses of some of our fellow citizens—it can't help but have the debilitating effect of shaking us all to our core. It's no wonder we're no longer as certain as we used to be about what's right and what's wrong.

Some will undoubtedly think that what I have to say is pure hyperbole, but nevertheless...I believe this is a perilous moment for America. When an *individual person* literally no longer feels confident about his shared reality with others, when he is wracked with self-doubt to the point of losing his decision-making abilities—in short, when his psychological life is in total, literal chaos—that's textbook clinical psychosis. When a *whole society* moves in a direction of no longer feeling confident about its shared reality, to the point of self-doubt and the rest, that society is inching closer to societal psychosis. Together with the intense racist, gender-bashing and religious-discriminating bigotry so endemic to our country, this is an intolerable psychic weight that no nation can ultimately survive. The tide needs to turn right now if there's to be any hope for us.

It's my view that one of the many things we'll need to do to move back in the right direction is to re-commit ourselves to the cause of political correctness. Minimally, we'll need to stanch the bleeding from the violent conservative assaults against PC. Advocates of political correctness need to bring new arguments to the table to underscore its virtues.

What Makes PC A Concept Well Worth Saving?

So, what exactly are those virtues? In a phrase, *good citizenship*. Recall from Chapter 1 that the meaning of political correctness comes into being at the nexus of where people, ideologies and the society's predominant public institutions (culture, politics, judiciary) all meet. At that nexus point, a person's behavior, attitudes and beliefs are said to be politically correct when they are consistent with the prevailing ideologies embraced by "the people" (in the form of the mores and traditions of the culture-at-large), by the political institutions of the nation (its political leaders and enacted legislation), and by the judicial system (in the form of its relevant legal decisions). In short, when a person lives in line with the prevailing ideologies promoted by the reigning forces of the world she lives in, she is living a politically correct life. PC anchors who she is as a political actor. Moreover, the politically correct individual is being a *good citizen* because she lives out the behavior, attitudes and beliefs that flow from the ideological life defining her society. Since good citizenship is a *sine qua non* of any well-functioning society, political correctness is a condition or state of being toward which all members of any well-functioning society ought to aspire. And so, when, contrariwise, people behave in ways aimed at denigrating and ultimately eradicating political correctness, they are acting against the best interests of their society. All good citizens ought to oppose this kind of behavior for the sake of a well-functioning society.

I'll stop here for a moment and briefly anticipate and respond to a possible objection to my claim about the virtue of PC. I can imagine someone arguing that surely it is appropriate for us to denigrate "political correctness" as practiced by the good citizens of Hitler's Nazi Germany. If Nazis were politically correct in supporting their national Nazi ideologies, there's obviously something wrong with the idea of political correctness.

My view is that such denigration aimed at PC *per se* is wrongheaded. If someone wants to claim that Nazi ideology was an abomination that needed to be defeated and that, therefore, so too should the very idea of political correctness have been eradicated—because, after all, it was the politically correct acts and attitudes of the "good German" masses that fed the Nazi war machine—that person is mistaken. Yes, one wants to change offensive *ideologies* and one wants to change the behaviors and attitudes that support those ideologies. But one shouldn't want to eradicate the idea of political correctness altogether; rather, one should aim to replace the content of offensive ideology that people had been PC about with more praiseworthy prevailing ideologies that they could then go on to be PC about. For example, after the War, Germans' politically correct behaviors and thinking of Democracy came to replace the politically correct behaviors and thinking of Fascism and Nazism; the content of the prevailing ideology changed, but not the concept of being PC. The idea of political correctness *per se* is always positive in the context of the smooth functioning and citizen vitality of a nation. It is what bonds people as good citizens around prevailing ideologies. And that's surely a good thing for the health of a nation.

Undoubtedly, the rejoinder here would be that my view of political correctness would have us believe that, since politically correct Germans were bonded around their shared Nazi ideology, they were being good citizens; and that that surely was a good thing for the health of the German nation. Well...yes, they were being good citizens, happily following their Nazi ideology; and it did bond them together. Now, from our perspective, we don't like people to feel good about Nazism and we don't want them to bond over it. But that's not a problem for the concept of political correctness *per se*; it's a problem for anyone opposing *Nazi ideology*. In this situation, we would need to mount *moral arguments* against fascism. And indeed, there are whole bodies of literature devoted just to that.

I made the point in Chapter 5 that for a good part of America's history, many kinds of bigotry were considered socially acceptable. And when we, as American citizens, acted in accordance with the prevailing national ideologies that sanctioned bigotry, we were being politically correct. But ultimately through moral persuasion, we replaced our bigoted and racist ideologies with the prevailing ideologies of social justice and minority liberation. When we, as citizens, have acted in accordance with these newer ideologies, we have been politically correct. Truthfully, during the eras when bigotries were popularly embraced, bigoted behavior did bond most of the large majority of the citizenry (obviously, not those who were being discriminated against). And this did in fact add to the health of our nation in ways we might not find acceptable today. But large swathes of our citizenry eventually came to detest bigoted ideologies. Moral arguments won the day. And so we changed. But that didn't require that we do away with the idea of political correctness.

So, yes, because being politically correct entails being good citizens, I am arguing that we need to champion the idea of political correctness rather than try to destroy it. You may try to mount persuasive arguments against a prevailing ideology if you don't like it; but don't throw away the idea of being a good citizen in the process.

What I've said thus far in this section concerns the general reason why PC is worth saving—namely, that it's a key component of good citizenship. But there is another reason why political correctness should remain an important, respected functioning concept. Political correctness has been the primary backstop for the championing and enforcement of minority liberation ideology and for this reason too, it's worth saving. PC has been the *counterweight against the forces of bigotry* of all varieties. Therefore, it must be maintained as a sacrosanct concept in political discourse as a powerful rhetorical device in fending off public displays of racism, misogyny, homophobia, religious discrimination, etc. which are no longer in favor with most Americans. When the principled or bigoted conservative goes overboard in his criticism of PC, this has the consequence of licensing these bigoted public displays, whether or not that was the intent of the principled conservative. And a counterweight here is what's called for.

Here's a specific case that illustrates why PC as a counterweight to bigotry is important. Consider those people who wax on about returning America to the good old days (Make America Great Again). One hears, for example, people yearning for the time before "our neighborhoods were overrun by minorities." When the prevailing racial makeup or religious preference of a neighborhood changes, many of the white people (often Christian but not always) who grew up there feel abandoned by their country; there no longer is anything comfortably familiar for them in their surroundings; things aren't what they used to be. Inasmuch as the old neighborhood is where these people carved out their personal life stories, it feels to many of them that parts of those histories have been erased. And that indeed is a devastating psychological condition to experience. Of course, were new white Christian people moving there instead, that would seem at least to be a "natural" acceptable state of affairs, because the old inhabitants of the neighborhood could at least identify with the new inhabitants and the values they imagine they share. But when the complexion or religious preference of the neighborhood changes, shared identification and community bonding can be difficult.

The same sorts of complaints—wanting to return to the "good old days"—are made about women in the workplace and LGBTQ people being "out" in public. The fact that women have become a large part of the workforce simply offends the sense of identity many men hold deeply, as the workers and primary breadwinners in the family. The same also can be said about heterosexuals who don't identify with LGBTQ people at all, certainly not with their public displays of affection. The ever-changing American social landscape does have the effect of erasing some of a "traditionalist's" personal history having to do with race, religion, culture, gender and sexual preference. The America that was part of this person's personal history is no more and that is simply too much to bear. So, he is uncomfortable and resents those whom he holds responsible for his discomfort.

This kind of bigoted nostalgia and white male entitlement is all too front and center today, with "Make America Great Again" the battle cry of those who oppose politically correct minority liberation. The MAGA crowd wants to challenge the stability of the culture-at-large with outrageous ruptures and disturbances that take the form of name-calling and, more and more, violent attacks against minority peoples. They proclaim war on what we have become as a nation and actively try to destroy the *zeitgeist*. They could care less about the prevailing ideologies of our culture-at-large and "the people."

It's only the counterweight of political correctness around minority social liberation ideology that can save us here and play to our better angels as citizens. Complaints about "the old neighborhood," "the war on Christianity," women in the workforce, LGBTQ people coming out of the closet, etc. are emblematic of the strong forces in our country that are all about defeating and replacing minority social liberation as a preeminent ideology in our nation's conscience. The bigot's actions, attitudes and beliefs are solemnly trained on defeating the current cultural passion for social liberation for all Americans. So we end up with a country divided, at war with itself. Indeed, that's why we call the conservative assault on PC part of the ongoing "culture wars."

Moreover, the PC war isn't just aimed at minorities and their rights claims; it's aimed at all of us. We're told, for example, that we don't all have a right to affordable healthcare or an affordable college education (or even the right to expect clean air and water). We're told that it's just political correctness that makes us think we do. Soon we'll be hearing that we don't have a right to Social Security and Medicare and that those who think otherwise are being "just *too* PC." To defend our democracy, we must, as I've said, insist on political correctness as a counterweight. In a democracy, we simply must ensure that all good citizens behave in accordance with the prevailing ideologies of the majority, of "the people" and the political and judicial powers-that-be, even if they disagree with them. If, as is their right, they refuse to embrace those ideologies, we need at least to expect from them that they show respect for the rest of us who do embrace those ideologies by their behaving in accordance with the ideologies. Moreover, if there are political leaders who would exhort their followers to swim against the tide of prevailing ideologies embraced by the culture-at-large in order to suit their own bigoted ideologies, these leaders must be strenuously opposed and duly—peacefully and Constitutionally—replaced. Responsible citizenship requires as much. Political correctness requires no less from us.

Let me have one more go at this last point. I can't emphasize enough that the forces aiming their sights at destroying the PC concept *per se* are doing the nation and themselves a disservice. If a nation's prevailing ideologies and the PC conceptual glue that holds them in place can't assume at least the *respect* if not the wholehearted embrace of all citizens, then we are at an unhappy moment. While not everyone will agree with every ideology that happens to be in fashion at a given point in time; and while we would expect the critics to argue their case passionately against those popular ideologies and argue for the ones they prefer; we would also expect that these arguments be respectful. That's part of good citizenship, too. When, instead, rancor gets so intense that respect flies out the window and is replaced by the destruction not only of a reigning ideological (enemy) view but also the very idea of citizens being politically correct about that reigning ideological view, then we are in deep trouble...for then, we would be allowing that it's no longer important for citizens to act in ways that promote our reigning ideologies, no longer a requirement to respect "the will of the people" or our political and legal institutions. That certainly threatens an end to civil society.

Moreover, this kind of behavior weakens the bonds of good citizenship. And I think that many of these people are quite aware of this, reveling in the idea of weakening those bonds because of their total antipathy for and lack of any sense of kinship with citizens who champion political correctness and minority liberation. I think they come from a place of "take no prisoners" and "better to tear the whole thing down" if this minority social liberation is what our democracy has come to.

Are Americans becoming advocates of apartheid? Could fascism be far behind? I still believe that there is at least a chance we can right the ship. To achieve this, the conservative mob that is set against the idea of political correctness needs to have the bigots among them exposed and called out. But it is also incumbent upon anyone who cares at all about good citizenship, whether conservative-leaning or liberal-leaning, to think twice about allowing political correctness to fall into total disrepair. We need to resuscitate the concept or risk losing the very integrity of our democracy to the forces of chaos. We need to find ways to turn around the public's attitude toward PC, to make new concerted efforts to celebrate PC. We must demonstrate that there are positive, practical consequences that come from respecting the idea of political correctness.

Restoring the Good Name of Political Correctness

The simplest way to restore political correctness to its proper place among the ranks of concepts most cherished in our democracy is to suggest how an embrace of PC might actually enable more citizens—not only minorities—to thrive. I won't get into the weeds of suggesting specific programs; that's for public policy professionals and grassroots organizations to hammer out. I just wish to show, in this final section, that PC really is an important player in the progress of all Americans.

To get at the larger point—that being PC is in fact a condition that ultimately serves the well-being of *all* of us, I will first present a paradigm case where being PC can be seen to positively impact the lives of a segment of society that isn't a traditional minority population: poor working-class whites. As a springboard for this discussion, I wish to point to a piece written by Peggy Noonan in *The Wall Street Journal* awhile ago.[4] The article quite convincingly makes the case that there is a sizable poor, white working class that's been left behind, not only economically but culturally.

---

[4] Thanks to Frank Levi for pointing me to Peggy Noonan's "Shining a Light on 'Back Row' America." *The Wall Street Journal*, December 31, 2016.

The rest of us—those relatively favored in society—need to empathically pay special attention to this:

> The front row [the protected, advantaged citizens]...needs to learn
> two things. [Quoting traveling photojournalist Chris Arnade:] "One
> is how much the rest of the country is hurting. It's not just economic
> pain, it's a deep feeling of meaninglessness, of humiliation, of not be-
> ing wanted." Their fears and anxieties are justified. "They have been
> excluded from participating in the great wealth of this country eco-
> nomically, socially and culturally." Second, "The front-row kids need
> humility. They need to look in the mirror, 'We messed this up, we've
> been in charge 30 years and haven't delivered much.'"
>
> Of those falling behind: "They're not lazy and weak, they're
> dealing with bad stuff. Both conservative and progressive intellec-
> tuals say Trump voters are racist, dumb. When a conservative looks
> at a minority community and says, 'They're lazy,' the left answers,
> 'Wait a minute, let's look at the larger context, the availability of
> jobs, structural injustice.' But the left looks at white working-class
> poverty and feels free to judge and dismiss."[5]

In the name of minority liberation, minorities have received a lot of attention. Celebrating their accomplishments in politics, sports, the arts and in everyday life has been absorbed into popular culture. But we don't give the same amount of attention to the poor white working class. They have become the "forgotten Americans." Any celebration of their cultural heritage is dwarfed by comparison to the attention paid to minority cultures. This, many in the working-class whites complain, is especially true of the influence black culture has had on the culture-at-large *vis-à-vis* its music and literature, leading poor whites to feel culturally marginalized, of little value.

---

[5] *Ibid.*, p. A11.

This not only offends their sense of justice (where *every* American's heritage should be respected and celebrated), but it also offends their unconscious sense of white privilege. Taken together, those two perceived offenses leave the white working-class citizen with a relative sense of "meaninglessness, of humiliation, of not being wanted" by the broader culture-at-large.

This is where the white supremacists try to fill a void—around the issue of a sensed injustice—in the life of the poor white working-class citizen. They tell him that it's okay to celebrate and take pride in his white cultural heritage. I say that, of course, it's okay for anyone to celebrate their heritage and to expect the culture-at-large to respect and celebrate it, too. However, that the white supremacist has an agenda more far-reaching than assuaging this sense of injustice is glaringly apparent. He promotes a social agenda of bigotry that would have the poor white working-class citizen unthinkingly slide into accepting bigotry as the only way to get back his sense of value in the culture-at-large. The deceptive efforts of the white supremacist need to be made crystal-clear to the public and dealt with accordingly. But so should the culture-at-large take responsibility for having marginalized the poor white working-class citizen's sense of meaning; feeling unworthy and forgotten creates a very serious mental health issue that our nation needs to confront head-on. So not only does there need to be a genuine re-kindling of popular respect and celebration for the parts of the white working-class citizen's heritage that don't offend the rest of the nation,[6] but, as an example, there is also a need for public monies to help those among the poor white working class who might benefit from psychological therapy. Difficult to carry out? Yes. Nevertheless—and here's my main point—it's the *politically correct* way for our society to behave. Just

---

[6] Pointedly, there still will be no room at the inn for a celebration of anyone's cultural heritage of bigotry.

as we champion liberation rights of minorities by insisting that all citizens be politically correct around those rights, so too should we champion the cultural liberation rights of the white working-class citizen by insisting that all citizens be politically correct about those rights; that they do all they can do to support those rights. How else (beyond just providing monies for psychological therapy) this gets spelled out practically in terms of specific social programs that would foster respect and celebration for the cultural heritage of the white working class is another matter, well beyond the scope of this book. But once we can see that the plight of the white working-class citizen pertains to certain rights of cultural liberation that have long gone unacknowledged and that any suggested solutions to this problem must be consistent with our culture-at-large embrace of liberation ideology, then we will also see that our embrace of the rights of the white working class will be tantamount to being politically correct.

Beyond championing the political correctness of cultural respect and celebration as well as making psychotherapy more readily available, though, perhaps even more important is to remedy the economic pain of the white working poor as referenced by Noonan. That is, the poor white working-class citizen's sense of meaninglessness is not only about the lack of respect for his cultural heritage; it's about the issue of work—about his having lost his place as an economically productive member of society. Politicians, economists and sociologists have certainly covered this ground intensively in the past decade. How to provide meaningful work for those who have been left behind? Many have offered solutions, but still with no appreciable results. Here are my thoughts:

It's just a fact that part of most people's sense of purpose has to do with feeling that they are productive members of their family and, more broadly speaking, of society. The unfortunate reality, though, is that economic forces have caused many of the jobs that used to go to poor working-class whites to be out-sourced to other countries for pennies on the dollar. (That's capitalism for you.) There's an obvious clash between two claims to rights; the capitalist's right to maximize profits lawfully along-side the right of any citizen *qua* worker to earn a living. Currently, the capitalist and his ideology are winning the day. There's not been nearly enough people publicly championing the worker's side of the issue, although I think most people would say that the worker does have a right to work. This right is part of what we might think of as our national *ideology* of "fair work," also encompassing ideas like the worker's right to safe working conditions, a fair living wage, humane treatment on the job, and more.

Here is where political correctness once again becomes relevant. I think this ideology of fair work is ingrained in the American psyche. But we have something of a divide in our nation between what "the people" (the culture-at-large) favor in this regard and what's favored by the political and judicial powers-that-be. If voting patterns in Congress and recent rulings of the Supreme Court tell us anything, it is that the political and judicial powers-that-be are still on the side of capitalist ideology. However, since the culture-at-large seems to favor the idea of fair work that includes the worker's right not to have his or her job pulled out from underneath her, then it would behoove "the people" to advocate for political correctness on behalf of the worker. So, ra-ther than disparaging political correctness, what we really need is a resurgence of praise for the concept and its re-emergence as a cru-cial tool in championing the cause of the dispossessed poor white working-class people. We have a long way to go before this can be-come a positive force for the poor white working class. More attention must first be paid to their cause so that the political and judicial powers-that-be will begin to *really* hear the voice of the people. Until recently, there has been hardly a peep from the nation's institutional powers regarding this ideological predicament; until Mr. Trump, that is. To give credit where credit is due, he is a member of the political class who came out of the gate swinging for the dispossessed worker. He promised to bring American jobs home and has argued for a very large infrastructure project in Congress to put America back to work. He promoted the idea of border taxes as a mechanism for protecting the current worker and he touted tariffs as a way to encourage American companies to bring back jobs from abroad for the working-class citizen who has lost his job. Many would argue with the motives and the efficacy to date of these attempts to help the American worker. The one thing you can't fault Trump for is that at least he is trying. As much as he would hate to hear this, Mr. Trump in fact has been championing a politically correct view that is backed by "the people." In general, he has taken politically correct steps in the right direction toward supporting the national ideology of fair work.

This is where my approval of Mr. Trump ends…because, along with his white supremacist followers, he is hell-bent on playing poor white working-class men *against minorities*—playing white working-class liberation against minority liberation—in a zero sum game, all to press his underlying bigoted agenda. He has injected race and gender into the issue of the forgotten American worker's plight. He suggests that for the jobs that *haven't yet* been offshored, the forgotten (white) American worker has to compete (unfairly) with people of color and women. Adding this race and gender layer to his zero sum game atop of the white working-class citizen's misfortune due to jobs being shipped overseas is a travesty. One can only hope that clearer minds than his can disentangle this false choice that he's provided the nation—that either it's the white population or the populations of women and people of color who will thrive in our society, but not both.

Assuming that clearer minds *will* eventually prevail, one can only hope that political programs to reinvigorate fair work for the currently dispossessed white working class will in due course be devised and agreed upon by both liberals and conservatives. Of course, accomplishing this won't be the end of the problem for the poor white working class. Not only does the riddle of outsourcing and offshoring vs. domestic manufacturing have to be solved, but the additional fact that technology has made many previous working-class jobs obsolete must be dealt with, too. Replacing human workers with computers and machines surely has been the cause of much of the anxiety and a sense of meaninglessness among dispossessed workers. It's also undoubtedly the central reason behind the alarming spike in hard drug addiction and crime among their ranks. And, as Ms. Noonan recounts in her article, liberals need to be just as understanding about the mitigating reasons why many poor whites appear to be lazy and weak and prone to a life of drug dependence and crime as they are about the mitigating reasons why some people of color might seem lazy and weak and susceptible to drugs and crime. A core problem for both groups is that there is not enough work available to them and that the few available jobs do not entail meaningful work. Waking up each day with the promise of purposeful work is a not-so-secret balm that soothes most souls.

New solutions for these occupational ills must be found: new ways to keep jobs in America; to celebrate the progress of technology while at the same time not allowing technology to replace human workers; and to create new and meaningful work opportunities. The government's investing in a national infrastructure project would go a long way toward solving the last of these problems. Training people to work in tech is a step in the right direction, although clearly not all workers have the capacity to fit in seamlessly with new technologies, given the galloping AI strides we keep making in this area. One can only hope that President Trump (or his successor) and the Republican Senate (or its successor) will redouble their efforts to figure out how to keep American jobs at home while at the same time not offending our nation's capitalist sensibilities too much. Whatever ideas they finally come up with, what can't be disputed is that these solutions will define a new set of politically correct behaviors, attitudes and beliefs that are consistent with the ideology of fair work; and that all good citizens will pull together to promote the ideology's cause.

But while the current spotlight for solving these problems is on the Republicans, the onus should not be entirely on the conservatives who happen to be in political power at this time. The ability to deal with the plight of the forgotten American worker is most naturally in the liberal's wheelhouse. Politically correct liberalism has always been concerned with taking care of the socially, economically and politically dispossessed. Until recently, that has meant the minority populations. The poor white working class— the forgotten American worker—is another dispossessed group that liberals need to include in their efforts. An *exclusive* focus on minorities serves neither genuinely liberal interests nor American interests. We need to broaden the politically correct ideology of minority liberation to encompass liberation for all Americans. Liberalism requires that we figure out policies and programs that will do as much for the kinds of people that are chronicled in Ms. Noonan's article as we've tried to do for minorities.

Creating and promoting as-yet unthought-of policies and programs would be the height of political correctness. My view is that if we, as liberals and conservatives, can work some magic in this regard, not only will we help people who have been genuinely suffering, but we also will have gone a long way toward restoring PC to its rightful laudatory place on the American liberation frontier. So if, for example, one could show the 40-year-old white worker who's been unemployed for 3 years with no possibilities on the horizon that there is some politically correct set of actions that would reinvigorate him and his possibilities in life, then the PC concept would once again take on a laudatory connotation and begin to regain its place of praise and pride in our nation. Who knows, even conservatives might start to see its value. Hope springs eternal, I guess.

The white, middle-aged unemployed worker who, rather than embracing this celebration of political correctness and instead rails against it (because he sees it as only championing the rights of minorities) has been sold a bill of goods by bigots, racists and misogynists who relish his antipathy toward minorities. They promote the idea in his mind of another one of those zero sum games we discussed. They get him to do their bigoted bidding. To overcome this anti-minority strategy of the bigots, it's on all of us to show the dispossessed white person that political correctness applies just as much to support him as it does to the ideologies supporting minority causes. What really needs to happen is for minority citizens to rally in great numbers to the cause of workers' rights (the rights of all workers, no matter their race, gender or religion). With the help of minorities, the cause of workers' rights—perhaps à la the Democratic Socialist views of Bernie Sanders—can become a centerpiece ideology, embraced by the culture-at-large as well as the political and judicial powers-that-be. Since the general citizenry naturally champions the culture's centerpiece ideology, the more citizens become enamored of that ideology, to the point where much of their behavior, attitudes and beliefs consistently promote it, the prouder they will become about being politically correct about that ideology. PC will then eventually be accepted as the central organizing principle for solving our societal problems. Like I say, hope springs eternal.

Okay. So what I've just been arguing is that if the idea of political correctness can be extended beyond the cause of minority liberation to also encompass the cause of the ideology of fair work, that would be so much the better for the overriding cause of political correctness. But I would not want the advocates of PC to rest there, satisfied that they have done enough to bring the concept back to its proper laudatory place in the public arena. PC and the liberation ideology of fair work for the poor white working class is just one example of where the discussion of PC needs to extend its reach.

In closing, let me point out that there is in fact no limit to the number of new possible ideological arenas where political correctness might be the very thing needed to defend against their (the ideological arenas) detractors. I would remind the reader of our earlier discussion (Chapter 2) of the ever-expanding liberation rights frontier. There are undoubtedly areas of rights liberation that none of us have thought about yet. Rest assured, though, it's inevitable that, in our nation of indefatigable liberationists, there will always be new rights expansions on the horizon. And as these ideologies are absorbed into the culture-at-large and into the political and judicial power structures representing "the people," the good citizens of our nation will express their advocacy of these ideologies through as-yet unimagined behavior, attitudes and beliefs that will be consistent with these ideologies.

Finally, I end by making what I consider an obvious point (though maybe not so obvious to everyone) about PC. It is that there are the endless numbers of ideologies that have nothing to do with liberation but about which we can nevertheless expect the American citizenry to be politically correct. The idea of Democracy is probably the most ingrained of such ideologies, where, among other things, the politically correct good citizen embraces and advocates for the importance of holding fair elections through which we vote for the leaders we would have represent us in government (even with mail-in balloting). In other times, citizens of other countries have been known to be politically correct about different reigning political ideologies, most notably Communism and Fascism in the 20th century. Then, too, there are the religious ideologies of Christianity in our country and Islam in many others, whose advocates work hard at being politically correct. Outside the realms of politics and religion, our nation has gone through periods where we've also had reigning ideologies of social Darwinism, free trade, multiculturalism and much more. When any of these ideologies are popularly accepted by the culture-at-large and the powers-that-be, good citizens have behaved as politically correct actors. This no doubt accounts for the periods of domestic tranquility any nation enjoys for periods of time in the life of that nation's history. These are the periods when a nation's central ideological institutions (the culture-at-large, etc.) and their citizenry are as one. What could be better? Of course, on the other hand, when political correctness is challenged by competing ideologies—through ruptures or disturbances either from abroad or from within a nation—tranquility and civility all too often are seen to break down as that nation fights for its life.

Political correctness, then, is no small thing. From where I sit, PC is one of the most important conditions that any nation could hope its citizens aspire toward. Attempting—as so many conservatives have—to send it to the junk heap of historically useless concepts is worse than a fool's errand; it's an insult to the life and vitality of a nation.

AFTERWORD

I know there are many people who would agree with everything I've laid out in this book about the cause of PC minority liberation, but nevertheless would ask me why I'm so wedded to restoring the good name of the exact term "political correctness." I've been told by many people sympathetic to the *ideas* behind the concept of political correctness that the *term itself* has been so thoroughly damaged by both the incessant attacks of its critics and the careless misuse of it by some of its liberal advocates (Chapter 1) that a better strategy might be simply to coin a new term that captures all of what I've assigned to the definition of PC, and go from there in celebrating and arguing for the new term's virtues.

That certainly was a possibility I had considered. However, when it became eminently clear to me that the disparagement of PC terminology was purposeful and part of a much larger war strategy to defeat the minority liberation ideology that is so central to who we are as a people, I just couldn't let it go. If the term "political correctness" could be destroyed so easily by incessant verbal disparagement and slippery logic, then so could any other terminologies that are sacrosanct to the idea of a liberal democracy in general and minority liberation in particular be subjected to the same treatment. Heaven knows, there have already been far too many successes of conservatives cleverly disparaging important concepts of liberal democracy through very intentional linguistic programs aimed at destroying the terms that captured

291

those concepts. As I said in the Introduction, compared to Dem-ocrats, Republicans are pretty good political street fighters and they're particularly good at disparaging wordplay. In their war against all liberalism, conservatives have intentionally tried to co-opt the moral high ground by changing the meaning of cer-tain terms, focusing on terminologies that favor their ideologies and deflecting from the harm that they are intent on doing to liberalism. For example, they talk about "family values" and "the moral majority" as a way to undermine liberalism's embrace of modern views of open sexuality. Similarly, "estate tax" becomes "death tax" in the conservative lexicon. This general phenome-non, known as "messaging wars," is really a way to avoid head-on confrontations with liberals (with the conservative messaging czar Frank Luntz seemingly always leading the charge). Turning political correctness into an *ad hominem* pejorative is just an-other of the many moves that conservatives use in their attempts to undermine liberalism indirectly; focusing on their favored ter-minologies while twisting or disparaging their disfavored ones.

Of course, it's not as though *both* sides of the ideological divide haven't been involved in creating messaging wars. People champi-oning an ideology hardly ever describe it in a value neutral way—a way that describes the sheer facticity of some phenomenon. We're forever *evaluating* ideologies through the words we use to desig-nate and describe them—the words we use to favor or disfavor them. So, liberals refer to "a woman's right to choose" (they are "pro-choice") while conservatives refer to "the right to life" (they are "pro-life"). Both sides focus on certain words that favor their case while twisting certain other words out of shape in the battle to change the prevailing ideologies of our culture. A pox on both their houses! Incessant talking points exist only to confuse people and ul-timately trick them into accepting ideological positions that have no argument behind them other than that they are antithetical to some other term that has thoroughly been disparaged on the cheap. This behavior is flat-out incompatible with a democracy that respects—indeed, requires—an informed citizenry. If some conservative were to write a book pointing out how liberals have engaged in these same egregious linguistic practices in order to disparage conservative ideologies, I would be all ears and generally sympathetic with her case. But that's for conservatives to decide. This book is the result of my decision to defend the linguistic faith around an important concept that works not only in favor of liberals but in favor of all prevailing ideologies of our democracy.

*   *   *

I would be remiss in my discussion of political correctness if I didn't bring it back around to the present political circumstances in our country. Mr. Trump has been our president for three-plus years as of this writing; and he and his cohort have continued to make political correctness a centerpiece issue. At the heart of matters for them is the belief that political correctness is a destructive force. Most pointedly, they rail against advocacy for the rights of illegal and legal immigrants, the rights of women to control their own bodies, the rights of citizens to be protected from easy access to guns, and much, much more. President Trump complains that liberal America has been "*too* PC" about all of these matters. I hope I've made it clear in this book what I think we should say to him about his particular racist, xenophobic, misogynistic and homophobic version of the anti-PC credo.

Fool Me Once....

President Trump, the politically incorrect emperor has no clothes. Get dressed, already!

ACKNOWLEDGEMENTS

Thanks to my friends and colleagues who looked at earlier versions of this manuscript and offered sage advice: Alex Miramontes, Jay Gerber, Estelle Shane, Manny Schreiber, Laura Smith, Fred Busch, Chris Messenger, Gary Schwartz, Frank Levi, Father Greg Boyle, Mark Doeffinger, Asher Seidel, Christine Schultz and John Economos. Thanks to Arnie Richards and IPBooks for believing in the worth of my project. A large THANK YOU to Carol Skolnick, an editor extraordinaire who worked tirelessly on improving the final product. Special thanks to Donald Trump for being the prime motivator behind my thinking as deeply as I have about the absolute importance of political correctness.

Howard Kamler is both an academic philosopher and a clinical research psychoanalyst. He received his doctorate in philosophy from the University of Michigan, studied and trained as a psychoanalyst at the Michigan Psychoanalytic Institute and at the Los Angeles Institute for Contemporary Psychoanalysis, where he received his Psy.D. He is the author of numerous articles about philosophy and psychoanalysis, two books of philosophy and one of psychoanalysis. Retired from these pursuits now, he spends his days sculpting large stones on his patio, "playing" the tenor sax, practicing his bridge game, running his dogs in the park, reading wonderful novels and watching Rachel Maddow.

CPSIA information can be obtained
at www.ICGtesting.com
Printed in the USA
LVHW042307261020
669824LV00001B/68